Cut!

Cut!

MOVIES
IN FIFTEEN
MINUTES

Cleolinda Jones

First published in Great Britain in 2005 by
Gollancz
An imprint of the Orion Publishing Group
Orion House, 5 Upper St Martin's Lane, London WC2H 9EA

This edition published in Great Britain in 2007 by Gollancz

1 3 5 7 9 10 8 6 4 2

A CIP catalogue record for this book is
available from the British Library

ISBN-13 978 0 57507 989 2

Printed in Great Britain by
Clays Ltd, St Ives plc

The Orion Publishing Group's policy is to use papers
that are natural, renewable and recyclable products and
made from wood grown in sustainable forests. The logging
and manufacturing processes are expected to conform to the
environmental regulations of the country of origin.

www.orionbooks.co.uk

*For my mother, who always believes in me,
and for Vladimir, who was always there.*

ACKNOWLEDGEMENTS

In order to get my thank-yous out properly, I'm going to have to tell you a little story. I would worry about boring you, but you and I both know that no one reads this part in any book, so that's all right.

I've been writing ever since I was old enough to hold a crayon, but until last year, all I ever wrote was fiction and bad poetry. I was fortunate enough to have teachers who supported and encouraged me from first grade onward, but to spare those of you who have accidentally stumbled onto this page and don't know how to get out, I'll skip to my high school years and thank Lynn McGuffey and Jennifer Mouchette in particular for always encouraging my writing. I also managed to finish two very bad, very florid novels about this time, and I would like to thank a certain large and reputable publishing house for rejecting them out of hand and sparing us all the horrors of a fifteen-year-old novelist.

Fortunately, by the time I hit college, I had greatly improved. Dave Ullrich taught me how to get tough with my writing, which was probably the most valuable thing I ever learned; Peter Donahue was a gentler influence, and with his help I put together about two-thirds of a decent novel. In grad school, Dennis Covington and Brad Watson were always supportive of my fiction; I was having a lot of fun with a fourth novel about Victorian steampunk vampires that friends and classmates actually liked, and life was good.

In the meantime, I had gotten myself one of those newfangled Livejournals online. The people who read my movie news website, dailydigest.net, and my other blog were kind enough to migrate over to Livejournal and continue reading me over there as well; I met a lot of great people and made some fast friends. And then one Sunday last year I went to see *Van Helsing*. I came home and started writing up a journal entry that turned into a 2500-word parody. I tended to write 'funny' entries here and there, but I didn't particularly think of myself as any kind of comedy writer. For whatever reason, people loved 'Van Helsing in Fifteen Minutes', but I have to thank fellow LJer Ferrett Steinmetz (theferrett.livejournal.com) for posting about it, because that's what really brought my work to a larger audience.

And then the next Sunday I went to see *Troy*; naturally, 'Troy in Fifteen Minutes' followed, but it ended up taking on a life of its own. To make a long story short, Simon Spanton at Orion Books emailed me the following Thursday and asked if I would like to do a book, the book that you are now holding in your hands, and if not for him, it wouldn't exist at all. I said yes, and then started running around in circles panicking, so I ended up going to Tony Crunk, another professor who had been helping me with poetry and (at that particular time) a children's book, and asked him what to do. His immediate advice was to get an agent, and he pointed me towards some online listings. Of course I had no idea who to choose, but there near the top was a listing for Ginger Clark at Writers House that said she could sell, among other things, pop-culture nonfiction, children's books, historical novels, and steampunk. It was destiny, I decided, and thus I found myself an agent. Together, in their infinite patience, she and Simon were mother and father to the book, or midwife and obstetrician, or some other, less clumsy metaphor of your choice. Once the initial draft was finished, Gillian Redfearn and Lisa Rogers at Orion were invaluable in the editing process. Everyone at Orion, in fact, was incredibly supportive of and patient with a first-timer who staggered in from the wilderness of the internets, and for that I can't thank them enough.

In the course of actually writing the book, I had several steadfast beta readers on Livejournal, including Andy Perrin, Anne Martinez (anne_jumps), Emily Self (The Lovely Emily), Evangeline Savage (aralinde), Kate Petruccelli (agentsculder), Laura Moody (shoiryu), R.A. Bartlett, Shannon W. (edda), Sharyn Kazarian (snacky), Sharon Miles (restriction), Wyndi Elyzabithe Anderson (deoridhe), Vladimir Cvetkovic Sever, and the members of a certain Cabal, all of whom were my international test audience. The readers of Occupation: Girl (cleolinda.livejournal.com) pitched in as well, researching this or that detail by committee for me here and there. Moreover, they kept reading the new parodies I put online, sent them to friends, linked to them on their journals, and kept the *Movies in Fifteen Minutes* name alive. Most importantly, they didn't abandon my journal when I couldn't update as frequently as I wanted to (which is to say, at all). At the end of the day, this book is for them, and for everyone who loves movies – so much that they can laugh at them anyway.

CONTENTS

JURASSIC PARK (1993)

Isla Nublar, Just Far Enough Away from Costa Rica to Not Get Sued

The Jurassic Park geneticists have spent weeks carefully, painstakingly nurturing a velociraptor hatchling to maturity. The process is not only highly experimental and, in fact, unprecedented, but also bitch-ass expensive. Now Safari Dude – that's MULDOON to you; MR MULDOON if you're nasty – is overseeing the relocation of the raptor to its exhibit pen.

The raptor immediately knocks the gate open and eats some guy.

MULDOON: Ah, shoot the bitch, see if I care.

The Comedy Mines of Risa de Dios

FOREMAN: Faster! We must dig up the jokes faster!

MINER: 'Why is this fool gringo lawyer coming to see us about investor troubles?'

FOREMAN: That doesn't even have a punchline! Dig deeper!

MINER: 'You'll never get Sam Neill out of Montana, since that's the place he said he wanted to see before he died'?

FOREMAN: Ah . . . with polishing, that could be a beauty. We must find the other half of that movie reference! Back into the shafts, men!

Some Badlands, Montana

SOME BRAT: Raptors suck!

DR SATTLER: Oh Lord, here it comes.

DR GRANT: Raptors suck? Yeah, they do, actually. See this giant fossil claw? They rip you open with a claw just like this, and then they suck out your intestines like spaghetti. But they don't kill you, so you get to watch. *Sucks, don't it?*

SOME BRAT: *has nightmares for the rest of his life*

[For the rest of the film, DR ALAN GRANT will be referred to as 'GRANT' or 'DR GRANT', because he is a professional. DR ELLIE SATTLER will be referred to as 'ELLIE' because she is a girrrrrrrl.]

ELLIE: Whose kid *is* that, anyway?

GRANT: Not my kid, clearly, as I hate all kids, and I mock you for ever wanting to have kids of your own.

ELLIE: You know, you're overlooking the one supreme advantage of having kids.

GRANT: What's that?

ELLIE: The *making* of the kids.

GRANT: This is . . . you mean . . . SHIT, WHO'S THAT IN THE HELICOPTER?

[GRANT runs off screaming at the helicopter as all their hard work is blown to the four winds, only to discover that they have a visitor:]

JOHN HAMMOND: I like you, so I want you to come down to my death-trap dinosaur park.

GRANT: GIVE ME ONE REASON NOT TO GUT YOU WITH MY CLAW.

HAMMOND: I fund your dig?

GRANT: That's . . . shit, that's a really good reason.

HAMMOND: So come certify the safety of my park?

ELLIE: But . . . we study bones. You know, dead things. I can't think of anything you could possibly have at your park that might be in our line of expertise. Because the things we study? Dead.

HAMMOND: Hey, just think of it as a weekend getaway. PS – I will fund your dig for three more years. I spare no expense!

ELLIE: What were we saying about making kids . . . ?

GRANT: I say we do it on a pile of money.

Some Nonexistent Beach, San Jose, Costa Rica

DODGSON: Hello, *Nedry*.

NEDRY: So, let me stop being loathsome for five minutes so you can tell me the plan!

DODGSON: Well, it involves you smuggling out frozen embryos in this super-spiff I Can't Believe It's Not Shaving Cream gadget.

NEDRY: Ooo, gadgets! I'm gonna be just like James Bond!

DODGSON: Nedry, this is *industrial* espionage.

NEDRY [*narrowing eyes*]: Does that mean there aren't going to be any spy babes?

DODGSON: No . . . there are totally going to be spy babes. Waiting for you . . . at the dock. Yes. Go have fun stealing embryos now!

Hammond's Private Plane

HAMMOND: So . . . I bring two clean-cut professionals at the top of their respective fields, and you bring . . . a rock star.

HAMMOND'S LAWYER, GENNARO: . . . Yes.

IAN MALCOLM: Fresh off my 'Rock the Cosine' tour, baby.

Some Concert Arena

ANNOUNCER: Ladies and gentlemen, put your hands together for . . . IAN MALCOLM AND THE STRANGE ATTRACTORS!

IAN MALCOLM [*rocking the mic*]: HOW Y'ALL FEEL?

Hammond's Private Plane

MALCOLM: Have you heard of chaos theory?

GRANT: Even though we are scientists, no.

MALCOLM: Not even the butterfly effect?

ELLIE: You mean that movie with the kid who punks people?

MALCOLM: Really, it doesn't do justice to the profession at all.

Isla Nublar

The helicopter lands on a lush, secluded island . . .

HAMMOND: We spared no expense!

  [. . . locked up like a maximum-security prison.]

MALCOLM: Kinky.

GENNARO: So, John, you have a weekend to convince me that this park will work, or all the investors are pulling the plug.

HAMMOND: Five bucks says you'll be apologizing to *me* after you see the main attraction.

GODS OF IRONY: *thunderclap*

GENNARO: Look, if they're not convinced, I'm not convinced.

HAMMOND: Donald? That doesn't even make sense.

Some Meadow

Whee, brachiosaurus!

GENNARO: I'm convinced.

HAMMOND: Don't you want to see the—

GENNARO: CONVINCED.

  [ELLIE and GRANT simultaneously paleogasm.]

ELLIE: Was it good for you?

GRANT: My God! The CGI is seamless!

ELLIE: How did you do this?

HAMMOND: I'll show you!

Exposition Time at the Visitors' Centre

SOME CRAP CARTOON CHARACTER: Howdy, folks! I'm Cowboy Dan the DNA Strand!

HAMMOND: Okay, look – we had to skimp *somewhere*.

GRANT: But where did they get the DNA?

ELLIE: I don't know, you'd think there would be gaps in DNA that old—

MALCOLM: But how did they fill them?

GENNARO: Shhhhh, people are *trying* to watch *the movie*!

COWBOY DAN THE DNA STRAND: We used summa that there am-phi-bean frawg DNA, because there's no way that could bite us in the ass *at all*! Look how purty them li'l dogies turned out!

ELLIE: Babies? STOP THE RIDE!

Jurassic Nursery

ANNOUNCEMENT IN BACKGROUND: All employees who don't want to die should be at the dock by 1900 hours.

[The SCIENTISTS have broken out of COWBOY DAN'S thrall and crashed the nursery to ooh and aah over the hatchlings.]

ELLIE: Babies! I love babies!

GRANT [*apologetically*]: She's a girl.

DR WU: Actually, so are all of our dinosaurs. That way they can't knock boots in the wild.

5

MALCOLM: Oh, trust me. With all that phallic vegetation out there? They'll find a way.

HAMMOND [*tickling baby dinosaur*]: Who's an ickle raptor-waptor? Yes she is!

GRANT: YOU BRED RAPTORS?

Feeding Time at the Raptor Pen

MULDOON: Surly bitches, the lot of 'em. Ought to be destroyed.

MULDOON'S SHORTS: *are concerned*

MALCOLM: They're that bad?

MULDOON: Well, they've got cheetah speed, systematic problem-solving skills, vicious intelligence, the jumping muscles of a cat and constant PMS.

   [A STEER is lowered into the paddock.]

SOME STEER: MRRRRRRRRRRRRRR— [*gobble snort snurfle crunch*]

HAMMOND: So who's hungry?

Jurassic Dining Room

ELLIE: Mmm, Chilean sea carnage.

HAMMOND: All right, everyone's opinions! You first, Donald!

GENNARO [*with dollar signs in eyes*]: This is the best idea anyone has ever had, ever.

MALCOLM [*banging table*]: This is a rape of the natural world, and it does not rock!

ELLIE: Also, the ferns in the foyer gave me a shady look on the way in.

HAMMOND: WHAT IS WRONG WITH YOU PEOPLE? Dr Grant, you're on my side, right?

GRANT: Well . . . not really, no.

Outside the Visitors' Centre

TIM AND LEX: GRANDPA!

HAMMOND: KIDS!

GRANT: AHHHH!

HAMMOND: Here they are – electrical cars that you can't drive, stop or lock! We spared no expense! Everyone pile in!

MALCOLM: Can I ride with Ellie?

GRANT: No.

LEX: Can we ride with you?

GRANT: No.

TIM: Can I talk to you about dinosaurs?

GRANT: No.

ELLIE: Are you going to let anyone have *any* fun?

GRANT: No.

The Control Room

MULDOON: There's a storm coming, so—

HAMMOND: Start the outdoor tour programme!

Welcome to Jurassic Park!

The tour cars approach a giant wooden gate.

MALCOLM: What's in there, King Kong?

Somewhere on Skull Island

ANN DARROW: Hon? Were we supposed to be somewhere tonight? Meet someone for dinner, or something?

KING KONG [*shrugging*]: Uh-ruh.

Enjoy Fine, Dinorrific Rides Such As: The Spittosaurus Pen!

THE VOICE OF RICHARD KILEY: The spittosaurus is a beautiful but deadly dinosaur not unlike a rabid gecko, which blinds and paralyzes its prey so that it may munch its guts at leisure. Tubby computer geeks are its preferred food.

TIM: AWESOME.

LEX: But . . . where is it?

HAMMOND [*on radio*]: Uh . . . see, kids . . . it's *sleeping*.

The Control Room

HAMMOND: Why does nothing work?!

NEDRY: Because I'm an underpaid jerk plotting to betray you?

MULDOON: SHUT UP! T-REX!

The T-Rex Paddock!

EVERYONE: Ooooooo.

RAY [*on radio, while smoking*]: Deploy the handsome show goat!

HAMMOND [*on radio*]: We spared no expense!

LEX: It's gonna eat the goat?

GENNARO: Nah, he's bringing out tyrannochow in a barrel around his neck – of COURSE it's gonna eat the goat.

[They wait.]

GRANT: . . .

ELLIE: . . .

MALCOLM: . . .

GENNARO: . . .

TIM: . . .

LEX: . . .

CROAKING FROGS: . . .

GOAT: Meh.

HAMMOND: *facepalm*

In the Science Car

MALCOLM: You can't count on a T-rex to show up for work. This? This is chaos theory.

ELLIE: I still don't understand what chaos is, because clearly I never had access to a dictionary as a child.

[Observe the wild flirtosaurus in its natural habitat, as it explains simple concepts to a strangely dense blonde.]

GRANT: OMG TRICERATOPS!

ELLIE: OMG I'M GOING WITH YOU!

MALCOLM: Again: gotta love chaos theory. Or you would if you were still here.

The Triceratops Habitat!

Everyone jumps out and follows GRANT and ELLIE to see the only actual dinosaur on the tour so far. While TIM yammers on about birds and meteors and diamond dust, LEX trips and GRANT helps her up.

GRANT: You okay?

LEX: I love you.

GRANT: Ellie, *help*.

[Meanwhile, the TRICERATOPS is doing its best dead-roach impression.]

ELLIE'S SHORTS: *are concerned*

SOME PARK RANGER: We can't figure out what's wrong with her at all.

ELLIE: Well, for starters, there are weird sores on her tongue, which is lolling out of her head in plain view, and her pupils are dilated.

SOME PARK RANGER: Really?

ELLIE: Dude, I figured that out and I'm a *botanist*. Seriously, do you know anything about animals at all?

SOME PARK RANGER: Shut up.

ELLIE: Wait, you've got West Indian lilac growing in their paddock?

SOME PARK RANGER: Well, we know it's poisonous, but we figured, you know . . . girl dinosaurs.

ELLIE: What?

SOME PARK RANGER: You know . . . girls like flowers. You wanna check their droppings for toxins?

ELLIE: No, I've seen enough bullshit for today, thanks.

The Control Room

HAMMOND: Our tour sucks.

RAY [*puffing on cigarette*]: Seriously? It could've been a lot worse. What if someone had hacked the system and all the fences went down and the T-rex started eating people?

HAMMOND: Yes, that *would* be bad.

NEDRY [*clutching 'shaving cream'*]: Hey, uh, guys? I think I'm, uh, gonna go get something to eat, maybe something sweet, except I've been eating sweets all day, so maybe something salty, although you know some things are sweet AND salty but we ran out of caramel corn last week, probably because I ate it all, so you really should have them restock that, maybe I can write a code for that, but then I'd probably have to debug it, oh hey, I debugged the phones, which is cool, of course the phones are going to go off in a few minutes because the system is going to go down, I mean, not all of the system is going to go down, because I sure didn't hack it or anything, just some of the system, the systems that are minor, while the system is compiling, because I debugged it like you asked me to, but it shouldn't take too long, maybe eighteen to twenty minutes, here, let me set my stopwatch so we can time it, you know, just for kicks. Also, I have to go shave. See you guys later!

RAY: O . . . kay.

Back in the Science Car

MALCOLM: So, chaos theory. Yeah. Anything can and does happen, particularly if you invest in inferior forms of birth control, if you see what I'm saying. Hey, is Ellie single? I've always got room for another set of alimony payments.

GRANT: *MY* BABIES! SHE'S NOT HAVING *MY* BABIES, GOT IT?

Tubby Espionage!

RAY [*blowing smoke rings*]: Weird – door security to our cherished stockpile of embryos just went off.

HAMMOND: Should we look into that?

RAY: Nah.

[NEDRY ~~ninjas~~ sumos on into cold storage and gleefully pilfers embryos.]

HAMMOND: The tour cars have stopped!

MULDOON: The fences are failing!

RAY: But the raptor fences are still on!

MULDOON: Which means he turned the other fences off on purpose!

RAY: The phones are also out, so we can't tell anyone!

HAMMOND: What could it *mean*?

[NEDRY speeds off towards the docks, completely unconcerned that the dinosaurs can break out, all the guests are trapped and there's nothing anyone can do about it, because it never occurred to anyone to have an easily accessible back-up generator or, for that matter, a cellular phone.]

HAMMOND: Wait . . . where did the cars stop?

The T-Rex Paddock

MALCOLM: So . . . we're just going to sit here . . . not being scared.

GRANT: You keep talking and I'll *give* you something to be scared about.

[Because, somehow, you're not going to see a frillion-ton dinosaur until it creeps up on you, no one notices anything's wrong until cups of water start vibrating.]

FILMMAKERS ACROSS THE LAND: We'll be able to spoof *this* for the next ten years!

[The T-REX flings great big gobs of greasy grimy goatly guts on the Kiddie Car. GENNARO, like any lawyer worth his salt, flees. And then the T-REX flosses her teeth with the fence and rumbles on out into the road.]

MALCOLM: That? That's chaos theory.

GRANT: SHUT UP AND DON'T MOVE. IT CAN'T SEE THINGS THAT DON'T MOVE.

The Kiddie Car

LEX: Let's wave the flashlight around!

TIM: Let's shut the door in its face!

LEX: I KNOW! LET'S FLAIL IN TERROR!

THE KIDS: WAHHHHHHHHHHHHHHHHHHHHH!

Ride #1: Kiddie Car Turnover!

In search of a main course, the T-REX flips over the Kiddie Car and starts sampling tires.

T-REX: DAMMIT! *PTUUUUW!*

GRANT: It's crushing the car!

MALCOLM: They're sinking in the mud!

GRANT: Even *I* know we have to save them!

[GRANT finds flares in the back of the Science Car and leaps out at his own peril, carefully attracting the T-REX, then throwing his flare away and standing absolutely still. MALCOLM, unable to let anyone show him up, leaps out with his own flare. But he doesn't . . . quite . . . grasp the concept.]

GRANT: And now you have to freeze! Freeze! Any time now . . . !

T-REX: Mmmm, flailing chaotician.

MALCOLM: Didn't think this through! Didn't think this through!

[Meanwhile, in a bamboo port-a-potty:]

GENNARO [*writing*]: Your client, Tyrannosaurus Rex . . . is required . . . to remain five hundred feet . . . from . . . AHHHHH-HHHHH!

[The T-REX throws MALCOLM at the port-a-potty to bowl a strike, and then eats GENNARO to celebrate.]

GRANT: THAT'S CHAOS THEORY!

13

Ride #2: Bobbing for Children!

GRANT: I've got you! I've got you!

LEX [*weeping*]: Dad! Dad!

GRANT: Look, we'll deal with your weirdo issues later! Tim! Are you in there?

TIM: I'm stuck!

GRANT: We'll get you out! Lex! How's the T-rex?

LEX: WAHHHHHHHHHHHHHHHHHHHHHHHHHHHHHHHHH-HHHHHHHHHHH!!!

GRANT: That's bad.

Ride #3: The Merry-Go-Round!

GRANT: Can't! see us! if! we don't! move!

> [The T-REX blows this plan out of the water by spinning the Kiddie Car around in search of a ~~can~~ car opener.]

Ride #4: Rappelling!

GRANT: Over the side! Down the wall! Grab the cable, Lex!

LEX: What about Tiiiiiiim?

GRANT: SCREW TIM!

> [The T-REX punts TIM and the Kiddie Car over the wall in carnivorous frustration.]

GRANT: AHHH! I DIDN'T MEAN IT!

The Control Room

RAY [*lighting cigarette*]: So . . . basically, for whatever nefarious reasons of his own, Nedry has screwed up our computers.

HAMMOND [*wringing hands*]: Why in the world would someone so underpaid and disgruntled betray us this way?

MULDOON: That's it, I'm going out there to get everyone!

ELLIE: I'm coming with!

RAY: Well, as the only people wearing shorts in the room, clearly you're the only ones qualified to go.

Ride #5: The Petting Zoo!

Brilliant computer hacker falls afoul of rogue road sign, film at eleven.

NEDRY: Hey, do you know which way the dock is?

SPITTOSAURUS: *shakes death frill*

NEDRY: Niiiiice spittosaurus . . .

SPITTOSAURUS: PTUUUUUUUUUW!

NEDRY: MY EEEEEEEYES!

Ride #6: Treetop Adventure Climb!

GRANT: Timmy? Timmy!

[TIMMY is dead from tree. GRANT climbs down from the wall and MacGyvers a raft out of car and tree wreckage and sails away with poor traumatized LEX to a nearby dinosaur-free island where they live out the rest of their natural lives in a tropical paradise where GRANT forgets all about that horsey blonde doctor chick and he and LEX do . . . adult stuff. Whatever that is. You know, like you see on TV. There may or may not also be unicorns.]

THE AUDIENCE: Wait . . . what?

[TIMMY is only slightly bruised from tree.]

LEX: Aw, damn.

[After stowing LEX in a convenient drainpipe, GRANT begins the long climb upwards.]

GRANT: I hate climbing . . . I hate trees . . . I hate kids . . . Oh, hi, Tim!

TIM: I threw up.

GRANT: I hate that, too. I mean . . . uh . . . that's cool?

TIM: I hate trees.

GRANT: Hey, maybe we do have something in common. Come on, let's get down now.

TIM: I can't do this. I want to stay up here and be very, very small.

GRANT: Come on, you can do it! Didn't your dad ever build you a treehouse?

TIM: No, my dad hates us.

GRANT: Oh.

Now with Bonus Freefall!

GRANT AND TIM: WAHHHHHHHHHHHHHHHH!

Ride #7: Tyrannosaurus Race!

ELLIE: In my forensic paleontological opinion, bad shit went down here. Also, Gennaro apparently ran away and got smeared for his trouble.

MULDOON [*disgusted*]: He was not worthy of the wearing of shorts.

[They manage to find a slightly mangled MALCOLM in the port-a-potty wreckage . . . but no one else, even after they climb down over the wall and find the wrecked Kiddie Car.]

ELLIE: Their mangled bodies aren't here! How are they going to survive at large in the park?

MULDOON: Well, I mean, the kids are conveniently with the one man on this entire island who knows everything there is to know about dinosaurs.

ELLIE: But he's also the one man who hates kids!

MULDOON: I'm sure he'll figure out some thematically appropriate way to resolve that.

PUDDLES: *vibrate*

MALCOLM: CAN WE LET HIM RESOLVE IT LATER?

ELLIE: But according to your chaos theory, there are a million different things that could happen—

MALCOLM: NO, I'M PRETTY SURE THAT A KID-HATING GUY STUCK WITH KIDS IN A MOVIE IS GONNA FIND A WAY TO WORK IT OUT. CHOP CHOP!

Ride #8: The Observation Tower!

TIM: I hate trees!

LEX: I hate monsters!

GRANT: Look, I hate KIDS, so *suck it up*.

[They settle down – or up – in a tree in brachiosaur country for the night.]

GRANT: Listen! They're singing!

TIM: Singing what?

GRANT: 'Some Enchanted Evening', it sounds like.

LEX: Is this going to be our song, Dr Grant?

GRANT: . . . No.

Ride #9: The Gift Shop!

Please remember to buy these fine 'Jurassic Park' products before you leave the shopping centre in which your theatre is situated. Free lunchbox with your fifth plushiesaurus!

HAMMOND: Any news?

ELLIE: Malcolm's kind of chewed up, but he's tripping the light fantastic now. Your grandkids are still missing, your lawyer is a bloody smear and I may never get to make baby Grants now. How about over here?

HAMMOND: My ice cream is melting.

ELLIE: . . .

HAMMOND: You know, the first park I ever built was a motorized flea circus, full of invisible trapeze fleas and seesaw fleas and acrobat fleas and carny fleas. Ever since, it's been my dream to build a flea circus that was *real*.

ELLIE: Okay, John? The difference here? Is that now you have giant two-ton fleas *that eat people*.

HAMMOND: You scientific types can't ever think positive, can you?

Ride #10: Hall of Plot Points!

LEX: AHHH MONSTER HELP!

TIM: It's okay, Lex! It's a veggiesaur!

LEX: Like me? Wow!

TIM: No, you're a loser.

GRANT: Did you know that dinosaurs can get colds?

BRACHIOSAUR: ACHOOOOOOOOOOOOOOOOOOOOOOOO!

LEX [*dripping*]: . . . Yes.

TIM: Great! Now she'll never leave her room again and try anything new!

GRANT: Tim? What does that have to do with anything? I mean, quite frankly, after this trip, *I'm* never leaving *my* room again.

TIM: It was . . . I just . . . to get across the point that she's a computer dork?

GRANT: Oh.

LEX: *Hacker!*

TIM: No, you're a *loser*, and nothing will change my tiny mind on this point, not even a heroic use of your l33t h4x0r skillz in the third act.

GRANT: Look! Dinosaur eggs!

INSIDE GRANT'S HEAD: *We used summa that there am-phi-bean frawg DNA! Am-phi-bean! FRAAAAAAAAWG! D-N-A! Problem-solving strange attractors! THAT'S CHAOS THEORY!*

GRANT: Man, I could use a drink right now.

The Control Room

For reasons best known to ELLIE, she is treating MALCOLM'S mangled leg by making him lounge around bare-chested.

HAMMOND: We have to shut down the system entirely to reboot it!

RAY [*stubbing out cigarette*]: BITCH, YOU CRAZY.

MALCOLM: Well, you could always upload a virus into the system and give it a cold and—

EVERYONE: NO.

MULDOON: What about that thing with the lysine?

ELLIE: Say what?

RAY: Yeah, yeah, we don't give 'em their lysine kibble, they die. Faulty genes, can't leave the island, blah blah blah. And that's great and all, but it's kind of moot because the lysine-kibble distribution runs on the same programs that Nedry hacked, so . . .

HAMMOND: MY BILLION-DOLLAR DINOSAURS – I mean, uh, my friends and family – WILL DIE!

RAY: Well, I don't have a better idea, so . . . whatever.

[RAY turns off the power and tries to reboot the system. It works. Kind of.]

ELLIE: Everything's still off.

MALCOLM: That's c—

HAMMOND: DON'T EVEN SAY IT.

RAY: Look, I'll just mosey on down to the maintenance shed conveniently located at the other end of the world and flip the breakers. Strap a carton of Marlboros to my back and let's go.

Ride #11: Gallimimus Rumble!

LEX: I'm hot . . .

TIM: I'm dirty . . .

LEX: I'm tired . . .

TIM: I'm hungry . . .

LEX: I love you . . .

GRANT: LOOK, DINOSAURS.

   [A herd of galliwhointhewhatsis thunder past.]

GRANT: Wow! Just like a flock of birds evading a predator! I wonder why they would do that!

T-REX: ROOOAAAARRRRR! *CHOMP*

GRANT: RUN!

The Emergency Bunker

ELLIE: Something has happened, and that something is WRONG and BAD.

HAMMOND: Oh, stop your bellyaching! Nothing went right when Disneyland opened!

MALCOLM: Okay, see, there's 'nothing going right' and there's 'tourists being eaten'. You don't exactly get that on Pirates of the Caribbean!

DISNEY EXECUTIVES: *hide plans for new *Pirates of the Caribbean: Dead Man's Chest* ride*

THE NATIVES OF BATAKA: HEY!

ELLIE: No, I mean that Mr Arnold hasn't come back yet, and he left *three hours* ago!

HAMMOND: Oh. Well, then . . . yes, someone should go look into that.

MULDOON: Come on, Ellie. It's up to us as comrades-in-shorts.

HAMMOND: It ought to be me going!

ELLIE: Why? Because it's your grandkids? Because it's your park? Because it's your fault?

HAMMOND: No, because I have a . . . and you *don't* have a . . .

ELLIE: OH, WHATEVER, OLD MAN.

MULDOON: Come! The Fellowship of Shorts must go.

Ride #12: Maintenance Shed Run!

MULDOON: And in our attempts to get the park back online, we did the one thing Nedry could not.

ELLIE: Which was . . . ?

MULDOON: Be stupid enough to turn the raptor fences off. RUN!

[ELLIE turns . . . and promptly trips over a log and falls on her face. It's all part of the fun here at Jurassic Park.]

Ride #13: The Tingler!

The electric perimeter fence appears to be off, so GRANT lays hands on it – and is promptly fried, violently, to death. The CHILDREN are eaten by the nearby T-REX and HAMMOND dies, a lonely alcoholic, blaming himself for the deaths of his grandchildren.

GRANT: HA HA!

LEX: Dr Grant? I am totally breaking up with you.

[Back in the bunker, HAMMOND and MALCOLM are consulting building plans to tell ELLIE where to go to turn the power back on. Meanwhile, GRANT and the KIDS are scrambling to climb the fence.]

GRANT: Take it easy – it's not a race. It's not like Ellie's going to magically turn the fence back on and fry the loser. I mean, Ellie doesn't even know how to turn the power on.

HAMMOND [*on radio to Ellie*]: . . . and so, if you flip these switches and push these buttons, that will turn the power back on.

THE FENCE: WHOOP WHOOP WHOOP WHOOP!

HAMMOND: All right, Ellie – you have to turn each park system on individually, for maximum suspense.

ELLIE: Here we go!

VISITORS' CENTRE: *is on*

GRANT: JUMP, TIM!

TIM: No!

HERBIVORE FEEDING COMPOUND: *is on*

GRANT: JUMP, TIM!

TIM: No!

MEATOSAUR FEEDING COMPOUND: *is on*

GRANT: JUMP, TIM!

TIM: No!

VELOCIRAPTOR FENCE: *is on*

GRANT: JUMP, TIM!

TIM: No!

T-REX FENCE: *is on*

GRANT: JUMP, TIM!

TIM: No!

CONTROL ROOM: *is on*

VISITORS' TOUR: *is on*

EMBRYO COLD STORAGE: *is on*

VENDING-MACHINE MATRIX: *is on*

ICE-CREAM GENERATOR: *is on*

ELLIE: Wow, you guys sure do have a lot of systems.

GRANT: JUMP, TIM!

TIM: Well . . . okay.

WARNING LABEL: Please Confirm That No Small Children Are Dangling From Perimeter Before Turning On Fence.

ELLIE: Man, they've got warning labels for everything these days.

PERIMETER FENCE: *is on*

TIM: *is fried*

LEX: WAHHHHHHHHHHHHHH!

  [Back in the maintenance shed:]

ELLIE: Huh, what's 'Raptor Jump-Scare'?

RAPTOR JUMP-SCARE: *is on*

RAPTOR: EEEEEEEEEEEH!

ELLIE: AHHHHHHHHHHHHHHHHH!

[Suddenly RAY'S arm, still holding a lit cigarette, falls out of nowhere onto ELLIE'S shoulder.]

ELLIE: AHHHHHHHHHHHHHHHHHHHHHHHHHHH!

MALCOLM [on radio]: . . . and that's chaos theory!

Ride #14: Raptor Hunt!

Waiting for ELLIE to return, MULDOON plays cat and mouse with a hiding RAPTOR.

MULDOON: . . . And I have so much respect for raptor intelligence that I actually believe putting my hat on a log will fool you.

RAPTOR #2: *chews on his head*

MULDOON: Oh, *damn*.

The Visitors' Centre

GRANT has successfully revived TIM, because if you thought the cute kid was going to bite it in a Spielberg blockbuster, you need to go back to movie school. Finally they reach the Visitors' Centre, where TIMMY 2: ELECTRIC BOOGALOO wobbles over to the buffet and starts two-fisting desserts while GRANT goes to find help.

GRANT: Ellie?

  [ELLIE magically appears limping from the maintenance shed and flings herself at him.]

ELLIE: I LOVE YOU.

GRANT: OH GOD, NOT YOU TOO.

The Emergency Bunker

GRANT: So we're thinking we have time to swing by and pick up some weapons before the kids get eaten.

ELLIE: Yeah, unless the raptors figure out how to open doors.

EVERYONE: AHAHAHAHAHAHAHA!

Ride #15: Hall of Mirrors!

RAPTOR OF IRONY: *opens door*

[The KIDS have made a run for it to the kitchen, where terror has magically combed TIM'S electric hair. The RAPTOR barks for a SECOND RAPTOR, who sidles in with *To Serve Man* in one claw. While the RAPTORS argue over slow-roasting the KIDS or doing a nice fricassee, the KIDS scramble. LEX'S raptor-avoidance strategy seems to involve gasping really loudly every time one gets close. After knocking over tons of spoons and pans, the KIDS find hiding places: a cupboard for LEX –]

LEX: AHHH! IT WON'T CLOSE!

[– and a storage closet for TIM:]

TIM: Hey, it's cold in here, and – there's a lamppost?

SOME FAUN [*slamming door*]: Get your own!

[The KIDS are saved by the fact that the RAPTORS can't quite hack (1) the concept of reflections and (2) icy floors, and run screaming from the room into the arms of ELLIE and GRANT.]

LEX: MY HERO!

GRANT: *eyeroll*

The Control Room

ELLIE: We have to reboot the system before we can call for help! Unfortunately, I'm just a botanist who can barely understand the concept of 'chaos'—

GRANT: And we've got a raptor at the door!

ELLIE: I'm coming to help you hold the door!

GRANT: But who will reboot the door locks? WHO, I ASK YOU??

LEX'S SHINING MOMENT: *arrives*

LEX: Hey! I can totally manoeuvre this system you call 'Unix', because I am a 'hacker'!

GRANT: We need more weight against the door! Approximately that of a small boy!

ELLIE: I can't reach the gun! Oh, if only there was a fourth person in the room who could help us!

TIM'S SHINING MOMENT: . . .

TIM: Come on, Lex! My chair-pounding should make you hack faster!

LEX: Door locks are go!

GRANT: My hero!

LEX: Dr Gr—

GRANT: Don't push it.

The Emergency Bunker

HAMMOND [*on phone*]: Grant! Is that you? Do the phones work? How are my grandchildren?!

GRANT [*on phone in Control Room*]: We found a few scattered toes.

HAMMOND: WAHHHHHH!

GRANT: I'm kidding! Lex is crusty with veggiesaur snot and Tim's ear is melted to his head, but other than that, they're fine. But Ellie and I are totally holding them here for ransom until you get us a damn helicopter. NOW.

ELLIE [*in background*]: *They're coming through the window!*

HAMMOND: WAHHHHHHHHHHHHHHH!

Ride #16: Escape from Meatosaur Island!

Now there are two RAPTORS, so GRANT, ELLIE and the KIDS climb up into the ceiling air ducts, which LEX'S stunt double LEX promptly falls out of, and GRANT has to haul her back up by the ass before the RAPTOR can snack on her feet.

LEX: *Dr Grant!*

GRANT: Lex, don't even START.

[They emerge in the Visitors' Centre, right on top of the Giant Dinosaur Skeletons of Irony, which they end up trying to climb down and destroying completely. Then, just as the two RAPTORS close in to eat everyone—]

T-REX: THAT WAS MY GRANDMAAAAAA! *CHOMP*

TIM: Didn't she spend half the movie trying to kill us?

GRANT: Tim? When a T-rex saves your ass, don't ask questions.

[GRANT, ELLIE and the KIDS book it on out of the Visitors' Centre to the road, where HAMMOND and MALCOLM-ON-A-STICK are waiting to pick them up. Back inside, the Gods of Irony drape a handsome WHEN DINOSAURS RULED THE EARTH banner over the conquering T-REX.]

The Helipad

GRANT: Okay, roll call! Malcolm?

MALCOLM: Somewhat gnawed, but still sexy.

GRANT: Nedry?

ELLIE: I saw a spittosaurus picking its teeth with a pocket protector. Make of that what you will.

GRANT: Gennaro?

ELLIE: Cowardly tyrannochow.

GRANT: Tim?

ELLIE: Slightly fried, but still truckin'.

GRANT: Lex?

LEX: I love you.

GRANT: Still? *Damn.* Muldoon?

ELLIE: Went down bravely, in a manner befitting the shorts.

GRANT: Ray?

ELLIE: *sob*

GRANT: Hammond?

HAMMOND: Not a scratch.

GRANT: Mmm-hmmm. That's about a sixty-per-cent survival rate, and that's not even including injuries. So . . . I'm thinking about writing a strongly worded letter to the Better Business Bureau, is what I'm saying.

HAMMOND: Sigh. Well, all my hopes and dreams are crushed, but I've got my grandkids, so I'll be fine.

THE KIDS: *snuggle against Grant*

HAMMOND: You are a merciless, merciless man, Dr Grant.

GRANT: Look, you can have 'em. I got kids of my own to make.

ELLIE: Awwwwww *yeah*.

FIN.

BRAVEHEART (1995)

Beautiful Scotland

Scotland: full of misty green hills and valleys, craggy peaks and rolling rivers, Scotland is so picturesque and visually pleasing that you will be able to watch its landscapes for hours on end. Three, to be exact. The next time *you* are planning to shoot your own big-budget historical Oscar-bait epic, please think of lovely, inexpensive Scotland for all of your slo-mo, time-killing scenery needs. Scotland: cheap and beautiful, like your slutty best friend after a round of free drinks. In conclusion: Scotland.

Formative Moments in the Childhood of William Wallace

YOUNG WILLIAM: Daaaaad, I wanna go to the gathering!

MALCOLM WALLACE: GET BACK TO YOUR CHORES OR I'LL TEACH YOU NEW LESSONS IN PAIN!

YOUNG WILLIAM: Jeez, Dad.

MALCOLM WALLACE: I HEARD THAT.

A Gathering Goes Awry

MALCOLM WALLACE: Aw, hell, they're all dead.

JOHN WALLACE: *Again?*

[YOUNG WILLIAM has sneaked after his father and brother anyway, only to discover a house full of hanging Scotsmen. He starts shrieking his fool head off and totally gives himself away. His father tries to grab him, but rather than run out the door through which he came in, WILLIAM starts running through the dead bodies, flailing like a muppet the whole way.]

MALCOLM WALLACE: Son! Son! It's all right – it's all right!

JOHN WALLACE: If by 'all right' you mean 'totally not, because everyone's dead'.

MALCOLM WALLACE: John? You're not helping.

The Wallace Homestead, Later That Night

MALCOLM WALLACE: . . . And so I say we fight!

MacCLANNOUGH, DAD OF MURRON: . . . And I say they'll pound our kilted asses into the ground.

MALCOLM WALLACE: Yes, but it's the *fighting* that's important.

EVERYONE ELSE: Suicide? YAY!

The Wallace Homestead, the Next Day

MALCOLM WALLACE: So, William, your brother and I are going to another gathering.

YOUNG WILLIAM: . . . You mean, like the one where everyone died?

MALCOLM WALLACE: Uh . . . no. This time we're actually going to fight before they kill us.

YOUNG WILLIAM: Oh. I can fight!

MALCOLM WALLACE: I know. But it's our wits that make us men. You know, mental faculties? Critical-thinking skills? Ability to plan ahead and learn from your mistakes? That kind of thing.

YOUNG WILLIAM: So. . . you're going to do exactly the same thing that got everyone else killed.

MALCOLM WALLACE: William? This is the last time I'm ever going to see you, and I really don't want to backhand you again.

William and Hamish Are Best Friends 4Evah

YOUNG WILLIAM: I LIKE ROCKS!

YOUNG HAMISH: WHEE!

The Men Return

OLD CAMPBELL, DAD OF HAMISH: Well, it's a good thing we dug some graves before we left.

MURRON'S DAD: Yeah . . . sorry about that.

YOUNG WILLIAM: *tear*

The Wallaces' Funeral

YOUNG MURRON: William? I . . . I plucked up all my courage to brave your cooties and the possible disapproval of my family so I could bring you this thematically important thistle.

YOUNG WILLIAM: Yeah? Well, my *entire family* is still dead.

YOUNG MURRON: *runs away crying*

SOME ONE-EYED GUY: *smacks William upside the head*

WILLIAM: OW! Who are you?

SOME ONE-EYED GUY: I'm your Uncle Argyle. You know, like the sock.

YOUNG WILLIAM: The English won't let us have socks.

UNCLE ARGYLE: Son, I am going to expand your horizons. I'm going to teach you to read *and* speechify in fifteen different languages. I'm going to take you on a pilgrimage to Rome so that you can see the world. And then I'm going to teach you to be the greatest warrior this land has ever seen.

YOUNG WILLIAM: Will you teach me basic hygiene, such as how to brush my hair or, you know, bathe?

UNCLE ARGYLE: Shpffff, we won't have time for *that*.

Later That Night

YOUNG WILLIAM wakes up from a bad dream about his dead father ('Your heart is free . . . but your body is apparently underground in my grave. Sorry about that') to find a group of men gathered around his father and brother's graves playing bagpipes by torchlight.

UNCLE ARGYLE: They're saying goodbye in the traditional Scottish way, which has been outlawed by the English.

YOUNG WILLIAM: Maybe they outlawed it because it sounds like dying cats.

UNCLE ARGYLE: *smacks William upside the head*

Le mariage royale de la princesse Isabelle et le prince Edward

LONGSHANKS: Hey, Isabelle, you sure look hot for a little kid.

ISABELLE: Well, I heard there would be sexing, so I went ahead and grew up.

PRIEST: You may now kiss the bride.

PRINCE EDWARD: Ewwwwwww, *girls*!

ISABELLE: WHAT? I WAS PROMISED SEXING!

LONGSHANKS [*leering*]: Oh, that can be arranged.

ISABELLE: *L'EW!*

Longshanks Hatches a Plan

Many scholars will tell you that relationships between men were not stigmatized in the past the way that they are today. In fact,

Renaissance playwright Christopher Marlowe's play *Edward the Second* makes clear the idea that the nobles resented Edward II's relationship with a male favourite not because it was 'homosexual', but because Edward lavished land and titles on the favourite – a commoner – that the nobles believed should have been theirs. In short, this film's portrayal of royal homophobia, in particular that of Longshanks (King Edward I), is not just incorrect; it's anachronistic.

LONGSHANKS: WHERE'S PRINCESS PANSY GONE NOW?

ISABELLE: He sent me in his place, my lord.

LONGSHANKS: Son of a . . . FINE. WHATEVER.

SOME LORD: So . . . what are we going to do about Scotland?

LONGSHANKS: Well, I figure we'll give first sexing rights to you English lords, and I know what dogs you all are, so you'll probably rush over to Scotland in a mass exodus and hop to it. *Voilà*, no new Scots.

SOME LORD: Ah, yes, *prima noctes* – 'First night', a lord's right to sleep with a new commoner bride before her rightful husband does.

SOME OTHER LORD: Thank you for explaining a concept with which we are already familiar, man.

LONGSHANKS [*leering*]: It's too bad you've already had *your* wedding night, Princess.

ISABELLE: Yeah, you'd think so, wouldn't you?

Council of Scottish Nobles, Edinburgh

ROBERT THE BRUCE meets the LORDS CRAIG and MORNAY wearing the pelt of Snuffleupagus.

ROBERT THE BRUCE: So I hear Longshanks gave the English lords *prima noctes*.

LORD CRAIG: Yeah, sucks for the plebes. How's your dad?

ROBERT THE BRUCE: Totally in France, and not rotting away from leprosy in that tower up there.

LORD CRAIG: Good to hear it, man.

The Wallace Homestead

WALLACE: Ach, so good to be back. Unfortunately, my house is completely in ruins. How could this have happened? I mean, I only left it to rot for twenty years!

Ye Olde Renaissance Faire

Ragged peasants wander around gnawing on turkey legs and dancing around maypoles and doing authentic medieval activities like throwing large rocks. Everyone's wearing their best garb for the day's centrepiece – a real live wedding!

FATHER OF THE BRIDE: Hey, get those vampires outta here!

OLD CAMPBELL [*kicking out Goth posers*]: JUST BECAUSE IT LOOKS MEDIEVAL DOESN'T MEAN IT IS!

HAMISH: BIG ROCKS ARE AWESOME!

WALLACE: NUH-UH, SMALL ROCKS RULE!

HAMISH: OW!

WALLACE: WHEE!

MURRON [*to* FRIEND]: Ooo, who's that hottie with the rocks?

MURRON'S DAD [*to* BRIDEGROOM]: Hey, you heard about that whole 'first night' thing, right?

MORRISON THE BRIDEGROOM: What?

MURRON'S DAD: Yeah . . . here comes Lord Rapington. I'll let *him* tell you about it.

The MacClannough Homestead, The Next Day

WALLACE rides up in the pouring rain to ask MURRON out on a date.

WALLACE: Murron, can you go for a ride?

MURRON: I don't know . . . it's kind of nasty wet out and stuff . . .

MURRON'S DAD: NO WAY IN HELL IS SHE GOING OUT IN THIS WEATHER!

MURRON: . . . I would *love* to go!

MURRON'S DAD [*shaking fist*]: Hey! HEY! YOU COME BACK HERE! DAMN THIRTY-YEAR-OLD KIDS!

Secret Dating Glade

WALLACE takes MURRON to a beautiful sunset forest glade where the weather is fine, their clothes are dry and their freshly blow-dried hair ripples in the breeze.

WALLACE: So, I can read and I can speak fifteen languages and I've seen Rome.

MURRON: I'm . . . happy for you?

WALLACE: So . . . how'd you recognize me?

MURRON: I didn't. I just saw you staring at me at the wedding. Who are you, again?

The MacClannough Homestead

WALLACE brings her back home to the rain and the wet hair and the damp clothes.

WALLACE: . . .

MURRON: . . .

WALLACE: . . .

MURRON: . . .

MURRON'S MOM [*from inside hut*]: Murron, you come in now! The weather forecast says there's an eighty-five-per-cent chance of kissing out there!

WALLACE: . . .

MURRON: . . .

WALLACE: Oh, by the way, here's a twenty-year-old thistle.

MURRON: Okay, you're getting warmer, but 'kiss' only has one syllable, and it starts with a 'k' . . .

WALLACE: *rides off*

MURRON: . . .

MURRON: . . .

MURRON: OMG THISTLE.

The Wallace Homestead

WALLACE is rethatching his brokedown, busted-ass cottage when OLD CAMPBELL and MURRON'S DAD ride over.

WALLACE: Uh, about the other night, and the riding, and the whole Murron thing, and . . . please don't hurt me?

OLD CAMPBELL: Oh, whatever. We're here about the secret rebel meeting, young Wallace!

WALLACE: What meeting?

OLD CAMPBELL: Well, that's why it's a *secret*. Duh!

WALLACE: Well, I'm not coming. I just wanna be peaceful and grow my crops and be mellow, dude.

OLD CAMPBELL: You're a damned dirty hippie, young Wallace!

WALLACE: HEY! I'm not any dirtier than you are!

MURRON'S DAD: Look, if you can prove that you're just a peace-loving hippie, you can go out with my daughter.

WALLACE: But I just said I wasn't going to the secret rebel

meeting . . . doesn't that prove it?

MURRON'S DAD: No!

WALLACE: No?

MURRON'S DAD: No!

WALLACE: No?

MURRON'S DAD: No!

WALLACE: No?

MURRON'S DAD: No!

WALLACE: No?

MURRON'S DAD: No!

WALLACE: No?

MURRON'S DAD: No!

WALLACE: DUDE! THIS IS NOT MELLOW!

Secret Dating Glade

WALLACE: So, basically, I'm a dirty peace-loving hippie farmer who just wants to be mellow. Unfortunately, farm work is not mellow. But it'll be more mellow after my sons get here.

MURRON: Oh, shit, you have kids?

WALLACE: Well, no, but I was hoping you'd pump out a litter for me.

MURRON: Man, you didn't learn manners in any language, did you?

WALLACE: Oh, come on. I love you and I kept your thistle all these years and I want you to have my babies.

MURRON: . . .

WALLACE: *snog*

MURRON: So . . . when do we get started?

Secret Wedding Glade

MURRON sneaks out to meet WALLACE in her best nuptial pillowcase. They exchange rags as the priest recites the vows.

MURRON: I will love you and no other, for ever.

WALLACE: I will love *you* and no other . . . well, I mean, there are exceptions, right? I have my list right here . . .

PRIEST: AHEM.

WALLACE: . . . and no other, for ever.

PRIEST: You may now sex the bride.

WALLACE: YAY!

Market Day in the Village

SERGEANT PIGSTY: Hey, baby! I'd like to carry *your* cabbages, baby!

MURRON: That . . . that doesn't even make any sense.

LIEUTENANT PIGSTY: Hey, baby, you look so fine, baby!

MURRON: Ew!

SERGEANT PIGSTY: Hey, you remind me of my daughter, baby!

MURRON: EW!

  [SERGEANT PIGSTY and his men chase MURRON and corner her behind a hut, where SERGEANT PIGSTY proceeds to assault her.]

MURRON: Ew, dude, did you just LICK ME? FOR REAL?

  [Faced with no other options, MURRON Lecterizes the guy's face until WALLACE can get there and beat the soldiers off.]

WALLACE: Here! Ride off by yourself! I'm sure you'll be able to defend yourself if they catch up to you!

  [Unfortunately, MURRON has ended up with the one horse on the planet that can't outrun four flabby guys.]

The Village Square

While WALLACE is off playing soldier dress-up in the Secret Dating Glade, the English soldiers are tying MURRON to the Oppression Stake.

MURRON: William! Help!

THE MAGISTRATE: You know, I've *tried* to oppress you lot as fairly as possible.

MURRON: William . . . ? William . . . ?

THE MAGISTRATE: We only flog you every *other* day now; you get to keep *three-quarters* of the crops you grow; and we only make off with your wives on wedding nights and anniversaries.

SOLDIER: And birthdays.

THE MAGISTRATE: Yes, and birthdays. But do you *appreciate* this? Do you see all the *sacrifices* we've made for you? Can't we all just *get along*? Well, it looks like not. Biting one of the king's rapists is the same as biting the king himself, so [*pulling out Dagger of Throat-Cutting*] I'm sorry, but it's just got to be done.

SERGEANT PIGSTY: *tear*

MURRON: Oh, *whatever*.

[WALLACE does not make it back in time. Woe.]

Half an Hour Later

SOLDIER: Look, it's Wallace!

THE MAGISTRATE: Bring him to me so that I may righteously kill him! By which I mean 'make the rest of you do it for me'.

WALLACE'S HORSE: *steps forward*

WALLACE: *holds his hands up*

SOLDIER: So I'm gonna come closer, okay?

WALLACE'S HORSE: *steps forward*

WALLACE: *holds his hands up*

SOLDIER: I'm gonna take hold of your bridle.

WALLACE'S HORSE: *steps forward*

WALLACE: *holds his hands up*

SOLDIER: We're going to arrest you, you realize that, right?

WALLACE'S HORSE: *steps forward*

WALLACE: *holds his hands up*

SOLDIER: You're totally going to be executed and stuff, okay?

WALLACE'S HORSE: *steps forward*

WALLACE: *holds his hands up*

SOLDIER: Okay, have it your w—

WALLACE: *HIGHLAND FLAIL!*

[WALLACE pulls a flail out of his hair and initiates a village-wide English-soldier beatdown. Then he pulls a sledgehammer, three axes, two clubs, a scythe and forty-two knives out of his hair and arms the populace. MORRISON and the CAMPBELLS go to town breaking heads and severing limbs until nothing is left but a fine mist of soldier gristle.]

THE MAGISTRATE: Ohhhhhh *shit*.

ONE LAST SOLDIER: I'll protect you, my lord!

WALLACE: WHERE'S THE MAGISTRATE?

ONE LAST SOLDIER: Rightherehesallyourspleasedonthurtme.

THE MAGISTRATE: ASS!

[WALLACE approaches with righteous vengeance in his eyes.]

THE MAGISTRATE: So . . . should I just tie myself to the Oppression Stake?

WALLACE: Yeah, that'd save us some time, if you don't mind.

[WALLACE cuts the MAGISTRATE'S throat, leaves him in the mud and goes to brood on a nearby Hillside of Woe. The VILLAGERS are left staring.]

OLD CAMPBELL: MacAulish. MacAulish! MACAULISH! MACAULISH!

VILLAGERS: MACAULISH!! MACAULISH!!

HAMISH: Dad? Who's MacAulish?

OLD CAMPBELL: . . .

VILLAGERS: . . .

CAMPBELL: WALLACE! WALLACE!

VILLAGERS: WALLACE!! WALLACE!!

Murron's Funeral

MURRON'S MOM: WAAAAAAA!

MURRON'S DAD: Give me one good reason not to pound you into the dirt.

WALLACE: I loved your daughter –

MURRON'S MOM: WAAAAAAA!

WALLACE: – as evidenced by this mysterious rag I place on her body –

MURRON'S MOM: WAAAAAAA!

WALLACE: – and I avenged her d—

MURRON'S MOM: WAAAAAAA!

WALLACE: WOMAN, COULD YOU PIPE DOWN A MOMENT?

MURRON'S DAD: Man, I have wanted to tell her that for *years*. You're okay by me, son.

The Village, Night

Despite the fact that the VILLAGERS have taken time to prepare MURRON'S body and have a touching burial service, OLD CAMPBELL'S wounds have apparently not been tended until now. In the middle

41

of this, the MACGREGOR clan troops in.

OLD CAMPBELL: AHHHHHHHHH!

SOME MACGREGOR: The hell was that?

WALLACE: Oh, that's just Old Campbell, getting a wound cauterized with hot pokers and whisky.

SOME MACGREGOR: Anyway, we came because we heard that shit was going down, and there's no way in hell you're having fun without us.

WALLACE: FUN? YOU CALL THIS FUN? MY SECRET WIFE JUST GOT KILLED!

MURRON'S DAD: Wait, what?

WALLACE: Nothing! I mean – my secret fife! It just got billed!

MURRON'S DAD: Aw, that's a shame.

OLD CAMPBELL: AHHHHHHHHH!

SOME MACGREGOR: What, are they still cauterizing the guy?

WALLACE: Nah, that's Old Campbell finding out that that was the *last* of the whisky.

Lord Rapington's English Garrison

SOLDIER: The patrol's come back!

LORD RAPINGTON: So, what's new in the world of oppressing the hoi polloi?

[The leader of the patrol strides up and rips off his helmet and it's WALLACE. All the other patrol soldiers reveal themselves to be pissy Scots as well.]

WALLACE: He's all yours, Morrison.

MORRISON: I've got a big spiky ball of pain that's just *dying* to have a talk with you—

LORD RAPINGTON: AHHH! NO! HELP! I never hurt her! I just violated your bride's sacred wedding vows and took her virginity and . . . wait, can I start over?

MORRISON: *HIGHLAND FLAIL!*

WALLACE: The rest of you assholes can go back to England, and you tell your king that Scotland is free because we routed a single garrison. That'll show them *for sure.*

Prissypants Indoor Archery Open

PRINCE EDWARD and his 'stylist' PHILIP are shooting at a straw target for the amusement of the court. PRINCESS ISABELLE, wearing a lovely blue kirtle, is relegated to a corner with her handmaiden SLUTTANY, the Countess of Booty.

LONGSHANKS: Pop quiz, Miss Thing: a lord's been murdered and a garrison's been stomped by a Scottish rebel. WHAT DO YOU DO?

PRINCE EDWARD: I would have the magistrate put him in a corner and tell him to think very very hard about all the bad things he's done.

LONGSHANKS [*glancing at assembled company*]: Could I abuse my son in private, please?

SLUTTANY [*to* ISABELLE:] Oh, this is gonna be good.

THE COURT: *flees*

LONGSHANKS [*pimpslapping son*]: THE MAGISTRATE IS DEAD!

PRINCE EDWARD: *emits tiny girly shriek*

LONGSHANKS: LOOK HERE, YOU. I am going to FRANCE. You are going to SCOTLAND, and you are going to SACK UP, and you are going to take this rebel DOWN. AM I UNDERSTOOD?

PRINCE EDWARD: *snivels*

ISABELLE: Oh, Edward, I am so sorry!

PRINCE EDWARD: EW COOTIES GET AWAY! Philip! Convene my military fashion council!

ISABELLE: *cries*

SLUTTANY [*sotto voce*]: I hope that your husband runs into the Scottish rebel, and that the Scottish rebel *stomps* him.

ISABELLE: But then I'll *never* get laid! If Edward lives, there's at least a *chance* that his father might beat the straight back into him!

SLUTTANY: Oh, *chérie*. You're going to be the Queen of England, not the Nile.

Scenes of General English Burnination

SCOTTISH VILLAGER: And our Trogdor coverage just! ran! out!

SCOTTISH VILLAGER ON FIRE: Woe!

Chez Bruce

LEPER THE BRUCE: So, in conclusion, you support the rebellion and I'll condemn it. You can have all the crush on Wallace that you want, but in the end, he's going to be dead and you're going to be the one on the throne. You and me, we'll both come out smelling like roses.

ROBERT THE BRUCE: Well, not 'roses', exactly, Dad . . .

LEPER THE BRUCE: Hey, could you hand me my ear? I think it just fell off.

Scenes of General Scottish Burnination

SCOTTISH AUDIENCE: People are on fire, but that's okay, because we don't like the English!

AMERICAN AUDIENCE: Who's burning who, again?

ENGLISH AUDIENCE: Wait, I put down a fiver to see *this*?

PRINCE EDWARD: Philip, are we offensively limp-wristed enough yet?

PHILIP: Girl, *please*. We definitely need to check our threads.

PRINCE EDWARD: *Garçon!* Bring us a primitive mirror!

[Meanwhile, poor neglected ISABELLE strolls with her handmaiden.]

SLUTTANY: So, I got the scoop on Scotland.

ISABELLE: Really? How'd you manage that?

SLUTTANY [*smirking*]: Slept with a member of the War Council.

ISABELLE: Wow, you actually found one that likes girls?

SLUTTANY: Well, it was hard, but – heh. 'Hard.'

ISABELLE: He shouldn't be spilling state secrets in bed!

SLUTTANY: Yeah, well, Englishmen don't know what you're *supposed* to do with tongues.

ISABELLE: *Le gasp! Le shock!*

SLUTTANY: Wow, you really aren't getting any, are you?

ISABELLE: What about Wallace, the Scottish rebel?

SLUTTANY: Oh! Yes! Him! Well, he's this Scottish rebel with animal tails in his hair and he never wears pants.

ISABELLE: Ooo.

SLUTTANY: So he had some secret bom-chicka-wow-wow, right? So the English cut the throat of his woman for all to see, so then he massacred dozens of soldiers with his *bare hands*, and then he dug up her grave and, still covered with the splattered brains of his enemies, reburied her mouldering body in a secret place!

ISABELLE: *Le sigh!* That is the most romantic thing I have ever heard!

SLUTTANY: Hon? That's just kind of sad.

ISABELLE: *le sob*

That Irish Guy Is Batshit Crazy

STEPHEN THE IRISH: Hi! I'm totally batshit crazy, can I fight with you?

WALLACE: Well, how crazy are we talking here?

STEPHEN THE IRISH: All of Ireland belongs to me, but I left and came here because the Lord Almighty told me that this new guy over here is going to try to kill you while you're out hunting.

NEW GUY: HEY!

WALLACE: Yeah . . . that's pretty batshit.

STEPHEN THE IRISH: So . . . do I get to kill Englishmen?

WALLACE: That's really all we're here to do, pretty much.

STEPHEN THE IRISH: *Righteous.*

The Battle of Stirling ~~Bridge~~

HAMISH: I thought this battle was supposed to be on a bridge.

WALLACE: Yes, well, that's what we *want* them to think.

HAMISH: O . . . kay.

MORRISON: What's with the Smurfy face paint, boss?

WALLACE: Guineveira and the Woadettes were having a garage sale.

MORRISON: Oh.

* * *

All the other Scots are lined up on the battlefield, just hanging out. Then the English troops arrive.

SOME GUY: So . . . that's a lot of soldiers with armour and helmets and shit.

SOME KID: Yeah . . . what are we fighting for, again?

SOME GUY: So Scottish lords can make us work on their lands instead of the English lords' lands.

SOME KID: Man, screw that.

SOME GUY: Dude, for real. ALL RIGHT, MEN, MOVE 'EM ON OUT!

WALLACE: No! Don't leave! I am William Wallace!

SOME KID: No you're not! William Wallace is—

WALLACE: I know, I know, he's ten feet tall and ruggedly handsome and slightly Australian and never runs out of bullets and rides around on flaming tanker trucks. I AM WILLIAM WALLACE!

EVERYONE: Ooooo.

WALLACE: You've come here to fight as free men!

SOME GUY: Well, actually, we came here to fight because the lords told us to—

WALLACE: But don't you want to fight, so you can be free in your hearts?

SOME GUY: Hell no! We'd rather run away and live!

WALLACE: Sure, you'll live for a while. And then you'll die old in your beds with your family all around you and you'll wish that you could come back here! You'll just wish you were back here with a sword in your hand and mud in your eyes and blisters on your feet so you could tell the English that they can never! take! away! YOUR FREEEEEEEEDOMMMMM!

SOME GUY: Well, actually, they can – clap some irons on, throw us in a dungeon . . . it's pretty easy, actually—

WALLACE: Hamish? Kill that guy.

HAMISH: *THUNK*

WALLACE: Let's try this one more time, all right? They can never! take! away! YOUR FREEEEEEEEDOMMMMM!

THE SCOTS: WOOOOOOOO!

WALLACE: STABNATION GU BRA!

THE SCOTS: RAAAAAAAAA!

* * *

LORD TALMADGE: So what happened?

CHELTHAM: Well, the lords rode up to negotiate, you know, like we were expecting, and then this cracked-out blue dude in a kilt rode up and insulted us with filthy uncouth profanities and said that if we didn't go back to England and apologize to every single Scot on the way back, he'd kill us all, even though he has no cavalry and his men are fighting with, like, sharp sticks and no armour.

LORD TALMADGE: AHAHAHAHAHAHAHAHA!

* * *

WALLACE: So when the fighting gets bad, you lords take all your men and make it look like you're running away.

LORD MORNAY: Yeah, I don't think that's gonna be too hard.

* * *

THE ENGLISH: . . .

THE SCOTS: . . .

THE ENGLISH: . . .

THE SCOTS: . . .

THE ENGLISH: . . .

THE SCOTS: RAAAAAAAAA!

THE ENGLISH: . . .

WALLACE: RELEASE THE NAKED BITS!

[All the SCOTS flash the ENGLISH with great enthusiasm.]

LORD TALMADGE: NOOOO! NOT BODY PARTS ALL OF US HAVE ANYWAY!

THE ENGLISH INFANTRY: *swoons*

WALLACE: UNLEASH THE BARE ASSES!

LORD TALMADGE: Okay, I've had just about enough of this. ARCHERS!

[Half the mooning SCOTS are shot in the ass, and manage to somehow be surprised by this.]

LORD TALMADGE: CAVALRY!

[The ENGLISH ride towards the SCOTS and the SCOTS just stand there.]

WALLACE: HOLD!

HORSES: *ride*

WALLACE: HOLD!

HORSES: *ride*

WALLACE: HOLD!

HORSES: *neigh*

WALLACE: HOOOOOOOOLD!

HORSES: *ride*

WALLACE: STABNATIOOOOOOON!

[The SCOTS pick up their giant tree-length spears, which they have cleverly been hiding on the ground right in front of them, in plain sight, and skewer all the horses.]

THE RSPCA: *dies*

LORD TALMADGE: INFANTRY!

THE ENGLISH: *charge*

THE SCOTS: *charge screaming*

[The two armies crash together in the middle of the battlefield. Arms and legs and heads and brains and jets of blood go flying. WALLACE breaks at least three guys' skulls like raw eggs, and just to make sure we understand how crazy STEPHEN THE IRISH is, he slashes some guy up the crotch. Then the SCOTTISH LORDS come back with their army and the ENGLISH run away shrieking like little girls.]

ENGLISH AUDIENCE: HEY!

SCOTTISH AUDIENCE: WOOOOOO!

AMERICAN AUDIENCE: MORE BRAINS PLEASE.

Council of Lords, Edinburgh

LORD CRAIG: I dub thee Sir William of Brainsmash. Please give these necklaces to your crazy, crazy friends as a token of our esteem.

EVERYONE: YAY!

ROBERT THE BRUCE: What side is Wallace on? What're his politics?

LORD CRAIG: Dude, that's the problem – he doesn't *have* any. 'Kill the English', that's about it.

BALLIOL: Sir William! Support my clan!

MORNAY: NO, MY CLAN!

BALLIOL: YOUR CLAN DROOLS, MY CLAN RULES!

WALLACE: Whatever, bitches. I'm taking over England. Peace out.

[Stunned, ROBERT THE BRUCE chases WALLACE and his posse outside.]

ROBERT THE BRUCE: Say *what*?

WALLACE: You heard me. I'ma go to England and kill them all there, and then they'll leave us alone.

ROBERT THE BRUCE: Scot, *please*. And don't piss off the nobles – you need them, or you'll end up dead with enemies on both sides.

WALLACE: Whatever. We all die. Besides, men don't follow lords, they follow scruffy warriors. Hell, if you would get off your ass and fight, I would follow *you*.

ROBERT THE BRUCE: Really?

WALLACE: Well . . . maybe if you ditched the muppet cloak.

The Battle of ~~Stirling~~ Bridge

THE DUKE OF YORK: OMG THE SCOTS ARE COMING!

THE PEASANTS OF YORK: RUN AWAY!

[WALLACE and the SCOTS form a turtle shell of shields around their battering ram, because apparently they, too, have seen all those movies about Roman warriors.]

THE DUKE OF YORK: Loose the mid-sized rocks!

SOME PEASANT OF YORK: They're not making a dent, my lord!

THE DUKE OF YORK: Fire a few half-hearted arrows!

SOME PEASANT OF YORK: Not really doing anything either, my lord!

THE DUKE OF YORK: Well, then – uh – RELEASE THE FLAMING TAR!

THE SCOTS: AUUUUGHHHHHHH!

WALLACE: You just HAD to have a battle on a bridge, didn't you?

HAMISH: Shut up, man.

Meanwhile, Back at the Palace

PRINCE EDWARD: I'm gonna stand up to him, Philip! I'm going to tell him what's what! My days of cowering are over! That's right! I'm going to— DADDY, HI.

LONGSHANKS: So, how's York? Not sacked or decimated or on fire or anything, I presume . . . ?

PRINCE EDWARD: Everything's just peachy, Dad! I ordered conscriptions to replace the troops that totally didn't just get stomped up north. Have I told you lately that I love you?

SOME MESSENGER: My lord, there is a message for you, and I would really like to set it down and flee for my life as soon as possible, if that's all right with you.

LONGSHANKS: Make it so.

PRINCE EDWARD [*reading letter*]: '. . . and then we dumped flaming tar on them but that only set the battering ram on *fire*, and then the *bridge* was on fire, and then the *castle* was on fire . . .' The writing gets kind of blurry here, I can't really— OH MY GOD THERE'S A SEVERED HEAD IN MY BASKET.

PHILIP: Thy own nephew, my lord! And we ordered that from the Fruit of the Month Club!

LONGSHANKS: THINE.

PHILIP: What?

LONGSHANKS: 'THINE own nephew', you HALFWIT. Who is this person who abuses the King's English thus, Edward?

PRINCE EDWARD: Philip is my chief counsellor and military stylist!

PHILIP: I am a master of the arts of love *and* war.

LONGSHANKS: . . .

Outside the Palace Window

PHILIP comes sailing out the window to his stylish death. The GUARDS look up; the GUARDS look down; the GUARDS run like hell.

Back Inside the Palace

PRINCE EDWARD: DADDY! NOOOOO!

[PRINCE EDWARD rushes at his father with a fashionable poniard and gets backhanded like whoa for his trouble. He falls on his ass with a shriek, revealing his princely red tights and black Mary Janes.]

LONGSHANKS: Nancy, put on some pants! *Damn.*

PRINCE EDWARD: *sobs*

LONGSHANKS: Well, this is a fine mess we're in. Someone's got to go out there and buy this heathen off before he burns down all of England, but [*hack hack, cough cough*] I'm exhausted from all my adorably homophobic exertions and the illness that will eventually kill me. Hmmm. Who do I send? Someone who actually has balls . . .

The English Arrive to Buy Wallace Off

ISABELLE: I am the Princess of Wales.

WALLACE: But you're French.

ISABELLE: And you're *Mel Gibson*. You wanna make something of it?

WALLACE: Touché.

[Hesitantly, WALLACE follows ISABELLE and her guards into the tent.]

SLUTTANY: Ooo, *girl*.

ISABELLE: Don't even start. [*To* WALLACE]: So, why are you so mean to us and stuff?

WALLACE: You were mean to us first!

ISABELLE: Nuh-uh!

LORD HAMILTON: Uh . . . about that . . .

ISABELLE: So . . . wait. Were we, Hamilton?

WALLACE: DUH.

LORD HAMILTON: Don't listen to him!

WALLACE: [*in Latin*]: I think she can listen to whoever she wants, Hamhock.

ISABELLE: Gasp!

WALLACE: [*in French*]: Oh, I've got more where that came from.

ISABELLE: *Le squee!*

WALLACE: [*in Spanish*]: And you can tell your king where to stick it, too.

ISABELLE: Eeeee!

WALLACE: [*in German*]: Where is the bathroom?

ISABELLE: What?

WALLACE [*in English*]: Look, I don't know a lot of German. My point is, your king's a jackwad and you know it.

[ISABELLE sends everyone else away.]

ISABELLE: Listen, you seem like a nice guy. Tell you what, I'll give you all this gold and lots of land and more titles than you can shake a stick at, and we can call it a day. Also, I'm sorry about your woman.

WALLACE: Wife, actually. I loved her, and I married her, and they killed her, and I killed them, and, basically, that's why York's a smoking crater right now. I don't know why I'm telling you this, except that you're kind of foxy, too.

ISABELLE: Could you excuse me a moment? I have some swooning to do.

Back at the Palace

ISABELLE reports for debriefing in a mustard-yellow kirtle, a purple surcote with an awful pattern and a clashing silver braid wrap. PHILIP THE STYLIST'S only been dead a week, and already the household is falling apart.

LONGSHANKS: Thanks for [*hack hack*] being our stooge, Izzy. Now they'll never see my [*cough cough*] vast armies coming!

ISABELLE: HEY!

Sluttany, Countess of Booty, Courier of Love

SLUTTANY: The princess asked me to ask you to ask Wallace if he likes her. Oh, and the English are on their way to surround Edinburgh.

HAMISH: OMG!

SLUTTANY: Hey, you're kinda cute.

HAMISH: *kicks dirt shyly*

WALLACE: HAMISH, COME ON! WE GOTTA GO!

On the Way to Edinburgh, That Irish Guy Is Still Crazy

STEPHEN THE IRISH: Whee!

Council of Scottish Nobles, Edinburgh

LORD MORNAY: Dude, we have to negotiate.

WALLACE: Don't you even want to try to fight?

LORD LOCHLAN: Not really, no.

WALLACE: Robert the Bruce! You're not lame like these fools! Unite us!

ROBERT THE BRUCE: . . .

WALLACE: UNITE US OR I STAB YOU.

ROBERT THE BRUCE: Okay!

The Battle of Falkirk

The KING and the mysterious MAN IN THE IRON PAIL MASK watch from a hill.

WALLACE: Deploy the fickle Irish!

THE FICKLE IRISH [defecting from English army]: Whassup, you guys?

STEPHEN THE IRISH: *beams crazily*

WALLACE: Activate the flaming tar!

ENGLISH CAVALRY: AHHHHHHHH!

WALLACE: Yeah, that's right! We took notes at York, bitches!

[The battle begins in earnest. WALLACE starts waving a flag to signal the SCOTTISH LORDS to bring in their troops. The SCOTTISH LORDS do not move.]

WALLACE: Hey, guys!

[The SCOTTISH LORDS ride away.]

WALLACE: Okay, guys, the whole 'pretending to flee' thing was just for Stirling! Guys . . . !

HAMISH: William? I don't think they're pretending.

[The KING's archers shoot everyone on both sides, but particularly WALLACE, MORRISON and this one kid who dies twice. OLD CAMPBELL gets chopped in the gut. Then the English reinforcements charge out, and the battle really starts to suck.]

Wallace Pursues the Retiring Victors

WALLACE: I KEEL YOU, LONGSHANKS!

THE MAN IN THE IRON PAIL MASK: I'll protect the king!

WALLACE: MY HORSE IS FAST!

THE MAN IN THE IRON PAIL MASK: My horse is armoured!

WALLACE'S HORSE: Dude, I'm not faster than *armour*, could we reconsider this . . . ?

WALLACE: MY SWORD IS LONG!

THE MAIN IN THE IRON PAIL MASK: My lance is longer!

WALLACE: MY RAGE IS MIGHTY!

THE MAN IN THE IRON PAIL MASK: Again, man: the armour.

[The two collide and WALLACE goes flying and lands on his kilted ass. When THE MAN IN THE IRON PAIL MASK leans over him, WALLACE rips off the Iron Pail Mask to reveal – ROBERT THE BRUCE, DUN DUN DUN.]

WALLACE: Adda . . .

ROBERT THE BRUCE: I'm sorry, Wallace! I had to do it!

WALLACE: . . . wibba . . .

ROBERT THE BRUCE: Get up! You've got to get up! They're coming for you!

WALLACE: *drools tragically*

ROBERT THE BRUCE: Help! Help! Someone get Wallace out of here!

[STEPHEN THE IRISH rides up at this moment to haul WALLACE'S stunned carcass out of there.]

STEPHEN THE IRISH: Hey, next time you're so worried about saving Wallace? TRY NOT TO BETRAY HIM IN THE FIRST PLACE, OKAY?

ROBERT THE BRUCE: SHUT UP, MAN!

Camp Kaput

MORRISON seems to have recovered from that arrow pretty well. STEPHEN THE IRISH gets everyone water. OLD CAMPBELL dies. HAMISH cries. WALLACE drools.

Bloody Muddy Battlefield of Woe and Weeping Women

ROBERT THE BRUCE: *cries*

Chez Bruce

ROBERT THE BRUCE: I am a liar and a traitor and I hate myself!

LEPER THE BRUCE: Oh, son, you and your silly 'ethics'.

ROBERT THE BRUCE: I HATE YOU AND THE ENGLISH AND I WILL NEVER FIGHT FOR ANYONE BUT THE DOWNTRODDEN SCOTTISH EVER AGAIN!

LEPER THE BRUCE: *makes 'whatever' fingers*

'WHATEVER' FINGERS: *fall off*

LEPER THE BRUCE: Hey . . . a little help here?

The Legend of William Wallace

LORD CRAIG [*stuffing face with mutton*]: And so you pissed Wallace off so bad that he's running around the countryside with nothing but a kilt and a dream, killing dozens of traitors with his bare hands. Hell, I think he killed Mornay in his *dreams*. You know, like that guy with the knives on his hands? I love that movie.

ROBERT THE BRUCE: AHHHHHH! SHUT UUUUUP!

> [And then LORD LOCHLAN falls from the rafters onto their dinner with his throat cut.]

ROBERT THE BRUCE: AHHHHHHHHHHHHHHHHHHHHHHHH-HH!!

Back at the Palace

LONGSHANKS: . . . so we'll send the princess and tell her she's on a peace mission, and that's how we'll trap Wallace.

LORD HAMILTON: What if she gets killed?

LONGSHANKS: Eh.

SLUTTANY, COUNTESS OF EAVESDROPPING: OMG!

The Princess's Hut of Faux Peace, Scotland

WALLACE ninjas on in without ISABELLE noticing.

WALLACE: Seriously, are you out here alone in the highlands? Where are your guards?

Ye Olde Starbuckes

SOME ENGLISH GUARD: Should we be getting back to the princess?

SOME OTHER ENGLISH GUARD: Nah, it's not like Longshanks cares if she dies anyway. You want another mochaccino?

The Princess's Hut of Faux Peace

WALLACE: Why are you helping me, again?

ISABELLE: Because . . . because of the way your cat's tail is looking at me now.

THE CAT TAIL IN WALLACE'S HAIR: Rrrrrrrowr.

[And then there is sex.]

A Romantic Glade the Next Morning

WALLACE: Bye, Isabeau.

ISABELLE: Isabelle!

WALLACE: Whatever.

The Lords 'Beg' for 'Pardon'

LORD CRAIG: Come and have a talk with the Bruce! He sends your dead wife's bloody embroidery as a pledge of his honesty.

WALLACE: GIMME!

HAMISH: But it's a trap!

MORRISON: It's a trap, William!

STEPHEN THE IRISH: It's a trap, Wallace!

ADMIRAL ACKBAR: IT'S A TRAP, STUPID!

WALLACE: But we've got to try!

STEPHEN THE IRISH: Should I come with you?

WALLACE: No, because it's a trap.

HAMISH: GAHHHHH.

The Meeting of the Bruce, Edinburgh

WALLACE rides up carefully disguised with a wad of tartan flung over his head. LORD CRAIG and ROBERT THE BRUCE meet him in the castle courtyard, whereupon a dozen English soldiers almost immediately leap out and start laying down ye olde smacke.

ROBERT THE BRUCE: NOOOOOOOOOO!

LORD CRAIG: Not the Bruce! Don't hurt the Bruce!

ENGLISH SOLDIER: Hey . . . what *is* a 'Bruce', anyway?

LORD CRAIG: I . . . I don't know.

Chez Bruce

Bruised, bleeding and furious ~~that no one knows what a bruce is~~, ROBERT THE BRUCE rushes up to his father's tower and starts choking the life out of him.

ROBERT THE BRUCE [*shaking father*]: DIE!!!!!!!!!

[LEPER THE BRUCE quivers a little, then collapses into a pile of miscellaneous body parts.]

ROBERT THE BRUCE: . . . I have to go now.

Wallace Is Charged With Treason

MAGISTRATE: Confess, and you may die quickly.

WALLACE: I deny that I did anything wrong, or that Longshanks is even my king, and I'd spit on him if I saw him right now. YOU JUST BRING HIM DOWN HERE AND SEE IF I DON'T!

MAGISTRATE: Right . . . so I'm gonna put you down for 'excruciating torture', does that sound about right?

Wallace's Prison Cell

ISABELLE: Confess your treason and they will let you die quickly!

WALLACE: Nope.

ISABELLE: Or maybe even live in a tower!

WALLACE: Nothin' doin'.

ISABELLE: Who knows what could happen! The king's going to die! Hell, I already wear the pants in this family! We could put a secret sexing door up there and everything—

WALLACE: No dice.

ISABELLE: FINE, BE THAT WAY WITH YOUR STUPID PRINCIPLES!

WALLACE: *shrug*

ISABELLE: At least drink this, okay?

[ISABELLE pulls out a vial of medieval Vicodin and makes him drink it. Then they make out for five minutes. After she tears up and leaves, he spits it out on the floor, having somehow held it in his mouth the whole time.]

ISABELLE [*outside in the hall*]: Ey, ma mouf feew kina num.

Longshanks' Deathbed

ISABELLE: My lord, I come to beg for Wallace's life!

PRINCE EDWARD: Shpfff, whatever. And don't even bother asking *him*, he can't even speak now.

ISABELLE: Oh, really? [*Whispering to* LONGSHANKS]: I got three words for you: William. Wallace. Junior.

LONGSHANKS: NNNGHHHFFFGGGHHHH! [*Dies.*]

PRINCE EDWARD: I don't know what you said to him, but *damn*, you should've said it years ago!

Executioner Square

The ROMANS lead WALLACE out, bound to a cross. The PHARISEES throw cabbage and rotten eggs at him.

MAGISTRATE: Stand your ground, and you'll get lots of sharp things for hours! Beg for mercy, and we'll let you have one sharp thing right now!

THE CROWD: WOOOO!

WALLACE: . . .

[They hang him with ropes and stretch him . . . in a cross.]

WALLACE: . . .

[They disembowel him . . . on a cross.]

HAMISH: This seems familiar, somehow . . .

STEPHEN THE IRISH [*blanching*]: *Jaysus.*

HAMISH: No, it's something else . . .

MAGISTRATE: BEG FOR MERCY, DAMMIT! YOU'RE MAKING US LOOK BAD!

WALLACE: fmmmfghghgmnnn

MAGISTRATE: Wait, what's that? He speaks! Say it again!

WALLACE: FREEEEEEEEDOMMMMM!

CROWD: . . .

MAGISTRATE: . . .

WOMAN IN CROWD: Hey! This isn't fun! We were told there would be fun death!

CROWD: FUN DEATH! FUN DEATH!

[An EERIE WOMAN walks through the crowd as WALLACE begins to lose consciousness.]

WALLACE: Satan? Is that you?

GHOST: *smacks Wallace upside the head*

WALLACE: Uncle Argyle?

GHOST: You get one more guess, and if you don't get it right this time, you are sleeping on the heavenly couch, mister.

WALLACE: MURRON!

[They cut off WALLACE'S head but that's okay because his soul leaves his body to go be with his beloved MURRON, as seen in the symbolic fall of her embroidered rag from his lifeless hand.]

ROBERT THE BRUCE: *tear*

William Wallace's Heavenly Reward

MURRON: Baby, who's 'Isabelle'?

WALLACE: Oh shit.

The Fields of Bannockburn

LORD CRAIG: So we're gonna eat crow . . .

ROBERT THE BRUCE: . . .

LORD CRAIG: . . . and we're all gonna go home . . .

ROBERT THE BRUCE: . . .

LORD CRAIG: . . . and this is all gonna be over.

ROBERT THE BRUCE: STABNATION GU BRA!

LORD CRAIG: *facepalm*

HAMISH: WALLAAAAAAACE!

THE SCOTS: RAAAAAAAAAAAAAAAAAAAAAAAAAAAAAAAAA

ENGLISH: Wha . . . ?

THE SCOTS: AAAAAAAAAAAAAAAAAAAAAAAAAAAAAAAAAA

THE WHITE KNEES OF SCOTLAND: *gleam*

THE SCOTS: AAAAAAAAAAAAAAAAAAAAAAAAAAAAAAAAAA

ROBERT THE BRUCE [*voiceover*]: They fought like warrior poets, like troubadour soldiers, like military balladeers . . . like pasty guys in skirts. And won their freedom. And then they went home to serf on my lands. Actually, Morrison ended up blowing stuff up for hire in Basin City, and Hamish got a pretty good gig teaching at Hogwarts. I heard something about Wallace being reincarnated as a megalomaniacal movie director with a Jesus complex, but I don't really know what's going on with that. And of course, I ended up king of Scotland, so, you know . . . all's well that ends well, I guess.

FIN.

Building the Perfect Sci-Fi Disaster Movie

Congratulations on your decision to make a sci-fi disaster movie! The two-genre combination can seem daunting initially, but with proper planning, your movie can rake in the cash, please crowds (if not critics) and become a perennial rental favorite.

Technically, you could argue that any disaster movie might involve at least a little pseudo-science and, being fictional, thereby automatically qualify as 'science fiction'. However, 'science fiction' is a term used here to denote 'aliens, with lasers, who want to kill us, and possibly suck our faces'. However, there is more to a good popcorn movie than death and destruction and lasers (which should be really big). Ideally, your film should utilize a complex mosaic of storylines designed to touch as many racial, ethnic, religious, political and sociological issues as possible. Feel free to use stereotypes if you start running out of time. Oh, and stuff needs to blow up real big.

To optimize your sci-fi disaster moviemaking experience, you may wish to keep the following suggestions in mind:

Name Your Film After a Holiday, And It Will Be Televised Yearly Without Fail

INDEPENDENCE DAY (1996)

Use Historical Events . . .

The 1969 moon-landing plaque – 'We Came In Peace For All Mankind' – is juxtaposed against the giant shadow of the approaching alien spacecraft. WOOO IRONY!

. . . And Legitimate Science to Give Your Film a Veneer of Realism.

Cut to: The SETI Institute, New Mexico. A ~~producer/screenwriter~~ TECHNICIAN takes time out from playing Putt-Putt and ironic modern rock to realize that . . .

TECHNICIAN 1: Oh my God, we're actually getting alien signals!

SUPERVISOR [*on phone*]: WHAT? That was just something we made up to get grant money!

TECHNICIAN 2: And they're coming from *the moon*!

SUPERVISOR: Well, how did they get there without us noticing? Do you people ever do any work at *all*?

ACTUAL SETI TECHNICIANS: They're so cutting our budget next year, aren't they?

When in Doubt, Call the Army.

GENERAL GREY: So . . . we don't know what it is, either?

SOME ARMY GUY: No, but we figure that it's really big. 'Quarter of the moon' big.

GENERAL GREY: That's bad.

SOME ARMY GUY: And slowing down . . .

GENERAL GREY: Well, that's good.

SOME ARMY GUY: . . . like it's looking for a parking spot.

GENERAL GREY: That's bad.

Introduce Your First Hero – the President!

PRESIDENT WHITMORE [*in bed, on phone*]: I'm a loving husband, father, President and former Gulf War pilot. Also, I put our daughter to bed on time. No, really.

MRS WHITMORE [*in hotel room, on phone*]: I'm a supportive wife, mother and First Lady. Also, you're really bad at lying.

PRESIDENT WHITMORE: Then how the hell did I get elected in the first place?

LITTLE PATRICIA WHITMORE: Daddy, can I be precocious?

PRESIDENT WHITMORE: Go back to sleep, munchkin.

PUNDIT ON TV: Everyone hates young President Whitmore, except for his family!

WHITMORE'S MOTHER [*on TV*]: No, I hate him too.

PRESIDENT WHITMORE: Sigh.

Get Bill Pullman And/Or Paxton If Possible.

CONSTANCE, THE PRESS SECRETARY: The bad news is, everyone thinks you're too young, inexperienced and wishy-washy.

PRESIDENT WHITMORE: Again: *why* was I elected?

CONSTANCE: The good news is, you've been named one of the ten sexiest men of the year.

PRESIDENT WHITMORE: *blinding smile*

CONSTANCE: . . .

PRESIDENT WHITMORE: What?

CONSTANCE: Which one are you, again?

PRESIDENT WHITMORE: Which . . . ?

CONSTANCE: Which Bill?

PRESIDENT WHITMORE: Oh. Pull . . . Paxton? No, Pullman.

CONSTANCE: Oh, that's right – Paxton's busy on the underwater salvage job.

Introduce Your Second Hero – the Science Geek!

DAVID: Dad, you're killing the Earth with your Styrofoam cup!

[Bonus points if the SCIENCE GEEK is of 'ethnic' origin:]

DAVID'S FATHER JULIUS: What, you want me to schlep a thermos everywhere I go? *Oy.*

[Double bonus points if you can work in some family issues:]

DAVID: Dad, smoking is unhealthy!

JULIUS: Unhealthy? Feh! You know what's unhealthy? Fixating on a woman you divorced four years ago, *that's* unhealthy.

DAVID: Well, it was great seeing you again, Dad, but I've beaten you at chess in three moves, so—

JULIUS: But . . . you just got here!

DAVID: Byegottago!

Be Sure to Include an Amusingly Gay Character.

DAVID bikes into the cable company where he works in case it's just not clear enough that he's Environmentalism Man.

EMPLOYEE ON PHONE: Ma'am, I'm sorry that the state-wide, alien-caused occurrences of static are preventing you from watching your ironically themed science-fiction show, but—

CUSTOMER ON PHONE: But I wanna see *The X-Fiiiiles*!

DAVID'S BOSS, MARTY [*flapping hands frantically*]: Daaaaaaaaaaaavid! Oh my Gaaaaaaaawd, *Daaaaaaavid*, all the satellites have disappeaaaaaaaaared! Do something about it, you big strong cable operator!

DAVID: NOT UNTIL YOU SEPARATE THE RECYCLABLES LIKE I TOLD YOU TO.

Got Time? Go for Broke With a Quirky, Downtrodden Hero!

Out in the California desert, poor studly, teenage MIGUEL is stuck taking care of his brother and sister because CRAZY RANDY QUAID is a drunk and a bad, bad father and their Hispanic mother is dead.

SOME DISTRACTINGLY HOT FARMER: MIGUEL! YOUR FATHER'S SCREWED UP MY CROPS AGAIN!

MIGUEL: No, really, I'm sure he's on his way to dust them, I promise!

RUSSELL [*veering wildly over fields in bi-plane*]: WOOOOOOOOOOOOO!!!

MIGUEL: RUSSELL, YOU MORON! THAT'S THE WRONG FIELD!

RUSSELL [*pitifully chugging whiskey*]: Aw, son, can't you even call me 'Dad, You Moron'?

MIGUEL: NO!

[Please add your extra 'ethnic characters' and 'family issues' points now rather than waiting until the end.]

Don't Forget the Actual Science Fiction And/Or Disaster.

The aliens approach the Earth in giant black discs.

Say What Everyone's Thinking: Government People Are BAD.

DEFENCE SECRETARY NIMZIKI: Let's blow it out of the sky!

PRESIDENT WHITMORE: But we don't even know what it is yet!

DEFENCE SECRETARY NIMZIKI: Upgrade to DEFCON 3 and blow it out of the sky!

GENERAL GREY: That's not your call to make!

DEFENCE SECRETARY NIMZIKI: BLOW! IT! UP!

SOME GUY FROM SPACE COMMAND: Uh, Mr President, the big thing has broken up into three dozen smaller things, which are still, themselves, really big things.

PRESIDENT WHITMORE: Like, how big?

SOME GUY FROM SPACE COMMAND [*spreading out hands*]: Like . . . FIFTEEN MILES BIG.

DEFENCE SECRETARY NIMZIKI: BLOW—

PRESIDENT WHITMORE: I KNOW, I KNOW!

Remind the Viewer That the Disaster Affects Everyone . . .

In the Iraqi desert, BEDOUIN in quaint garb stare as one of the alien ships enters the atmosphere through a wall of cloud-fire.

. . . But That We Really Only Care About Americans.

GENERAL GREY: Mr President, there are *two* confirmed sightings of big fiery things!

PRESIDENT WHITMORE: Turn on the TV news that we can't see too well, because God knows we're not actually in contact with other countries' diplomats or anything!

NEWS ANCHOR: . . . And now, live from Russia—

RUSSIAN REPORTER: It's fire in the sky and panic in the streets! Looting, mobbing, pillaging!

THE AUDIENCE: Yeah, sucks to be them. When does stuff blow up?

GENERAL GREY: OH MY GOD, THERE'S ONE HEADED FOR CALIFORNIA!

PRESIDENT WHITMORE: OH NO!

Remember, the President Is a Firm, Moral Hero.

GENERAL GREY: Mr President, we have an AWACS checking out the big thing on the West Coast!

AWACS AND EVERYONE ON IT: *are toasted*

GENERAL GREY: Oh, and more big things are heading for New York and DC. So basically, they're coming right for us.

DEFENCE SECRETARY NIMZIKI: WE HAVE TO LEAVE. NOW.

PRESIDENT WHITMORE: I'm staying here! Take the VP, the cabinet and the joint chiefs to a secure location, but leave me, the leader of the free world, here because I don't want to panic the people and cause riots. You saw Russia!

GENERAL GREY: Should we tell the American people to get to a secure location as well?

PRESIDENT WHITMORE: Nope, just tell 'em to sit tight. Calmness will protect them better than any bomb shelter!

Show the Science Geek Doing . . . Science. Or Something.

DAVID: Marty! I've got a signal pattern! I think I can block it out if I extricate the precise binary sequence and use the calculated spectra analyzer to employ a phase-reversed signal and isolate the specific sequential digital patterns. Actually, though, I think it'll be gone in about seven hours anyway, because the signal reduces itself every time it recycles, which is, you know, what I keep trying to get CERTAIN PEOPLE WHO WON'T SEPARATE THE CANS FROM THE BOTTLES TO . . . Marty?

MARTY: Oh my Gaaaaaawd, are you *watching* this?

CONSTANCE [*on TV*]: So, in conclusion, calmness will protect you better than any bomb shelter.

MARTY: EVERYONE DOWNSTAIRS TO THE BOMB SHELTAHHHHH!

Your Quirky Hero Can Also Be a Source of Comedy!

RUSSELL hunches over his beer at the diner counter as a group of MECHANICS saunter in.

MECHANIC: Hey, Russell! Your alien-abduction-induced alcoholism provides me with great entertainment and a much-needed self-esteem boost! I am amused by the possibility that you endured torturous sexual abuse at the hands of extraterrestrials!

THE OTHER MECHANICS: BWAHAHAHAHAHAHA!

RUSSELL: *cries into his beer*

Remind Your Audience That the Stakes Are High.

Giant alien discs rumble into the atmosphere, their shadows blotting out the Hollywood sign, the Lincoln Memorial and the New York skyline.

WILL SMITH'S GIRLFRIEND'S ADORABLE KID: Mommy, look!

PRESIDENT WHITMORE'S ADORABLE KID: Daddy, look!

TROY (RUSSELL'S YOUNGER KID): Hey, where's Dad?

MIGUEL (RUSSELL'S OLDER KID): Probably out getting shitfaced again. Everyone into the RV, let's go!

[While everyone else is busy wrecking their cars and running wild through the streets, DAVID goes to the roof of the cable-company building to watch the alien ship emerge, only to realize . . .]

DAVID: . . . my GOD.

[. . . something he won't tell us for several more minutes.]

Introduce Your Action Hero.

Your ACTION HERO should be well rounded: reasonably good-looking, romantic when necessary, able to carry off both comedy and tragedy. Athleticism is not actually all that important, as action scenes will be accomplished using blue screen and stunt doubles, but he should look ripped. Above all, however, audiences should admire him but also be able to identify with him as an Average Joe. If at all possible, hire WILL SMITH.

WILL SMITH: Baby, why's there a spaceship on our lawn?

The Science Geek Reveals the Threat!

DAVID: It's a countdown!

MARTY: Countdown! Countdown to WHAT? DAAAAAVID!

DAVID: To . . . checkmate, a metaphor I'm conveniently borrowing from my first scene in the movie.

MARTY: Daaaaavid, I don't play chesssssssssss!

DAVID: TO THINGS GOING BOOM.

MARTY: WAAAAAAAAAAH!

But No One Believes Him!

In a shocking twist, CONSTANCE turns out to be DAVID'S ex-wife! Wow! Who saw that coming?

DAVID [on phone]: CONNIE THEY'RE GOING TO ATTACK GET OUT NOW.

CONSTANCE [on phone]: Um, hi, I'm kind of working on matters of national importance and you're my ex-husband, thanks.

DAVID: Don't hang up . . . Don't— AHHH SHE HUNG UP.

[Behind CONSTANCE, PRESIDENT WHITMORE addresses the nation:]

PRESIDENT WHITMORE: Please, remain calm. If you feel compelled to evacuate the affected cities, please do so in an orderly fashion.

THE NATION: *starts looting*

DAVID: Dad, we gotta get out of New York! Can't this car go any faster?

JULIUS: In this *mishegas*? No, but let's banter about it.

PRESIDENT WHITMORE: Honey, you've got to get out of Los Angeles.

MRS WHITMORE: I won't be convinced until we banter about it.

WILL SMITH'S GIRLFRIEND: Baby, I don't want you to go to the base!

[WILL SMITH is actually 'STEVE', a fighter pilot. STEVE has a girlfriend, JASMINE. JASMINE has a son (DYLAN) and a dog (BOOMER). They don't want him to go to the base, either.]

~~WILL SMITH~~ STEVE: I gotta go, baby. But we can banter about it a while before I go.

RUSSELL [*on TV*]: You gotta listen to me! They're comin' to kill us all! I know! They abducted me and did experiments on me! Hey, don't put me in that police car—!

MIGUEL: *facepalm*

[MIGUEL knows that his family's too far gone for banter. He throws his brother and his sister (insert 'Our Last Night On Earth' scene with FRISKY TEENAGE BOY here) into the RV and prepares to hit the road – only to run into a drunk RUSSELL on the loose.]

MIGUEL: We're leaving without you!

RUSSELL: But I'm your father!

MIGUEL: Not any more! I do all the parenting around here anyway! I HATE YOU!

TROY: I hate you both AND my expensive medicine! [*Smash!*]

MIGUEL: GO TO YOUR BUNK BED, YOUNG MAN!

Singers Are More Than Happy to Go Hollywood.

~~HARRY CONNICK JR~~ JIMMY: Stevie, where you been? We're behind on our banter!

STEVE: I ain't got time for banter, Jimmy – NASA won't let me fly the space shuttle, which is my one great dream. Oh, and aliens are coming.

JIMMY: Let me try to cheer you up with *homoerotic* banter!

STEVE: Thanks, man, but I got too much on my mind. I'm also thinking about asking Jasmine to marry me. Oh, and aliens are coming.

JIMMY: Man, if you marry a stripper, you'll *never* fly the shuttle.

STEVE: What's stripping got to do with anything?

Speaking of Stripping, Sneak in Some Sexy If You Can.

JASMINE: WHY IS NO ONE WATCHING MY BOOTY?

TIFFANY, ANOTHER STRIPPER: No one cares about anything but aliens now, including me. In fact, I'm gonna go dance on the rooftops with all the lunatics tonight!

JASMINE: Good God, y'all crazy, crazy white people.

The Science Geek Can Always Figure Out What the Government Can't.

JULIUS: I can't believe you want us to walk up to the White House like a pair of *schlemiels*. You think you know everything? *Feh*.

DAVID: I think I know how to triangulate Connie's exact position in the White House, call her secret phone number and get us inside.

  [He does. However, the situation is awkward, because DAVID and PRESIDENT WHITMORE have met before, and . . .]

DAVID: I kind of punched him in the head. Because I thought he was having an affair. With Connie.

JULIUS: DAVID, YOU SCHMUCK! He's a *mensch*! A moral hero with a family! He'd never *touch* Connie!

CONSTANCE: HEY!

PRESIDENT WHITMORE: Look, Head-Puncher, I don't have all day. We're kind of dealing with the first signs of other intelligent life in the universe. What do you want?

DAVID: They're using our satellites against us!

PRESIDENT WHITMORE [*squinting heroically*]: My scepticism is manly.

DAVID: DO SOMETHING!!

Everyone Panics!

GENERAL GREY: Let's send helicopters to try to communicate with the big thing.

HELICOPTERS: *blow up*

PRESIDENT WHITMORE: EVACUATE TILL YOU CAN'T EVACUATE NO MORE.

But Not Soon Enough!

PRESIDENT WHITMORE: Where's my wife?

SOME CUTE AIDE: Still futzing around in LA.

PRESIDENT WHITMORE: DAMMIT!

NEWS REPORT ON RADIO: . . . And so everyone is advised to evacuate Los Angeles, but don't take the highway.

JASMINE [*on highway*]: DAMMIT!

TIFFANY: Wheeeee! Rooftop raves are fun! I hope the aliens come soon!

LAPD CHOPPERS: DAMMIT!

[With all of fifteen seconds left, the White House staff starts evacuating.]

PRESIDENT WHITMORE: Everyone on my plane! YOU TOO, PUNCHY McNERDENSTEIN!

Stuff Blows Up!

Get historic monuments, if possible. In lieu of monuments, rooftop raves attended by nutcases bearing professionally designed posters may be destroyed instead if the city has no important landmarks to speak of.

LOS ANGELES: HEY!

TIFFANY: Oooo, the giant death ray is so pretty!

ROOFTOP RAVE: *boom boom BOOM!*

TIFFANY: *BOOM!*

THE FIRST LADY: *BOOM!*

EVERYBODY: *runs*

CARS: *go flying*

LA: *is on fire*

Stuff Blows Up Big!

From multiple angles, if you can manage it. You may reuse your basic tower-blowing-up effect if your monuments are similar.

EMPIRE STATE BUILDING: *boom boom BOOM!*

MARTY: *BOOM!*

EVERYBODY: *runs*

CABS: *go flying*

NY: *is on fire*

Stuff Blows Up GOOD!

Go for broke! Surely there was something you didn't show in the trailer! And don't worry – there's no way the destruction of American landmarks could become a painful issue for future audiences. You have *nothing* to worry about.

THE WHITE HOUSE: *boom boom BOOM!*

THE WHITE HOUSE CHINA: *BOOM!*

CUTE AIDE'S HELICOPTER: *BOOM!*

THE CAPITOL BUILDING: *BOOM!*

THE LINCOLN MEMORIAL: *BOOM!*

THE VIETNAM VETERANS MEMORIAL: *does not go boom, because that would be in bad taste*

MONUMENTS: *go flying*

DC: *is on fire*

   [Air Force One somehow manages to outfly a massive city-wide fireball. Everyone else, everywhere, dies. That's what you get for not having a speaking part.]

Never, Ever Kill the Dog.

JASMINE is stuck in an LA underpass. She stops and looks back fifteen times, but she and DYLAN alone are able to hide in a tunnel maintenance room while thousands of other people die in a giant wave of fire. BOOMER is fried to a crisp.

THE AUDIENCE: OH MY GOD *THE DOG*?!? WE WANT OUR MONEY BACK RIGHT NOW!!

   [JASMINE is stuck in an LA underpass. She stops and looks back fifteen times, but she and DYLAN alone are able to hide in a tunnel maintenance room while thousands of other people die in a giant wave of fire. BOOMER leaps to safety at the last second.]

THE AUDIENCE: WOOOOOOO! BEST MOVIE EVER!!

You Must Always, *Always* Use the Statue of Liberty.

THE STATUE OF LIBERTY: *is dead from boom*

Don't Forget About Your Quirky Hero With Ethnic Kids and Family Problems!

RADIO ANNOUNCER: . . . And thus, all three cities are now just smoking craters.

RUSSELL [*driving*]: I told you! I TOLD YOU they were coming to get us!

MIGUEL: God, Russell, *shut up*.

RUSSELL: What'd I say?

MIGUEL: You're so busy being aggressively quirky and adorably drunk that you haven't even noticed that your KID is SICK.

TROY: *Baaaaaaaarrrrrrrrrrf.*

The *Real* Drama is on Angst Force One.

PRESIDENT WHITMORE: How's my daughter?

CONSTANCE: Sleeping and mostly unaware of terror rampaging below.

PRESIDENT WHITMORE: How's my wife?

GENERAL GREY: As far as we can tell? Toast.

PRESIDENT WHITMORE: *works jaw manfully*

* * *

CONSTANCE: You saved a lot of lives today, Mr President.

PRESIDENT WHITMORE: But we could have saved so many more if it had just occurred to us that all aliens are evil bastards who want to kill us! How many people died because we forgot about every alien movie ever made?

CONSTANCE: What about *E.T.*?

PRESIDENT WHITMORE: Don't start with me about that son of a bitch. The mother ship just picked him up before he could get anything started.

* * *

JULIUS: Never should you have broken up with my son, Connie.

CONSTANCE: We were different people in different places, Julius!

JULIUS: What, you think you can share the same molecules? *Feh.*

* * *

DAVID [*with airsick bag*]: *Baaaaaaarrrrrrrrrrrf.*

Lighten Things Up With Some Courageous, Multi-Ethnic Camaraderie.

Going into battle, all the FIGHTER PILOTS are cocky:

JIMMY: Let's kick the tyres and light the fires and drain the mires and burn the pyres and climb the spires and—

STEVE: Jimmy? Shut it.

JIMMY: Make me!

STEVE: Fine. No victory cigar for your punk ass.

JIMMY: Oh, you mean the phallic representations of our homoerotic rapport?

STEVE: . . . No.

[Let your AMATEUR ACTOR get a little hamming in:]

JIMMY: As the estimable Johnnie Cochran might say, 'If they're on your town, you must shoot them dow—' OH MY GOD.

STEVE: Yeah, ain't so funny no more, is it, Jimmy?

[The big alien thingy is big, and alien, and protected by giant force fields. The FIGHTER PILOTS find this out the hard way.]

FIGHTER PILOTS: *BOOM!*

[Don't wear out your SINGER-TURNED-ACTOR'S welcome. Remember, he has better, possibly more musical, things to do.]

JIMMY'S PLANE: *BOOM!*

STEVE: JIMMY NOOOOOOOOOOOOOOO!!!

[Coming out of the battle, all the FIGHTER PILOTS are dead.]

GENERAL GREY: I am astonished that aliens with the technology to travel all this way somehow also have protective shields!

PRESIDENT WHITMORE: GET THE REST OF OUR WOEFULLY LOW-TECH PILOTS OUT OF THERE!

[And then the base blows up.]

EL TORO: *BOOM!*

Big! Action! Sequence!

GENERAL GREY: Wait! There is still one more pilot!

PRESIDENT WHITMORE: My God! It's an action hero, invulnerable to all attacks! If I'd known that, I would have sent him in all by himself!

[STEVE banks and dives and swerves through the Grand Canyon, heckling his pursuers. This would perhaps be more effective if they could actually hear him. None of the ALIEN FIGHTERS are bad-ass enough to match STEVE'S leet flying skillz and go down in flames – except for one, which is slick enough to follow STEVE that far, but dumb enough to get taken down by a well-deployed parachute.]

Don't Forget the Comic Relief!

STEVE vents his rage at the only other survivor of the ordeal. Note:

this requires casting of WILL SMITH.

~~WILL SMITH~~ STEVE: *punches the alien out*

[It may take a few tries before you settle on an appropriate punch line.]

TAKE ONE: How's that for some *Contact*?

TAKE TWO: Yeah, who's the *Predator* now, bitch?

TAKE TWELVE: *Mars Attacks* this!

TAKE THIRTY-FOUR: There better not be no *Alien: Resurrection*!

TAKE FIFTY-SEVEN: Boy, I'll put you in a damn *Cocoon*!

TAKE EIGHTY-THREE: Now that's what *I* call a *Close Encounter*.

The Scrappy Heroine Overcomes All Obstacles.

JASMINE: Wow! An abandoned maintenance truck! I bet the owner left the keys right here in the visor!

DYLAN: Mommy, didn't we abandon our car?

JASMINE: Well, yes, sweetheart, we had to.

DYLAN: Where are the keys to our car?

JASMINE: Right here in my pocket.

DYLAN: Well then why—

JASMINE: Honey? No one likes a smartass.

There's Always Time for Humour.

STEVE drags his captive back to civilization.

STEVE: I can't BELIEVE I have to drag your STANK, INTER-GALACTIC ASS across DEATH VALLEY.

THE ALIEN: Could you pick up the pace a little? My dreads are drying out.

STEVE: GAHHHHHHHHHHHH!

Your Characters Begin to Converge!

Having gathered a small band of survivors on the maintenance truck, JASMINE gets out and deploys BOOMER, the Survivor-Sniffing Dog.

JASMINE: Someone help me! This lady pinned under the smoking helicopter is still alive!

THE FIRST LADY: Ack . . . help . . . your dog . . . prancing on my . . . ruptured spleen . . .

Everyone Loves Odd-Couple Humour.

THE ALIEN: Are we there yet?

STEVE: NO.

THE ALIEN: Are we there yet?

STEVE: NO.

THE ALIEN: Are we there yet?

STEVE: NO, WE STILL GOT THE REST OF THE MOJAVE DESERT TO HIKE THROUGH, WITH NO WATER AND NO SUNSCREEN.

THE ALIEN: OW! Hey, that was a rock!

Nukes Are Baaaaad.

DEFENCE SECRETARY NIMZIKI: NUCLEAR COUNTER-ATTACK NOW.

PRESIDENT WHITMORE: But . . . nukes are bad.

SOME AIDE: Mr President! The aliens have blown up NORAD and the joint chiefs and the VP!

PRESIDENT WHITMORE: Nukes are starting to sound good.

DAVID: NO NO NO! NUKES ARE ALWAYS BAD!

DEFENCE SECRETARY NIMZIKI: NUH-UH!

DAVID: YUH-HUH!

JULIUS: PUT A SOCK IN IT, ALL OF YOU! This is all your fault anyway, you *schnooks* in the government! You knew this could happen and you did nothing!

GENERAL GREY: Except for the part where we totally, totally didn't.

JULIUS: Yes you did! Don't act like you don't know anything about this! I watch that show with the redhead and the doo-doo-doo! The government's always known about aliens! They keep 'em at that place in the desert, you know, that Studio 51—

PRESIDENT WHITMORE: Mr Levinson, I assure you, there is no Area 51. We don't have any underground bunkers, and we don't have any alien spaceships that humans can conveniently fly, and we've recovered no alien bodies that would be of any use to us at the present time.

DEFENCE SECRETARY NIMZIKI: Uh . . . yeah. About that, Mr President . . . ?

You May Even Want to Consider a Spin-Off. Together, They Could Fight Crime.

STEVE [*kicking* ALIEN *savagely*]: YOU KNOW WHAT I'M MISS-ING BECAUSE OF YOU? BARBECUE! AND SLEEPING IN! AND ALL MY FRIENDS NOT BEING DEAD!

THE ALIEN: OW! Look – OW! – don't blame me, man, I'm just—

STEVE: THE ONE WHO BLEW UP MY TOWN?

THE ALIEN: Well, I mean, besides that!

[A fleet of trailers comes across STEVE and his ALIEN POW in the desert.]

RUSSELL: You need a hand, soldier?

84

THE ALIEN: Uh, this is just a domestic dispute, really, nothing to see here—

STEVE: Yeah, there's a super-secret government base around here, if me and the space octopus could get a lift . . . ?

Pop-Culture Legends? They're All True!

PRESIDENT WHITMORE: So . . . basically you've been hiding a super-secret, multimillion-dollar, twenty-five-storey research facility under a mountain out in the desert for fifty years? And you didn't even tell *me*?

DEFENCE SECRETARY NIMZIKI: E-zactly.

[PRESIDENT WHITMORE is then introduced to the RESIDENT NUTCASE-SAVANT. Sci-fi geeks will appreciate stunt casting. Just make sure they can tell which actor it is . . .]

DR OKUN: . . . Yeah, they mostly keep us down here under the mountain, where we collect *data* on the aliens. Ha! Ha ha! You know, *data*! Because I played . . . you know . . . on *Next Generation*, and—

PRESIDENT WHITMORE: I'd like to get a move on with seeing the aliens and whatnot, Dr Okra, if that's okay with you.

[DR OKUN leads the Angst Force One survivors to a spaceship that looks exactly like the one STEVE shot down.]

DR OKUN: And the coolest thing is that it turned on by itself yesterday! Is that not rad, or what?

PRESIDENT WHITMORE: Yeah, millions of people dying was *totally* boss, dude.

DR OKUN: Aww, really? Bummer. Hey, you wanna see our alien corpses?

PATRICIA: Daddy, he scares me.

PRESIDENT WHITMORE: Me too, munchkin.

Don't Blame the Government – Blame the *Shadow* Government.

GENERAL GREY: You were the head of the CIA! You knew about this base, and you knew they had aliens, and you knew they had alien technology! Did it never occur to you to, you know, SAY SOMETHING ABOUT THAT when the spaceships started showing up?

DEFENCE SECRETARY NIMZIKI: Well, no, because I didn't *realize* that our *armed forces* were going to *suck*.

[Before GENERAL GREY can tear DEFENCE SECRETARY NIMZIKI into confetti with his bare hands, PRESIDENT WHITMORE arrives to find out the extent of the damage.]

GENERAL GREY: Atlanta, Philadelphia and Chicago: destroyed. Our troops: down to fifteen per cent. The rest of the world: toast in thirty-six hours.

PRESIDENT WHITMORE: And we haven't had Nimziki shot already because . . . ?

GENERAL GREY: I'm saying, Mr President.

As If Things Aren't Bad Enough, Let's Torture Our Heroes Some More.

AREA 51 GUARD: Look, I don't know how you and five thousand RVs found us, but—

[STEVE throws back the parachute to reveal the ALIEN POW.]

THE ALIEN: Help! Help! I'm being oppressed!

AREA 51 GUARD: . . . You can all go right this way, folks.

DR OKUN: A NEW ALIEN, WHEE!

GENERAL GREY: Congratulations, Captain Hiller, on not getting dead, and actually being useful besides.

STEVE: So, uh . . . can I go back to the base and be reunited with my girlfriend and future stepson now?

GENERAL GREY: You mean they didn't tell you?

[At that moment, JASMINE and the survivors drive up to El Toro and also find out that it's just a smoking crater.]

STEVE: Well, there goes my hot stripper girlfriend and her adorable kid.

JASMINE: Well, there goes my ticket out of the booby hatch.

DYLAN: Now I'll never have a daddy!

BOOMER: *tear*

In the Midst of Tragedy, There's Always Time for Girl Talk.

JASMINE: . . . I mean, sometimes I get tired of shaking my money-maker just to have a nice house and a good school for my little boy, but mostly, the chafing is worth it.

THE FIRST LADY: Could you . . . throw another stick of debris . . . on the fire? I can't . . . feel my . . . extremities.

JASMINE: Sure thing, babe. Now, where was I . . . ?

Had a Good Jump-Scare Yet?

MAJOR MITCHELL, AREA 51 LIAISON: So, let's check in on Dr Okun and see how the desuitification process is going with that new alien, shall we?

[Behind glass walls, the operating room is a smoking wreck. Suddenly, DR OKUN'S body is slammed against the glass.]

EVERYONE: AHHHHH!

DR OKUN'S BODY: RELEASE . . . ME . . . PUNY . . . EARTH-LINGS!

MAJOR MITCHELL: You heard the man!

GENERAL GREY: No, wait! Are we sure that's really Dr Okun?

[They are clued in to the fact that it is not actually DR OKUN speaking when they see a tentacle wrapped around his throat. Oh, and when the ALIEN leaps down from the ceiling in all its betentacled glory.]

EVERYONE: AHHHHHHHHH!!

PRESIDENT WHITMORE: Look, I'm really sorry about that whole thing with you and Captain Hiller in the desAHHHH HHH-HHHHHHHHHHHHHHHHHHHHH! MY BRAIN! IT'S EATING MY BRAIN!

EVERYONE: *shoots the alien*

GENERAL GREY: What about Dr Okra?

MAJOR MITCHELL: Oh, the nutcase? I'm sure his crumpled body's around here somewhere. Probably under a shelf or something.

We Have Met the Enemy, And They Are Us. But With More Tentacles.

GENERAL GREY: What happened?

PRESIDENT WHITMORE: It . . . showed me . . . what they're going to do. They're going to take over our lands, kill all the natives, use up all our water, fresh air, forests and oil, and then move on when they're done.

GENERAL GREY: So basically, they're . . . us.

PRESIDENT WHITMORE: But they're not even going to put casinos on the people reservations!

GENERAL GREY: THOSE DAMN DIRTY LOCUSTS!

PRESIDENT WHITMORE: NUKE EVERYONE!

Action Heroes Can Always Break the Rules.

STEVE: I'm taking your chopper without permission, okay?

SOME BEEFY SOLDIER: Don't make me shoot you, Captain!

STEVE: . . .

SOME BEEFY SOLDIER: Oh, *all right*.

STEVE: Tell 'em I kicked your ass or something.

SOME BEEFY SOLDIER: Girl, *please*.

Nukes Are Baaaaaad.

GENERAL GREY: Nukes ahoy!

DEFENCE SECRETARY NIMZIKI: WOOOOO!!

[The nukes make no dent in the spaceship hovering over Houston.]

PRESIDENT WHITMORE: So . . . we just sent Texas into nuclear winter for nothing?

GENERAL GREY: Yeah, pretty much.

Have You Tugged a Heartstring Lately?

STEVE [*in chopper*]: Baby, I've come to save you!

JASMINE: I knew you'd come! Hurry, the First Lady is dying! But first, let's make out!

THE FIRST LADY [*beaming*]: *tear*

* * *

CONSTANCE: Why couldn't you ever do anything *important* with your life, David?

DAVID [*stone drunk*]: I thought I did when I married YOU!

CONSTANCE: *tear*

PRESIDENT WHITMORE: Sweetheart, it's about your mom . . .

PATRICIA: Mommy's going to get better, isn't she?

PRESIDENT WHITMORE: *tear*

Environmental Parallel or Classic Movie Allusion? Why Not Both?

JULIUS: David! What are you doing?

　[DAVID, on a world-class drunk, is busy throwing the Area 51 recyclables around while everyone else is sleeping on their lab tables and under their desks.]

DAVID: I'm trying to destroy the Earth so the aliens won't want it anymore! So we've got to burn the toxic waste and dump the rainforests and . . . Hey, these guys sure do drink a lot of Surge.

JULIUS: David! You're never going to accomplish anything stomping around here like a child! You might want to ask your friend the President for one of his nuclear weapons—

DAVID: GAHHHHH!

JULIUS: Oh, come on! Focus on the positive! At least you've got your health and you won't be sniffling when they come to suck our faces! Although this too could be a blessing – we all get colds, they suck our faces, they die of the flu. Heh.

DAVID: . . .

JULIUS: . . .

DAVID: Dad, I think you just saved the planet.

JULIUS: What'd I say?

DAVID: So, Major, take your gun and shoot the alien craft we all know is impenetrable.

MAJOR MITCHELL: Shoot it?

DAVID: Yes. Aim for the carefully product-placed soda can I have conveniently balanced on the wing and not, you know, a part of the ship you could actually hit.

[MAJOR MITCHELL fires and the ship's force shield deflects the bullet, sending it ricocheting around the lab while everyone screams and ducks.]

DAVID: Sorry, sorry. My bad! Everyone all right?

MAJOR MITCHELL: Actually, I think one of the interns is dead.

DAVID: Oops.

MAJOR MITCHELL: Eh, it's just an intern.

DAVID: Cool. Now . . . [typing on laptop] . . . shoot again.

ALL THE INTERNS: *hide*

[MAJOR MITCHELL blows the Soda That Shall Not Be Named away.]

GENERAL GREY: Wait, what?

DAVID: I gave it a cold! Or rather, a complex and destructive computer virus. Found it in an e-mail that said it could make my free iPod's penis very rich.

GENERAL GREY: Wait . . . *what*?

PRESIDENT WHITMORE: So . . . the aliens are Mac-compatible?

DAVID: Oh, yes. All higher life forms use Macs.

Remember, Kids: Government Types Are Cowardly and Nasty.

DEFENCE SECRETARY NIMZIKI: So, what you're saying is,

you're going to let some jug-eared, stripper-dating fighter pilot take a fifty-year-old alien craft into outer space, dock with the mother ship and sit there while Punchy McDrunkard infects them with *porn spam*?

GENERAL GREY: Sounds good to me.

PRESIDENT WHITMORE: You got a better idea?

DEFENCE SECRETARY NIMZIKI: Well, no – in fact, I vehemently protest against us doing *anything* to save ourselves! In fact, I will mention your wife's death in an attempt to bully you emotionally!

GENERAL GREY: WHAT THE HELL KIND OF DEFENCE SECRETARY ARE YOU?

PRESIDENT WHITMORE [*with bitch-slap*]: A fired one, that's what!

THE AUDIENCE: YAY! VOICES OF REASON ARE EVIL!

Nothing Gets Done If Americans Don't Do It.

SOME ARABIC GUY: The Americans want to launch a counter-offensive!

SOME BRITISH GUY: Well, it's about time! I was quite miffed at waiting over here to get my face sucked off.

SOME ARABIC GUY: What about the Russians?

SOME BRITISH GUY: Tally ho, I do believe they'll join us!

SOME ARABIC GUY: What about the Japanese?

SOME BRITISH GUY: Also them!

SOME ARABIC GUY: And the French?

SOME BRITISH GUY: Oh, they surrendered two days ago – the aliens have been using the Eiffel Tower as a radio transmitter for some time now.

Has the President Given His Big Inspirational Speech Yet?

MAJOR MITCHELL: All right! Anyone who can fly and doesn't mind dying, line up here!

RUSSELL: *perks up*

PRESIDENT WHITMORE [*taking microphone*]: Perhaps it's fate, or gimmicky screenwriting, that today is July Fourth. But here we are again, fighting not for our right to govern ourselves or drink reasonably taxed tea – but fighting for our right to live, and to kill *each other* in peace, and to party. The Fourth of July will no longer be known as just an American holiday, although God knows we do a good enough job of making everything about us as it is. This will be remembered as the day when the world declared with one voice, in English, that we will not go gently into that good night! Rage, rage—

THE VOLUNTEERS: *glaze over*

GENERAL GREY: Mr President, I don't think they know that one.

PRESIDENT WHITMORE: . . . And – that, uh – we will survive! We will not crumble! We will not lay down and die! We will grow strong, even though they've done us wrong! And we will stand up and tell them as one, 'Go on now! Walk out that door! Just get in your spaceships and turn around now, 'cause YOU'RE NOT WELCOME ANY MORE!'

THE VOLUNTEERS: WOOOOO!!

A Hero's Not a Hero Unless He's an Action Hero.

RUSSELL: I'm drunk and crazy, but I gotta fly!

PRESIDENT WHITMORE: I'm the leader of the free world and the only parent my little girl's got left, but I gotta fly!

STEVE: I actually am most qualified to fly this craft, so all y'all haters can step off.

DAVID: *Baaaaaaarrrrrrrrrrf.*

A Global Emergency Is the Best Way to Solve Everyone's Problems.

JULIUS: Now that I have given you airsick bags and you have given me a yarmulke, son, I feel that our relationship is repaired.

CONSTANCE: David! We never should have broken up!

STEVE: Jasmine, if I come back, let's get married.

DYLAN: Yay! Now I'll have a daddy!

RUSSELL: Now my kids will respect me –

MISSILES: WHOOP WHOOP WHOOP WHOOP!

RUSSELL: – unless I blow myself up first. Hey, you guys? A little help here . . . ?

No Alien Technology Is Too Weird For Humans to Figure Out.

STEVE: Hey, look – it's like they've got a gas pedal and a brake and a steering wheel and seatbelts and everything.

DAVID: It's a good thing that the aliens are quadrupeds with logical processes much like our own, and not, say, blobs of goo that primarily operate machinery using only the power of their minds, or their sixteen multidimensional tentacles.

STEVE: Shut it, Poindexter.

Your Heroes Are Always Prepared for Danger.

After a brief mishap involving some backwards directions, STEVE begins to get a feel for his new toy:

STEVE: Wheelie! Ollie Pop! Laser Flip! Hurricane! WOO!

DAVID: *Baaaaaaaaaaaaaarrrrrrrrrrrrrrrrrrrrrrrf.*

GENERAL GREY [*on radio*]: Uh, Mr President, I think the aliens have figured out that we're coming for them.

PRESIDENT WHITMORE [*in plane*]: What makes you say that?

GENERAL GREY: Well, they're kind of headed this way.

CONSTANCE: Uh, Major Mitchell, should we, you know, *bring all the civilians inside*?

MAJOR MITCHELL: Oh shit.

Reveal the Extent of the Alien Menace.

DAVID: Oh my God! Look at this thing! The mother ship is huge, and filled with millions of aliens ready for battle! What the hell are they doing?

STEVE: My guess would be 'invading', EINSTEIN.

There Must Always Be a Fakeout Before Triumph . . .

GENERAL GREY [*on radio*]: Porn-spam delivery complete, sir!

PRESIDENT WHITMORE [*in plane*]: Firing Fox Three!

[Fox Three bounces harmlessly off the alien shields. Everyone hangs their head in disappointment.]

PRESIDENT WHITMORE: GODDAMN PORN SPAM! NEVER DOES WHAT IT SAYS IT WILL!

[Outside, in the ersatz Area 51 trailer park:]

MAJOR MITCHELL: Hey, you guys . . . !

TRAILER PARK: *BOOM!*

[Meanwhile, up on the mother ship:]

STEVE: I think we're stuck.

DAVID: The jig, I think she is up.

STEVE: HIDE!

DAVID: Steve, I'm pretty sure they can still see us—

STEVE: SHUT UP AND GET BEHIND THE SEATS, FOOL.

. . . But a Hero Never Gives Up.

PRESIDENT WHITMORE: Wait, lemme try one more just in case Punchy McNerdenstein wasn't *totally* full of shit!

FOX FOUR: *BOOM!*

THE CONTROL ROOM: WOOOOO!!

Include a Pan-Denominational Religious Moment.

But nothing that will make anyone actually feel bad about not going to church.

JULIUS: Everyone hold hands and pray with me!

   [Little PATRICIA and little DYLAN and BOOMER hold ~~paws~~ hands.]

FORMER DEFENCE SECRETARY NIMZIKI: But . . . I'm not Jewish.

JULIUS: Well, clearly, or you'd be much less of a *schmuck*. PRAY!

It's Always Darkest Just Before Dawn. Well, Figuratively Speaking.

PRESIDENT WHITMORE: We're not blowing things up fast enough!

GENERAL GREY: The alien ship is going to blow our mountain up!

PRESIDENT WHITMORE: I have just come up with the brilliant idea to blow up their laser!

GENERAL GREY: But your rocket missed it!

PRESIDENT WHITMORE: And now I have no more!

GENERAL GREY: And no one else has any missiles, either!

PRESIDENT WHITMORE: Oh, whatever shall we do?

RUSSELL: Mr President! I, Russell Casse, have one missile left!

MIGUEL [*in control room*]: OMG!

[Unfortunately, crazy must be redeemed with DEATH.]

RUSSELL: Oh no! My missile is jammed! But there is no one else who can save the planet! I have to . . . I must . . . TELL MY CHILDREN I LOVE THEM.

MIGUEL [*in control room*]: NOOOOOOOO!!

[RUSSELL, raving about alien injustices to his ass to the very end, sacrifices himself to blow up the giant alien disc thingy hovering over Area 51.]

EVERYONE IN THE CONTROL ROOM: WOOOOOOOOOOOOOOO!!!

MAJOR MITCHELL: What's wrong with you, son? Cheer for the dead man!

MIGUEL: THAT WAS MY DAD, ASS.

MAJOR MITCHELL: Oh. Sorry about that. He was a good man . . . I mean, not that I knew him, but . . . Can I get you a posthumous medal or something?

[And then the falling alien ship thingy takes out five towns, a mountain range and the rest of the Area 51 trailer park.]

The Escape Is Narrow!

DAVID: So . . . I'm thinking we're pretty much going to have to blow ourselves up with the mother ship.

STEVE: Yeah, it's looking like that.

DAVID: We'll never see our women again.

STEVE: But we do have phallic tobacco.

DAVID: Well, that's something.

STEVE: So . . . bombs away. Thirty seconds and counting.

[STEVE fires an alien missile into the alien control tower inside the mother ship which . . . hey, what do you know, knocks their ship free. Twenty seconds later:]

DAVID: Shit! We still have thirty seconds to get out of here! GO GO GO!

[Thirty-eight seconds later, halfway into a thrilling alien fighter chase:]

DAVID: Faster, faster! We still have twenty-four seconds!

[Forty-one seconds later, STEVE squeezes their fighter through the rapidly closing mother-ship doors.]

STEVE: WOOOOO!

[Fifteen seconds later:]

DAVID: I LOVE YOU SO MUCH.

STEVE: And we still have nine seconds until the ship blows up!

The Climax of the Film: Stuff Blows Up So Big!!

Nine seconds later:

MOTHER SHIP: *BOOOOOOOOOOOOM!*

[Across the world, plucky survivors start shooting down the other ships, and we see a montage of happy people dancing around the spaceship-crushed remains of several mountain ranges, the Sydney Opera House and the Pyramids.]

No Matter Your Race or Religion, You Too Can Be a Hero to the Womenfolk.

PATRICIA: Yay! My daddy didn't orphan me!

[After being reunited with his daughter, PRESIDENT WHITMORE drives out into the desert with the other Angst Force One survivors, where STEVE and DAVID are sauntering away from their crash landing. JASMINE runs to STEVE and kisses him, with DYLAN and BOOMER hot on her heels. CONSTANCE, press secretary of the United States, flings herself at DAVID like a thirteen-year-old Backstreet Boys fan.]

DYLAN: Daddy!

BOOMER: Woof!

JASMINE: Steve! Now you can make an honest woman out of me!

CONSTANCE: SQUEEEEEEEEEEEEEE!

Everyone Lives Happily Ever After!

THE FIRST LADY: *is dead*

MIGUEL, TROY AND ALICIA: *are orphans*

ALL THE MAJOR CITIES OF THE WORLD: *are sizzling craters*

HOUSTON: *nuclear tumbleweed bounces past*

STEVE [to JASMINE]: Baby, let's get married!

DAVID [to CONSTANCE]: Baby, let's get remarried!

PRESIDENT WHITMORE: And you can marry Captain Hiller's stepson, munchkin!

PATRICIA: But Daddy, boys are gross!

PRESIDENT WHITMORE: Buck up, Patricia, we've got to repopulate the Earth somehow.

FIN.

TITANIC (1997)

Faux Newsreel Footage

Did you know this movie is based on a true story? It totally, totally is! Well, except for Jack and Rose. And Rose's mother. And Rose's evil fiancé. And all of the lower-class people they meet. And the fictionalized versions of real people they interact with. But the china is *exactly* replicated.

Under the Sea

Two subs weave among the various deep-sea divers, exploration teams and tour groups, kicking up clouds of sediment and disturbing debris as they go. What better way to preserve an historical century-old shipwreck than to film a movie inside it?

ROBERT BALLARD: HEY!

LOVETT: MOVE IT OR LOSE IT, BALLARD!

> [BROCK LOVETT, an intensely smarmy treasure hunter, is our hero. He and SEAMAN BODINE, a large, ebullient redhead who has taken time off from running his movie news site to play sidekick, cruise through the shipwreck.]

LOVETT [*smarming into video camera*]: I get choked up every time I see the beautiful, tragic *Titanic* lying on the ocean floor, looted and ravaged by . . . time. Yes. Time.

LOVETT'S EARRING: *smarms also*

BODINE: Snerk.

LOVETT [*turning off camera*]: All right, we've met the bullshit quota for today. Launch Dunkin, Mir 1.

MIR 1: ACH, LADDIE.

LOVETT: Mir 2? Snoop Dog in the heezy?

MIR 2: FO SHIZZLE.

LOVETT: All right, Dunkin, open that door and grab me some treasure.

DUNKIN: I CANNAE, CAP'N, I HAVE NAE GOT THE POWER!

LOVETT: Well, let's have Snoop Dog try.

[BODINE takes over Snoop Dog's controls and pilots him through the bedroom.]

BODINE: You want me to pick up any of these other valuable artefacts, boss?

LOVETT: *Shpfffff*, no one wants to buy *those*. LOOK! IT'S THE SAFE! GRIZZLE THE SIZZLE, SNOOP!

[BODINE manoeuvres Snoop Dog, which grabs the safe and floats back to the submersible while everyone cheers.]

Ship's Deck, the *Keldysh*

BODINE [spraying champagne]: Who's your daddy? Oh yeah! Who's your daddy?

[Once the safe has been cracked, LOVETT gleefully rifles through it and finds . . . rusty mud.]

LOVETT: RAAAAAAAAAAAAAAAAA!

BODINE: Me and the bubbly will take our questions of paternity elsewhere.

The Investor Phone Call of Doom

LOVETT: No, it wasn't in the safe, but . . . we can still find it! No, we totally can! In fact, we might find it in the mother's wardrobe, or the maid's bathroom, or the dog's parlour . . . OR ON A MUDDY OLD SKETCH OMG CALL YOU BACK.

[In a water tray, mud slides away to reveal a sketch of a naked chick wearing a diamond necklace.]

LOVETT: Fuck *me*.

LAB TECHNICIAN: Hey, I have a pen like that.

Chez Calvert

LIZZY: What would you like to watch, Grandma?

OLD ROSE: I don't know, dear. Turn it to the Coincidental Channel, there might be something interesting on there.

LOVETT [*on nearby TV*]: Everyone knows the stupid stories about the heroes and the band playing and blah blah noble sacrifices blah. *We* want to know about the trea— *truly*, I mean, uh, truly unknown stories of *Titanic*. So, uh, if this dirty, dirty sketch rings a bell for anyone, let us know—

ANCHORWOMAN: And that's Brock Lovett, treasure hunter and grave robber.

LOVETT: —call me! [*phone fingers*]

OLD ROSE: Well, fuck *me*.

LIZZY: GRANDMA!

OLD ROSE: Oh, put a sock in it, *Elizabeth*.

The Deck of the *Keldysh*

SOME GUY: Lovett, we got a phone call from destiny over here for you.

LOVETT: Look, man, we're about to launch the . . . destiny, you say?

Phone Call from Destiny, Deck of the *Keldysh*

OLD ROSE: Found the Heart of the Ocean yet?

LOVETT: WHO IS THIS?

OLD ROSE: You may remember me from such sketches as the one in your hand right now.

LOVETT: omg.

The Next Day, Aboard a Totally Different Ship. Okay, It's Still the *Keldysh*

BODINE: She's a liar, man! I checked her out! This Rose Something-Whateverthingy died on the *Titanic* at seventeen! And even if a brief, star-crossed romance with a teen idol somehow saved her life, the old bat here was an ACTRESS. You know? People who PRETEND for a living?

LOVETT: No, I don't, and I'm sure no one else in this movie appreciates your insinuations about that noble profession.

BODINE: Lovett, this is a scam!

LOVETT: What exactly do you think she's gonna *do*, Bodine?

BODINE: She could . . . she could totally go, like, friggin' ninja and hijack our ship and sell us out to bloodthirsty Filipino pirates!

LOVETT: We're in the *Atlantic*, Bodine.

BODINE: Or . . . she could waste a few hours of our time.

LOVETT: I'm saying, man.

Rose's Stateroom, the *Keldysh*

LOVETT: Everything all right?

OLD ROSE: Oh, yes. As long as I've got my dog and my fish and my pictures and my wheelchair and my Ensure and my knitting and my stories on the picture tube and my begonias and my potter's wheel, I'm fine.

THE *KELDYSH*: *groans*

LOVETT [*to* CREWMATE]: Go find something heavy to chuck overboard if you can, okay? [*To* ROSE] Is there anything else I can get you, ma'am?

OLD ROSE: Yes, my sketch, please.

LOVETT: Now? Right now?

OLD ROSE: I'm a hundred years old! Dying a little more with every passing moment here, people! Chop chop!

The Dirty, Dirty Sketch

OLD ROSE: Damn, but I had a rack back in the day.

LOVETT: The jewel in this picture is a priceless blue diamond once worn by Louis XVI until an unfortunate run-in with the guillotine in 1792, at which point it may have been re-cut into a heart shape, as this picture plainly demonstrates, and became known as—

OLD ROSE: The Heart of Exposition, I know, Mr Lovett. Believe me, the man who bought it wouldn't shut up about it.

LIZZY: Oh, Grandma, your pretends are so silly!

OLD ROSE: Cram it, Elizabeth.

LOVETT: About that man, Mrs Calvert . . . ?

OLD ROSE: Yes, that ass Hockley.

THE CREW: YUSS! THAT'S THE NAME!

LOVETT: And that's the man whose father filed the insurance claim right after the sinking, which means that the necklace went down with the ship, which means that I love you, Mrs Calvert.

OLD ROSE: Heh. Get in line, Mr Lovett.

Bodine Simulates the Shipwreck

BODINE: So, as you can see, Mrs Calvert, the iceberg rams the shit out of the ol' girl and she starts takin' on water and the compartments fill up and everyone's screaming and dying down below, all like [*imitation of high-pitched shriek*] 'OMG! HELP US!' but no one's helpin' 'em! No one's helpin' 'em! And then the ship goes ass-end up, and that's a big ol' ass, too, and then the ship breaks in half and we start to back that ass up—

LOVETT: *You're* an ass, Bodine. *Jesus.*

OLD ROSE: If I were a spry young thing of eighty, Mr Bodine, I would put you over my knee and give you what-for!

LIZZY [*grabbing wheelchair*]: I think it's time for someone's nap!

OLD ROSE: SCREW OFF, ELIZABETH.

LIZZY: HAVE IT YOUR WAY, GRANDMA! *GAH.*

LOVETT: Tell us every horrific, excruciating detail, Rose.

OLD ROSE: Well, it's been eighty-four years . . .

LOVETT: That's cool. You can just make stuff up if you don't remember—

OLD ROSE: Son, let me tell the damn story, all right? AHEM. It's been eighty-four years, but I remember *Titanic* as if it were yesterday. The paint was still wet and all the tags were still on the pillows. It was a ship of dreams, it was a ship of fools. It was the best of times, it was the worst of times . . .

Southampton Docks, 1912

The ship is huge and the people are tiny and you are impressed. YOUNG ROSE, stepping out of an old-fashioned automobile, rocks a big purple portrait hat like it's going out of style, which . . . technically, it did. She is followed by her mother RUTH, her fiancé CAL, his henchman LOVEJOY, two MAIDS, several VALETS, fifty-nine trunks, thirty-nine valises, fourteen hatboxes, five portmanteaux and A SAFE, DUN DUN DUN!

RUTH: So this is the unsinkable ship.

CAL: Indeed! God Himself could not sink it!

GOD: Awwww, *man*! Now I *have* to smite you.

YOUNG ROSE: Eh.

OLD ROSE: Everyone else was over the moon. For me, it was a slave ship and I was in chains.

ACTUAL SLAVES: Bitch, *please*. Laundry service and five-star food – throw us into *that* briar patch.

Some Pub, Also Southampton

JACK DAWSON, a scruffy young artist, and his sidekick FABRIZIO STEREOTIPO are playing poker with two SWEDES. The stakes are tickets on *Titanic*.

JACK: Full house! OWNED!

SVEN: FUGEBORG!

FABRIZIO: I go-a to America! Earna the low wages and live inna the immigrant slums! My dream, she come-a true!

JACK: WOOO! We're the luckiest guys in the world! A statement that will in no way become ironic two days from now!

BARKEEPER: Or even five minutes from now, when the ship has sailed and your tickets are rendered worthless.

[JACK and FABRIZIO race to the docks, but get held up at the terminal and miss the boat. ROSE throws herself off the back of the ship the night before it sinks, JACK becomes a wandering artist/bum who whores himself out for cheap booze and FABRIZIO never gets to America.]

JACK: We're passengers! Let us board! We've got a movie to catch!

CREW GUY: Sure thing!

THE CROWD ON THE DOCKS: Yay!

[JACK and FABRIZIO race to the deck railing, where they wave to the crowds.]

JACK: Come on, make like someone cares about us! GOODBYE! I'LL MISS YOU!

THE CROWD ON THE DOCKS: Goodbye! Whee!

FABRIZIO: Goodbye! I willa nevah forgetta you, whoever you are!

[*Titanic* sets off steaming from Southampton, mowing down five sailboats, a yacht, a handful of dinghies and most of the tugboats that pulled her out of the dock.]

THE CROWD ON THE DOCKS: Hooray!

Young Rose's Suite

ROSE: Apparently my room on the most luxurious ship ever built wasn't decorated sufficiently, so I brought a metric shitload of paintings by artists who will someday be famous. How do you say this man's name? 'Pick-a-so'?

CAL: I pronounce it 'You suck', myself. Famous my ass.

THE AUDIENCE: Wait, these famous paintings went down with the *Titanic*? So . . . how do we know they're famous now?

CAL: I TOLD YOU SO!

The Ship's Bow

FABRIZIO and JACK horse around on the prow to the cheerful stylings of Mannheim Steamship.

JACK: Look! Dolphins! They're swimming in front of the ship! They're so—

[The ship mows over half the dolphins in a churning bloodbath.]

JACK: Ohhhh . . . *oh.*

FABRIZIO [*covering eyes*]: Thatta gotta *hurt.*

[On the bridge, FIFTH OFFICER HORATIO HORNBLOWER brings the CAPTAIN his tea. JACK and FABRIZIO have recovered their spirits by climbing the railing and pretending to fly.]

JACK: WOOOO!

FABRIZIO: I canna see-a the Statue a' Liberty allaready!

JACK: WOOHOO!!

FABRIZIO: Jack? Heya, Jack!

JACK: WOOOOOHOOOOOOOO!!!

FABRIZIO: You listena to me, Jack? You listena, right?

JACK: I'M KING OF THE WOOOOORLD!

Some Dark Editing Room

JAMES CAMERON: *Man*, that is a great line. I gotta have that embroidered on something.

The Ship's Bow

JACK: WOOOOOOOOOOOOOOOOO!!

CAPTAIN THÉODEN: Hornblower, go scrape those plebeians off my prow. They're upsetting my tea.

Luncheon in the Dining Room, First Class

ISMAY: . . . And so our shipbuilder Mr Andrews built us the largest man-made moving object in the history of ever, and it OWNS.

ANDREWS: Well, it was *his* God complex; I just designed her and built her and stuff.

[ROSE lights a cigarette in her dandy Holder of Rebellion.]

RUTH: You know I disapprove of that, Rose.

ROSE: Hi, that's why I do it— Hey!

CAL [*stubbing out cigarette and addressing* WAITER]: The lady and I will have the sacrificial lamb, extra-rare.

MOLLY BROWN: You gonna chew it up and feed it to her like a mama bird, too?

CAL [*quietly putting away* ROSE'S *knife and fork*]: No! No, of course not! Don't be *absurd*.

MOLLY BROWN: So, who came up with the name *Titanic*? You, big boy?

ISMAY: Well, yes, actually. It connotes size and strength and girth and length and general manly endurance.

ROSE: Does the word 'overcompensation' mean anything to you, Mr Ismay?

ANDREWS [*snorting*]: It's funny because it's true.

Poverty Deck, Steerage

JACK sketches a MAN with his YOUNG DAUGHTER while a CREW-MEMBER walks several VERY IMPORTANT DOGS.

SOME IRISH GUY: Well, here comes first class to shite on us again.

JACK: Well, you know, class warfare blah impending tragedy blee. What's your name again, man?

SOME IRISH GUY: They call me Ill-Fated Tommy O'Ryan.

[ROSE stalks out onto the upper deck and glares out over the sea. JACK stares up at her longingly.]

CAL: Muffin, the lamb has arrived.

ROSE: I don't *want* the—

CAL: EAT THE LAMB, MUFFIN.

ROSE: Okay!

Later That Night

OLD ROSE: My entire life flashed before my eyes: an endless parade of parties and yachts and privilege and canapés. Woe. I felt like I was standing on the rail of a great ship's deck, about to commit suicide, with no one to care or talk me out of it.

YOUNG ROSE: *is standing on the rail of the ship's deck, about to commit suicide*

JACK: You're not really gonna jump.

ROSE: Yuh-huh!

JACK: Nuh-uh!

ROSE: You're a nasty boy and I don't like you! Go away!

JACK: Shit, that didn't work. [*Stripping off coat and shoes*] Ma'am, seriously, I'm begging you. Don't jump, because I'm gonna have to jump in after you.

ROSE: But . . . that would kill you. Which is why *I'm* trying to do it. I mean, *duh*.

JACK: See, you'd think so, wouldn't you? Actually, you'll probably just snap your spine in the fall, and then be left floating in the sub-freezing water while vengeful dolphins gnaw your toes.

VENGEFUL DOLPHINS [*shaking bloody flippers*]: EEEE! ACK-ACKACK EEEEEHEEHEEHEH! *CLICK CLICK CLICK*

ROSE: . . .

JACK: . . .

ROSE: So . . . I'm gonna climb back over now.

  [She takes JACK'S hand in a meaningful moment of poignant foreshadowing. And then ROSE slips for real.]

ROSE: WAHHHHHHHHHH! I DON'T WANT TO DIE!

JACK: OH, THE *IRONY*!

  [JACK hauls her back over the railing and falls on her in the rescuer missionary position right as several SAILORS come running.]

SAILORS: OMGWTF!

  [The SAILORS summon the MASTER-AT-ARMS, who summons CAL and his henchman LOVEJOY, who have JACK clapped in irons.]

CAL: HOW DARE YOU LAY HANDS ON MY PROPERTY!

JACK: Miss?

CAL: ANSWER, SCUM!

JACK: Miss Something-Whateverthingy?

CAL: I DEMAND THE SATISFACTION OF A GENTLEMAN!
Lovejoy, have him fed to the dolphins.

VENGEFUL DOLPHINS: HEEEEEEH!

JACK: A little help here . . . !

ROSE: Oh! Yes! Cal! It was an accident! It was *so* silly, really. Yes.
Uh. I was . . . uh . . . doing stuff and . . . I . . . fell over. Yes. And
this gentleman saved me.

MASTER-AT-ARMS: And that's what happened?

JACK: No, she was actually trying to . . .

ROSE: *gives Jack the stink-eye*

JACK: Yes, that's totally what happened.

CAL: Oh. Well. Fabulous. Spot the kid a twenty, Lovejoy.

ROSE: Oh, *whatever*. You spend more than that on eyeliner in a
week, Cal!

CAL: Aww, widdle hussy Rose is displeased. I know! We'll invite
him to dinner on the first-class deck and humiliate him completely!

  [Everyone else exits to drink brandy smugly . . . except for
  henchman LOVEJOY, who hangs back.]

LOVEJOY: She just suddenly fell in, but you had time to take off
your coat and shoes?

JACK: Yeah, I always go raping with my shoes off, man.

Rose's Suite

CAL: I've noticed your complete and utter depression, kumquat. I
don't pretend to know why you're so unhappy . . .

ROSE: Oh, I can *tell* you why—

CAL: So I guess it'll remain a mystery for ever. What do I have to do to make you happy, pork chop? I would never deny you anything, except personal freedom and autonomy.

ROSE: *eyeroll*

CAL: Oh, look! Here's a giant rare diamond that once belonged to kings! Surprise!

ROSE: Whoa.

CAL: *We* are the royalty now. Well, except for the part where we have no crowns and no thrones. But we RULE.

ROSE: Well, actually, we DeWitt-Bukaters are kinda broke. Why are you after me, again?

[CAL gets down on his knees and answers her query with these words of tenderness:]

CAL: Open your heart to me, Rose. By which I mean 'legs'.

ROSE: WAH.

Moodswing Deck, First Class

ROSE: Mr Dawson, I just wanted to thank you for not ratting me out last night. And for saving my life and all that jazz.

JACK: Well, anything I could—

ROSE: I know, I know, you must be thinking that a rich girl can't possibly have problems but—

JACK: Well, actually—

ROSE: But my impending nuptials keep speeding ahead like a giant steamship full of society matrons heading right for an iceberg and there's nothing I can do to stop it and sometimes I wake up at night screaming about how my five hundred wedding invitations are coming to paper-cut me to death—

JACK: Wedding, huh? Do you love this guy?

ROSE: OMG YOU ARE SO RUDE! HOW DARE YOU PRY INTO MY LIFE!

JACK: *gets whiplash*

ROSE: That's it! I'm leaving! No I'm not! You're leaving!

JACK: Heh. Rude!

ROSE: No I'm not, *you're* rude! [*Grabbing sketchbook*] YOINK!

JACK: HEY!

ROSE: Oh, wow! These sketches the director drew for you are amazing! You have so much fake talent! And— Oh. Goodness me. That right there is a hairy one-legged prostitute. You had a thing with her?

JACK: No, no – just a love affair with her hands.

ROSE: Yeah, I bet you did.

[JACK and ROSE bond over busted French whores and tinkly music on the soundtrack. Elsewhere, over in the dining room . . .]

RUTH: I don't see why Rose should go to university. She already has her MRS degree.

THE OTHER LADIES: Tee hee!

ISMAY: We have to make headlines! Bigger headlines! Faster! Harder!

CAPTAIN THÉODEN: Wow, Rose really was right about your dick, wasn't she?

[Back outside on the Rebellion Deck . . .]

JACK: . . . and then they made me chief of their tribe, but I got tired of all that savage adoration so I caught a ride on a squid boat to the Santa Monica pier and held off starvation by drawing ten-cent portraits.

ROSE: Why can't I be like you, Jack?

JACK: What – baby-faced, downtrodden and broke?

ROSE: No! Free to do whatever I want, whenever I want!

JACK: Hey, you wanna do stuff? We'll go do lots and lots of stuff. We'll vomit on roller-coasters and ride sandy, wet horses. But you'll have to ride like a man.

113

ROSE: With one leg on each side? No! No . . . I . . . Can you teach me how to do that?

JACK: Nah, I'm not supposed to show you that for another [*checks watch*] good hour or so. But I can teach you to spit like a man right now!

ROSE: You want me to *spit*?

JACK: Well, I'd really prefer if you sw— Yes. Yes I do.

   [JACK drags her over to a railing where he teaches her to hawk the Loogies of Love.]

ROSE: Ew! That's disgusting! MY TURN! *ptuuuw!*

JACK: That was *weak*, man. See, you gotta really hork it up, like this –SNNNNNNORRRRRRK . . .

ROSE: OH, MOTHER, HI.

JACK: *drips snot helplessly*

RUTH: *sniff*

ROSE: I . . . uh . . . well . . . I'll . . . see you at dinner tonight, Mr Dawson!

MOLLY BROWN: Oh, son – you and I need to have a talk.

Molly Brown's Unsinkable Stateroom

MOLLY BROWN: I knew this suit would fit you, Jack! It belongs to my son, who is conveniently not on this ship even though his clothes are! Look at you – you shine up like a new penny! Which is about what you're worth.

JACK: Whee!

Clock, Grand Staircase

ROSE, impressed with the way JACK cleans up, meets him wearing a beautiful sparkling dress of peach overlaid with black.

TEENAGE GIRLS IN AUDIENCE: If I buy a replica of this dress, I'll be the only girl wearing it at the prom for sure!

CAL: Oh, who's this, Rose? Someone you've been babysitting?

ROSE: You remember Mr Dawson, Cal.

CAL: I'll be damned! You can almost pass for a gentleman.

JACK: Thanks, man. You can almost pass for not an asshole.

The Dining Room

ROSE [*whispering*]: Look at all the nobles and millionaires! Long story short, they're all screwing.

JACK: Good to know . . . ?

[They sit down to dine. Every major upper-class character, including ANDREWS the shipbuilder, ISMAY – the head of the White Star Line, and the GUGGENHEIMS and the ASTORS just for good measure, are at the table.]

RUTH: Everyone, this is Mr Dawson from steerage. How do you like being poorer than dirt, Mr Dawson?

JACK: It's fabulous, ma'am. In fact, the *Titanic* is so nice that we have tiny white mice instead of rats.

ROSE: Yes, Mr Andrews, your ship is marvellous!

ANDREWS: *beams*

RUTH: Yes, yes. Back to your poverty, Mr Dawson. How did you end up here, again?

JACK: Well, I won my ticket in a poker game. That's how I live life, ma'am – I wake up each morning not knowing what's coming to me, and what does come, I enjoy the hell out of it.

ROSE [*raising glass*]: To enjoying the hell out of it!

EVERYONE ELSE: Bravo! I say! Well said, good chap!

RUTH AND CAL: Grrrrrr.

[The men exit for brandy and smokes. JACK passes ROSE a note.]

JACK'S NOTE:

> Hey Rose do you like me?
>
> ___ Yes
>
> ___ No
>
> ___ Maybe
>
> PS Meet me at the clock if you wanna crash a real party.

ROSE: Ooo.

Irish Steerage Stomp

After protesting that she doesn't know the steps, ROSE challenges JACK to a dance-off and wins. Then she downs an entire glass of beer, to JACK'S shock.

ROSE: What, you think first-class girls can't drink? Trust me, it's the only way we get through the day.

   [Across the room:]

ILL-FATED TOMMY O'RYAN: I can drink you under the table!

SOME SWEDISH GUY: I can beat your ass into next week!

ROSE: *I* can stand on my toenails!

EVERYONE ELSE: *Damn*, girl.

   [ROSE falls into JACK'S arms and is of course seen at that very moment by a spying LOVEJOY.]

LOVEJOY: Grrrrrr.

CAL: I was hoping you would come to me last night, Rose, and we would do the sex. But clearly you were too busy whoring it up with the plebeians—

ROSE: Oh, how like a man to complain that his fiancée is gallivanting around with other men!

CAL: HOCKLEY SMASH!

[CAL turns the breakfast table over, makes some extremely creepy threats to ROSE about 'honouring' him and storms off.]

TRUDY THE MAID: Miss Rose!

ROSE: Oh! Oh, Trudy! We had . . . we had a little accident! Nothing to worry about! I'm sure . . . I'm sure we'll have lots more once we're . . . we're . . . married . . . WAHHHHHHHH!

TRUDY THE MAID: Oh, Miss Rose! It'll be all right! If by 'all right' you mean 'a living hell for the rest of your life'!

ROSE: *sob*

Devotional Service

JACK: Hi, could I get in to see Rose?

STEWARD: I'm sorry, plebe, we don't recall your presence at dinner here last night.

JACK: But I didn't say anything about— HEY! Look, I just need to talk to Rose!

LOVEJOY: *Au contraire*, I think you need to have your ass kicked. [*Holding out money to* STEWARDS] Gentlemen?

JACK: Sigh.

Rose Tours the Ship

CREWMAN: Another ice warning, Captain!

CAPTAIN THÉODEN: Excellent. Full steam ahead!

ROSE: Um, Ship Daddy? I did the math, and . . . you totally don't have enough lifeboats.

ANDREWS: Well spotted, young Rose! Fortunately I have built you a good ship, strong and true, that would never run into an iceberg and take down fifteen hundred people with it!

ROSE: Oh, good!

[Suddenly JACK sneaks up in a stolen hat and overcoat and drags ROSE into an empty gymnasium.]

ROSE: Jack! What are you— Hey, we have a gym on this ship?

JACK: Rose, we have to talk. I know you're engaged to some guy who's richer than God and I'm dead broke and have no prospects and nothing to offer you, and you're a total spoiled brat who would curl up and die if she didn't have her weekly pedicure—

ROSE: Twice-weekly. And you're trying to convince me of *what*, here?

JACK: Just that . . . look, I want you to be happy.

ROSE: I'll be plenty happy! I'm happy right now! I'm so happy I could cry! Every night! Into my pillow so no one can hear! EXCUSE ME, I HAVE TO GO NOW.

Tea of Despair

RUTH: . . . and it was an utter disaster! We had to send the invitations back twice, and then the envelopes for the invitations, and then the seals for the envelopes, and then for some reason that stationer didn't want to do business with us any more! I never! And then Rose picked lavender for the bridesmaid gowns just to spite me, and . . .

[ROSE'S attention wanders away to a MOTHER and YOUNG DAUGHTER having tea.]

SOME MOTHER: Sit up straight! Spread out your napkin! Hold

your pinky out! YOU PICKED THAT COOKIE JUST TO SPITE ME.

Ship's Prow

ROSE: So . . . it was either come to you or stab my mother with the sugar tongs.

JACK: You made the right choice. Come on, Rose! Climb up on the rail, even though that's what nearly got you killed at the beginning of the movie.

ROSE: And how is this any safer?

JACK: Well, it's the front of the ship.

ROSE: So . . . if I fall I'll be immediately ploughed under, rather than slowly freezing to death in the backwash?

JACK: Don't forget the vengeful dolphins.

VENGEFUL DOLPHINS: EEH! EEH!

JACK: Don't worry! I'll hold onto you the whole time. Don't you trust me?

ROSE: . . .

JACK: We can pretend to fly! And then we can make out.

ROSE: I like the way you think.

Present Day, Back on the *Keldysh*

LOVETT: So this takes us up to the night of the sinking.

BODINE: Man, these people, who have no way of knowing then what we know now, are MORONS.

LOVETT: Well, the captain has a quarter-century of seafaring experience working against him. He's assuming that a giant ship will not be built with a tiny rudder, and that the lookouts won't lose their binoculars the moment the ship launches, and that corporate jerk-wads will actually stock enough lifeboats. He has no idea that his men will be completely outnumbered by a factor of thirty, and that the Haradrim will have giant elephants—

BODINE: Boss? Have you been smoking again?

Young Rose's Suite

ROSE: Jack, I want you to draw me like one of your French whores, wearing nothing but a giant diamond my fiancé bought me. You know, just to spite him. What do you say?

JACK: The word I am looking for here is . . . YES.

[ROSE drops her robe and, despite having sketched numerous naked women in the past, JACK is agog.]

JACK: So, lie down on the bed— I mean the cooch— I MEAN THE COUCH.

[We cut between JACK'S twenty-year-old face and JACK'S forty-year-old hands sketching ROSE.]

Back on the *Keldysh*

OLD ROSE: But since all I could see were the twenty-year-old eyes, it was the most erotic moment of my life.

BODINE: And . . . ?

OLD ROSE: You mean, did we do it?

THE CREW: Tee hee!

OLD ROSE: No, Mr Bodine. He was very professional for another half-hour.

Young Rose's Suite

ROSE writes a letter and puts it, the necklace and JACK'S sketch back in the safe.

ROSE'S LETTER:

Dear Cal,

Suck it,

'Love' Rose

Ship's Bridge

CAPTAIN THÉODEN: All clear?

SECOND OFFICER LIGHTOLLER: Yes.

CAPTAIN THÉODEN: Totally clear and disaster-free?

SECOND OFFICER LIGHTOLLER: You could not ask for better sailing weather.

CAPTAIN THÉODEN: Yep, not even a breeze.

THE CAPTAIN'S TEA: *thumbs up*

SECOND OFFICER LIGHTOLLER: You know . . . that *will* make the icebergs harder to see.

CAPTAIN THÉODEN: Good thing there are none of *those* around here!

Rose's Suite

JACK: Brrrr, it is so cold. Oh, hey, you look nice.

ROSE: Thanks! It's my winter chiffon— OMG IT'S LOVEJOY RUN!

LOVEJOY: I HEARD THAT!

The Boiler Room

ROSE and JACK flee LOVEJOY, laughing and cussing like drunks all the way. They run in a picturesque fashion through the boiler room –

STOKER: OI, WE'RE TRYIN' TO WORK HERE! DAMN KIDS!

The Cargo Hold

– and then find themselves in the cargo hold. To show JACK that she loves him despite the barrier of social caste, ROSE forces him to hand her into a car and pretend to be her chauffeur. Then she drags him into the back seat.

ROSE: Oh, Jack, that coal-shovelling really turns me on!

JACK: I could shovel some of your coal, baby.

ROSE: Okay, you've just taken the metaphor too far.

  [They both seem to understand that sex is inevitable at this point and – hey, it's a back seat. JACK gets nervous, so ROSE kisses his fingertips with her mad seductress skillz.]

ROSE [*huskily*]: Put your hands on me, Jack.

JACK: And you said you're . . . how old, now? Seventeen?

Back on the *Keldysh*

OLD ROSE: And *then* we did the sex.

LOVETT: In the back of a car?

LIZZY: Awww, Grandma, you too?

Back on *Titanic*

We are treated to an overhead shot of the massive ship coasting through the limpid, submissive waters.

JAMES CAMERON: Well, it's no train-going-into-a-tunnel shot, but it'll have to do.

Just Outside the Bridge

SECOND OFFICER LIGHTOLLER: Murdoch! Did you ever find the binoculars for the lookouts? You know, so they could be looking out, and stuff?

FIRST OFFICER MURDOCH: Nah. I think someone dropped 'em overboard at . . . the docks?

SECOND OFFICER LIGHTOLLER: What about the *Californian*? Heard anything from them?

FIRST OFFICER MURDOCH: Oh, we're ignoring the *Californian* so completely that it's not even in the movie.

Sex Car, Cargo Hold

ROSE'S hand smacks the steamy window like something out of a horror movie – *I Know What You Did Eighty-Four Years Ago*.

Rose's Suite

CAL is standing at the safe, having discovered the 'Dear Cal' letter and the nudie sketch.

LOVEJOY: Anything missing?

CAL: Oh, no, everything's here, locked up tight EXCEPT FOR MY FIANCÉE'S VIRGINITY!

Ship's Deck

ROSE and JACK run away laughing from STEWARDS chasing them through the hold. Apparently JACK laced up ROSE'S corset while they were on the run.

ROSE: Jack? When the ship docks, I'm getting off with you.

JACK: I thought we already—

ROSE: Off THE SHIP with you.

JACK: Oh. Oh! Yay!

ROSE: Let's make out!

LOOKOUT 1 [*watching them instead of the sea*]: Well, if that's what it takes to get warm, you and I . . . well . . . we . . . I AM TOTALLY NOT GAY.

LOOKOUT 2: ME NEITHER.

LOOKOUT 1: I'M GLAD THAT'S SETTLED.

LOOKOUT 2: IN A VERY HETEROSEXUAL WAY, YES.

ICEBERG: Hi.

LOOKOUT 2: OH SHIT!

LOOKOUT 1: BUGGER *ME*!

LOOKOUT 2: I THOUGHT YOU JUST SAID—

   [LOOKOUT 1 calls the bridge, setting off a chain of reactions:]

LOOKOUT 1: ICEBERG! RIGHT AHEAD!

SIXTH OFFICER MOODY: OH SHIT!

FIRST OFFICER MURDOCH: GODDAMMIT!

CHIEF ENGINEER BELL: JESUS JOSEPH AND MARY!

SECOND ENGINEER HESKETH: BLOODY HELL!

LEAD STOKER BARRETT: SWEET FANCY MOSES!

FIRST OFFICER MURDOCH: Turn!

THE SHIP: *does not turn*

FIRST OFFICER MURDOCH: Turn!

THE SHIP: *does not turn*

FIRST OFFICER MURDOCH: TURN, DAMN YOU!

THE SHIP: *does not turn*

FIRST OFFICER MURDOCH: Everyone lean to the left REAL HARD!

EVERYONE: *leaaaaaaaaans*

[The SHIP just manages to avoid hitting the iceberg head-on, which it might have survived. Instead, it grazes the hidden bulk of the iceberg, ripping open its side and flooding compartments and washing half the stokers in the boiler room away and drowning the Sex Car, oh noes.]

Andrews' Stateroom

ANDREWS: I feel a great disturbance in the ship, as if millions of rivets suddenly cried out in terror and were suddenly silenced.

Hey, What Was That?

STEWARD: Everyone please be calm. We've just thrown some completely non-essential piece of hardware that will not result in the damp, frosty death of hundreds.

MRS ASTOR: Oh, how entirely bothersome.

GUGGENHEIM: Eh wot?

TINY WHITE MICE: Abandon ship!

ILL-FATED TOMMY O'RYAN [*watching mice*]: Oh, that ain't good.

CAL: I demand that everyone drop whatever they're doing and arrest a man on false charges!

STEWARD: Well . . . I guess that *does* take priority over the lives of fifteen hundred people.

Rose's Suite

MASTER-AT-ARMS [*looking at sketch*]: You got a hot number there, sir.

CAL: Why, I ought to pay someone to slap you!

ROSE [*entering with* JACK]: Mother? Cal? Something serious has happened that you need to know about—

CAL: Yes! Right there! That man stole my girl and he stole my rock!

JACK: OH, WHATEVER, I ONLY STOLE HIS GIRL.

LOVEJOY: And the rock, which I totally just dropped in your pocket as you came in.

EVERYONE: OMGWTF!

JACK: This is bullshit! I'm not a thief!

CAL: And this coat! And this hat!

JACK: Oh . . . yeah, about that . . .

[The MASTER-AT-ARMS seizes JACK and drags him away.]

JACK: ROSE! ROSE! YOU KNOW I WOULDN'T DO THIS! YOU'VE KNOWN ME FOR . . . TWO DAYS . . .

ROSE: . . .

JACK: . . . Yeah, I'll go now.

The Ship's Bridge

CAPTAIN THÉODEN: I LEAVE YOU PEOPLE ALONE FOR TWO MINUTES, AND YOU WRECK MY SHIP.

FIRST OFFICER MURDOCH: *wibbles*

ISMAY: Yes, yes, unsinkable ship blah making headlines blee. Can we put a quickness on and get moving, please?

ANDREWS: THE SHIP IS SINKING, YOU ASS.

ISMAY: But that's physically impossible!

ANDREWS: Oh, really? Well, there's forty-six tons of iron here that would like to have a chat with you.

Rose's Suite

CAL slaps ROSE so hard that her head just permanently sticks back there. In fact, he slaps her all the way back to the beginning of the movie.

CAL: WHAT DO YOU HAVE TO SAY FOR YOURSELF, WHORE?

ROSE: I don't know! The beginning of the movie was a long time ago!

   [They are interrupted by a STEWARD who insists that they put on lifebelts and come up on deck.]

STEWARD: Don't worry, ma'am. This is only a temporary inconvenience. We'll return you to your domestic abuse as quickly as possible.

The Wireless Room

OPERATOR: You want me to say *what*?

CAPTAIN THÉODEN: That the unsinkable ship is sinking, yes.

OPERATOR: Jigga *what*?

CAPTAIN THÉODEN: I know, man.

Lifebelt Soirée, Grand Staircase

All the rich people are milling around drinking and laughing and being generally useless while the TRAGEDY QUINTET plays cheerfully. ANDREWS is horrified.

ANDREWS: Remember what you said about the lifeboats?

ROSE: Oh shit.

On the Deck

OPERATOR: So basically, the closest ship is four hours away.

CAPTAIN THÉODEN: OH MY GOD— I mean, uh . . . good. Excellent. Good man. OH MY GOD.

SECOND OFFICER LIGHTOLLER: So, should we load the lifeboats?

CAPTAIN THÉODEN: Uh-huh.

SECOND OFFICER LIGHTOLLER: Women and children first?

CAPTAIN THÉODEN: Uh-huh.

SECOND OFFICER LIGHTOLLER: Should we let steerage come up now, or later?

CAPTAIN THÉODEN: Uh-huh.

[The TRAGEDY QUINTET sets up and starts to play on deck to keep people calm.]

BANDLEADER HARTLEY: Take it to the bridge! Drop it in the water—

CELLO GUY: THAT'S NOT FUNNY.

Master-at-Arms' Office

LOVEJOY is guarding JACK, who is cuffed to a pipe.

LOVEJOY: Hey, you know what? I think this ship is actually going to sink.

[LOVEJOY gets up, punches JACK in the gut, pockets the key to the handcuffs and leaves.]

JACK: Man, are you just the most ironically named guy in the history of ever or what?

In the Movie Theatre

SOME GUY: I was sure there'd be an intermission after the iceberg hit.

SOME OTHER GUY: Well, the sinking hasn't really started yet. I'm sure we'll get one before then.

Steerage

ILL-FATED TOMMY O'RYAN: LET US OUT!

FABRIZIO: YOU LEAVA US DOWN HERE, WEESA GONNA DIE!

STEWARD 1: Did you hear something?

STEWARD 2: No, I don't think I did.

On the Deck

All the first-class women are milling around delicately.

RUTH: Goodness me, I do hope we aren't put in the same boat as the unwashed masses.

MOLLY BROWN: INTO THE BOAT, BITCHES! YOU TOO, RUTH!

CAL: So . . . any room in there for a gentleman? No? Well, that's all right. I'll pay my way onto another boat and live to weasel another day, propagating my loathsomeness unto the end of time.

MOLLY BROWN: Your turn, Rose!

ROSE: You know what? I think all y'all can go screw, is what I think. Except you, Molly.

MOLLY BROWN: No offense taken, babe.

CAL [*manhandling* ROSE]: OMG YOU WILL HONOUR ME AND SERVE ME AND SUBMIT TO ME AND BE MISERABLE WITH ME!

[ROSE fights back with the only weapon left at her disposal –]

CAL: ACK! THE LOOGIE OF LOVE! I'M *MELTING*!

[– and beats feet in search of JACK.]

Rose to the Rescue

ROSE: Where would you put someone under arrest? Help me!

ANDREWS: I . . . well . . .

ROSE: HELP ME.

ANDREWS: Crew passage! That way!

ROSE: I have to go downstairs! Help me!

ELEVATOR GUY: Oh, hell no.

ROSE: HELP ME, GODDAMMIT.

ELEVATOR GUY: Yes, ma'am!

Some Crew Passage

ROSE DEWITT BUKATER, ACTION HERO! swings from pipe to pipe through a flooded hall. Then she finds the crew passage. It goes both right and left.

ROSE: *Shit.* Jack?

JACK: Rose!

ROSE: Jack?

JACK: Rose!

ROSE: Jack?

JACK: Rose!

ROSE: Jack?

JACK: ROSE!!

The Master-at-Arms' Office

ROSE: JACK!! I came to save you!

JACK: How'd you find out I didn't steal the necklace?

ROSE: I didn't. I just realized you're the hero, that's all!

Some Crew Passage

ROSE: A man is trapped down there! Help me!

STEWARD [*panicking*]: Don't panic! There's no need to panic! No one's panicking!

ROSE: DON'T MAKE ME ASK YOU TWICE, BITCH.

STEWARD: *froths at the mouth*

ROSE: *punches him in the nose*

STEWARD: OW! SCREW YOU!

ROSE: WHY WON'T ANYONE HELP ME!

AXE ON THE WALL: Hey, baby.

ROSE: I LOVE YOU.

The Master-at-Arms' Office

ROSE must now chop the handcuffs in half, even though she's shaking with cold and her lumberjack licence has expired.

JACK: Hey, I'm just an artist, I don't need my hands anyway. GO!

> [ROSE CLOSES HER EYES and nails the chain in one blow anyway.]

ROSE: Hurry, let's go!

JACK: SHIT, THE WATER IS COLD!

ROSE: NO SHIT, ASSHOLE! GET A MOVE ON!

Lifeboats, Ship's Deck

The hoi polloi have fought their way to the deck and panic is setting in.

SECOND OFFICER LIGHTOLLER: Please, keep calm while we rip you from your loved ones!

ANDREWS: WHY ARE YOU PUTTING THE BOATS OUT HALF-FULL, BITCHES?

SECOND OFFICER LIGHTOLLER: I . . . because . . . we weren't sure how many they would hold . . . ?

ANDREWS: THEY CAN HOLD SEVENTY PEOPLE!

> [ANDREWS' guilt trip is interrupted by another outburst from the mob.]

SECOND OFFICER LIGHTOLLER: I'LL SHOOT YOU ALL LIKE DOGS WITH THE BULLETS I HAVEN'T LOADED IF YOU DON'T! STEP! OFF!

FIFTH OFFICER HORATIO HORNBLOWER: Seriously, guys, he crazy. Work with us here.

SWEET LITTLE OLD MAN: Get in the boat!

SWEET LITTLE OLD WOMAN: No! Where you go, I go!

CAL: Yeah, well, where I go, my money goes. Murdoch! Sneak me onto a boat of women and children?

FIRST OFFICER MURDOCH: Sure. Fine. Whatever. Jerkface.

LOVEJOY: I found Miss Rose! She's on the other side of the ship! WITH HIM.

CAL: ARGHHH! Revenge or self-preservation?

LOVEJOY: Your two defining moral principles, I know.

CAL: DAMMIT! WE HAVE TO FIND THEM.

LOVEJOY: *facepalm*

ISMAY: I'll take his spot, thanks.

FIRST OFFICER MURDOCH: You *asshole*.

The Curse of the Starving Class

CREW GUY 1: Don't jump out the windows and swim to the half-full lifeboats!

STEERAGE PASSENGERS: Grrrr!

CREW GUY 2: Lock the gates and don't let anyone out! Not even women and children!

STEERAGE PASSENGERS: Fnarrr!

CREW GUY 3: Go back to the main stairwell, which is also locked, and they will ignore you there!

STEERAGE PASSENGERS: ATTICA! ATTICA!

In the Movie Theatre

SOME CHICK: You know, it'd be really great if we got an intermission about now.

SOME CHICK'S BEST FRIEND: There's got to be one coming up in a moment.

JACK: Get on the boat, Rose!

ROSE: No, Jack!

JACK: Yes, Rose!

ROSE: No, Jack!

JACK: Yes, Rose!

ROSE: No, Jack!

JACK: Yes, Rose!

ROSE: No, Jack!

JACK: Yes, Rose!

ROSE: No, Jack!

JACK: Yes, Rose!

[This eloquent debate is interrupted by the arrival of CAL and LOVEJOY, who are pretending that they actually care about ROSE.]

CAL [*putting overcoat on* ROSE]: God, you look a fright!

ROSE: Yeah, and you look an asshole— Jesus, what are you doing, *petting* me? Get off me!

JACK: Get in the boat, Rose!

CAL: Yes, get in the boat, Rose. Look, I totally bribed an officer on the other side of the ship. We'll let Lovejoy drown –

LOVEJOY: HEY!

CAL: – and Jack can have his place, all right? Get in the boat, Rose.

[Reluctantly, ROSE gets in the boat. CAL and JACK gaze down at ROSE as the lifeboat is lowered to the sea. ROSE gazes up moistly at JACK. CAL and JACK gaze down at ROSE. ROSE gazes up at JACK. CAL and JACK gaze down at ROSE. ROSE gazes up at JACK. CAL and JACK gaze down at ROSE. ROSE gazes up at JACK. CAL and JACK gaze down at ROSE. ROSE gazes up at JACK. CAL and JACK gaze down at ROSE.]

JACK: You totally just screwed me over, didn't you?

CAL: That's about the way of it, yeah.

[CAL and JACK gaze down at ROSE. ROSE gazes up at JACK. CAL and JACK gaze down at ROSE. ROSE gazes up at JACK. CAL and JACK gaze down at ROSE. ROSE gazes up at JACK. CAL and JACK gaze down at ROSE. ROSE gazes up at JACK. CAL and JACK gaze down at ROSE. ROSE gazes up at JACK. CAL and JACK gaze down at ROSE. ROSE gazes up at JACK. CAL and JACK gaze down at ROSE. ROSE gazes up at JACK. CAL and JACK gaze down at ROSE. ROSE gazes up at JACK.]

ROSE: GERONIMO!

[ROSE leaps from the lifeboat to the sinking ship. She and JACK race across and down and through the ship to each other.]

JACK: ROSE! [*snog*] YOU MORON! [*snog*] WHY [*snog*] DID [*snog*] YOU [*snog*] COME [*snog*] BACK [*snog*] FOR [*snog*] ME [*snog snog snog*]?

CAL: I KEEL YOU, WHORE!

[CAL, hot on their heels, grabs LOVEJOY's gun and, after a brief interlude of falling on his ass, chases the young lovers down several floors, shooting all the way. After using up all LOVEJOY's bullets on moving targets, CAL stops and comforts himself with the following thought:]

CAL: AHAHAHAHAHA! They ran away into the depths of a sinking ship! WITH MY DIAMOND IN HER POCKET OMG.

LOVEJOY: You're right, that really *is* funny. FOOL.

Below Decks

SOME CRYING CHILD: WAHHH!

ROSE: Oh, crap, we've got to save that child!

SOME CRYING CHILD'S FATHER: How dare you save my kid?

ROSE: WHY IS EVERYONE INSANE?

MASSIVE WALL OF WATER: WIIIIIIIPEOUT!

[ROSE and JACK get trapped against one of the locked steerage gates. Rather than just hand them the keys, a passing STEWARD fumbles with them in the lock and panics and drops them and runs away. JACK manages to retrieve them with his super Chippewa Falls swimming powers and unlocks the gate himself.]

ROSE: Hurry, Jack! Jack! Hurry! Hurry, Jack! Jack! JACK!

JACK: WOMAN, WHAT DO YOU THINK I'M DOING?

In the Movie Theatre

SOME GUY: We're not getting an intermission, are we?

SOME GUY'S DATE: OH MY GOD I DON'T THINK WE ARE!

TEENS IN THE FRONT ROW: BUT HOW ARE WE GONNA HOLD IT FOR ANOTHER HOUR?!

EVERYONE IN THE THEATRE: *panics*

On the Deck

FIRST OFFICER MURDOCH throws CAL'S money back in his face. A small riot breaks out and ILL-FATED TOMMY O'RYAN lives up to his name by getting shot. FABRIZIO keens over his body. FIRST OFFICER MURDOCH feels so guilty about shooting people who were probably going to die anyway that he shoots himself, to the horror of all. There is not really anything funny you can say about this.

CAL: Aaaaaand now it's time for a change of plans.

[CAL goes back, scoops up some other CRYING CHILD and runs back to the lifeboats.]

CAL: Let me on the boat! I'm all the total stranger she has in the world!

SECOND OFFICER LIGHTOLLER: God, it's worth it just to get you out of my face. *Damn.*

136

In the Movie Theatre

Outside at Concession Stand 3, people are beating each
other to death with souvenir tumblers for the last box of Twizzlers.

Sad Scenes of Noble Martyrs

ROSE: Ship Daddy? Won't you take a life jacket?

ANDREWS: Thanks, I'll just go down with my ship.

SOME CREW GUY: Captain? Won't you take a life jacket?

CAPTAIN THÉODEN: Thanks, I'll just go down with my ship.

SOME VALET: Mr Guggenheim? Won't you take a life jacket?

GUGGENHEIM: Tally ho, I'll just go down for no reason at all!

BANDLEADER HARTLEY: Gentlemen, it was a privilege.

[As the TRAGEDY QUINTET disperses, HARTLEY picks up his violin
and starts playing again. Reluctantly, the other musicians come
back and join him.]

CELLO GUY: Dammit, Wally!

[A Monet painting dies for the sins of the White Star Line. We
don't see exactly how LOVEJOY dies, but it probably involves
decapitation by a predatory sheet of glass. But that's okay,
because he's evil. FABRIZIO is nailed by a smokestack. An IRISH
MOTHER reads a story about Tir-nan-Og, land of eternal youth
and beauty, to her YOUNG CHILDREN. The SWEET LITTLE OLD COUPLE
curl up on a bed to die as the water rushes in to drown them. I
could probably think of something funny to say if I thought hard
enough, but I don't like the idea of roasting in hell for eternity.]

The Ship's Stern

JACK drags ROSE up to the back of the ship, which is rising as the
bow sinks. Everyone is screaming and flailing and clinging and

generally freaking out. Death sounds like choral Celtic music.

JACK: I won't let go, Rose! I've got you! I won't ever let go! Don't let go, Rose! Don't ever let go!

ROSE: I won't, Jack! I won't ever let go!

PRIEST: The Lord is with thee as thou drown'st horribly because thy betters were too snotty to let thee have a seat on the lifeboat. Neither shall there be sorrow or crying or pain, unlike RIGHT NOW.

[We watch loving shots of the *Titanic* china smashing to the floor. TRUDY THE MAID slides away to the Great Tea Tray in the sky.]

SOME GUY: Not our underpaid hired help! Nooooo!

SOME OTHER GUY: Forget the maid, what about our CHINA?

EVERYONE: *weeps*

ROSE: What's happening, Jack!?

JACK: I think we're SINKING, ROSE!

In the Movie Theatre

SOME WOMAN: I'm not going to the restroom without you!

SOME WOMAN'S HUSBAND: It's only for a little while!

SOME WOMAN: I won't leave you here, Chad!

SOME WOMAN'S HUSBAND: *Someone has to save our seats, Jennifer!*

SOME CRYING CHILD: Bye bye, Daddy!

The Ship's Stern

The back half of the ship pitches all the way up and then falls back down and starts plunging into the sea and everyone still alive is in big, big trouble.

JACK: We're going to make it, Rose! Trust me!

ROSE: I trust you, even though trusting you has nothing to do with whether we drown or not!

JACK: You jump when I jump! Don't look down! Don't look back! Stay alive, whatever occurs! Do not let go of my hand!

ROSE: *lets go of his hand*

EVERYONE: WAHHHHHHHH!

[The back half of the ship goes under and it's every attractive teen idol for him- or herself.]

ROSE: Jack!

JACK: Rose!

ROSE: Jack!

JACK: Rose!

ROSE: Jack!

JACK: Rose!

ROSE: Jack!

JACK: ROSE!!

ROSE: JACK!!

[And then they hear . . . *the vengeful dolphins*.]

Back on the *Keldysh*

LOVETT: What happened?

OLD ROSE: Fifteen hundred souls went into the water. We didn't see the first dolphin for about an hour. What we didn't know was that our ship was considered so unsinkable that no distress signal was heeded. The idea was that a dolphin would come to the nearest man, and that man, he would start flailing and shrieking, and sometimes, that dolphin would go away . . . but sometimes . . . he wouldn't go away. Sometimes the dolphin would look right at you.

Right into your eyes. And the thing about a dolphin is that he's got happy eyes. Real happy eyes. Like a doll's eyes. A great big wet fishy doll. When he comes at you, he doesn't even seem to be angry . . . until he starts gnawing your toes, and those gleaming little button eyes glow red with righteous vengeance and then . . . then you hear that terrible high-pitched *EEH! EEH!* The ocean turns red, and despite all your flailing and your shrieking those dolphins come in and . . . they smack you with their flippers until you're soft enough to chew. So fifteen hundred souls went into the water. Seven hundred came out, and the dolphins and the cold took the rest, April the fourteenth, nineteen-twelve. Anyway, we delivered the bomb.

LOVETT: What?

Some Chunk of Debris, the North Atlantic

JACK: GET OFF HER!

VENGEFUL DOLPHIN: EEH! EEH!

JACK: *punches the dolphin in the nose*

VENGEFUL DOLPHIN [*rubbing nose with flipper*]: WEH WEH! WEHHHHH!

JACK: Oh yeah? So does your mom! Get outta here, and tell 'em Jack Dawson sent ya!

ROSE: Is it gone?

JACK: I think so – quick, climb on this plank, Rose! It's big enough for both of us!

FIVE HUNDRED TINY WHITE MICE: Get off our plank, bitches!

JACK: . . .

ROSE: . . .

JACK: Or you can get on this chunk of debris. Totally your call.

140

Some Chunk of Debris, the North Atlantic, an Hour Later

ROSE: You wanna take a turn on the debris?

JACK: No, no, I'm fine.

ROSE: Should I give you my lifejacket, then?

JACK: Nah, I'm good.

ROSE: You want my coat?

JACK: No, no, I won't freeze to death for another couple of hours at least. It's cool.

FLOATING CREW GUY [*blowing whistle*]: Return the boats! Return! Return, boats! C'monnnnnnn, *boats*!

JACK: See? The boats are totally coming back.

On the Lifeboats

CREW GUY: The hell we're going back!

The Next Two Hours

DROWNING PEOPLE: Help! Help!

LIFEBOAT PEOPLE: . . .

DROWNING PEOPLE: *thrash, scream, weep*

LIFEBOAT PEOPLE: . . .

DROWNING PEOPLE: *drown*

LIFEBOAT PEOPLE: . . .

DROWNING PEOPLE: *freeze*

LIFEBOAT PEOPLE: . . .

[Wash, rinse, repeat.]

ROSE: Jack, your lips are blue!

JACK: The whole movie's blue right now, Rose. I'm totally not dying of hypothermia, don't worry about it.

[ROSE believes this. Bless.]

ROSE: I l-l-l-l-love you, J-Jack.

JACK: Oh, don't you start with the speaking-our-true-feelings crap!

ROSE: It's so c-c-c-c-c-cold . . .

JACK: BITCH, I'M THE ONE IN THE WATER!

ROSE: I'm not gonna m-m-m-make it, J-Jack . . .

JACK: Yes you are! You're going to make lots of babies—

ROSE: That's it. You're getting on the debris, I'm freezing to death.

JACK: No! No! No babies, then! Maybe just a couple— Look, you'll die an old lady! Your heart is going to go on. Love was when I loved you. Which technically is right now. Near, far, wherever in fact you are, we'll stay forever this way . . . freezing to death in the middle of the Atlantic. So we've got that going for us. You see what I'm saying? So promise me you'll never let go, and do me the honour of not dying.

ROSE: Yeah . . . I think I can handle that.

On the Lifeboats

FIFTH OFFICER HORATIO HORNBLOWER: We have to go back, men!

[FIFTH OFFICER HORATIO HORNBLOWER organizes a search party to go back. However, everyone is already dead and frozen.]

FIFTH OFFICER HORATIO HORNBLOWER: Anyone out here? Raise your hand if you're dead!

CREWMAN: I don't think that's going to work, sir.

FIFTH OFFICER HORATIO HORNBLOWER: We waited too long! *Woe!*

VENGEFUL DOLPHINS: HEEEHEEEHEEEH.

ROSE [*hoarsely*]: Jack! Jack! They're coming to save us!

JACK: . . .

ROSE: Jack? Jack? Jack? Jack? Jack?

JACK: . . .

[JACK is dead. Heartbroken, ROSE lies down to die.]

GHOST OF JACK: WOMAN! I TOLD YOU TO LIVE!

ROSE: I'm sorry, Jack! You're right, Jack! I'll never let go, Jack! I'll never let go!

[In order to call the lifeboat back, ROSE has to . . . let go.]

ROSE [*blowing some dead guy's whistle*]: Come back! Come back! I changed my mind! Come back!

[FIFTH OFFICER HORATIO HORNBLOWER finally swings the boat around and fishes ROSE out.]

ROSE: My hero! You are a true Lancelot, sir.

FIFTH OFFICER HORATIO HORNBLOWER: Ma'am, you have no idea.

ROSE: Too bad you failed in your quest to save the other fifteen hundred people.

FIFTH OFFICER HORATIO HORNBLOWER: . . . I totally have to go live in the wilderness now, don't I?

Back on the *Keldysh*. Woe

OLD ROSE opens her eyes. Here endeth the sad story of Roseo and Jackiet.

OLD ROSE: There were twenty boats on the sea that night. Only one boat came back. That one boat saved only six people out of fifteen hundred souls adrift in the cold, merciless sea. Bitches.

[Everyone sniffles.]

OLD ROSE: I never told your grandfather, Lizzy. A woman's heart is a deep, suggestively undulating ocean of secrets, and he saved me in every way it is possible to save a woman, all night long until the break of dawn.

LIZZY: Grandma, ew.

That Night on the Prow

LOVETT: Man, I've been fishing around out here for three years and it never occurred to me that this is the grave of fifteen hundred people. I'm such an asshole.

LIZZY: Well . . . I mean . . . at least *now* you know it.

LOVETT: . . .

LIZZY: . . .

LOVETT: You know, it's a nice night. Good weather for getting up on a rail and pretending to fly. If you know what I mean. And I think you do.

LIZZY: So . . . wait. You mean that's not a gay earring?

That Night on the Stern

OLD ROSE scampers out in her nightgown clutching something to her chest. She climbs the rail and reveals that she has been hoarding the Heart of Exposition for eighty-four years. Then she throws it into the sea.

OLD ROSE: Hee hee! They'll never find it now! I could have been filthy rich! I showed all you bastards! Wait . . .

[Then OLD ROSE creeps back to bed and we see the photos she brought with her of all of the awesome things she did, like fly with the Wright Brothers and ride Seabiscuit and climb Mount Everest and vomit on roller-coasters. And then she goes to sleep. Or dies.

144

Pick one and argue about it with your friends or
something.]

Titanic Heaven

THE GOOD PASSENGERS: Now that you're reunited, we're all
happy!

ANDREWS: I don't care that I built a shitty ship any more, young
Rose!

CAPTAIN THÉODEN: I'm not depressed that fifteen hundred
people died on my last voyage!

FABRIZIO: Itta no matta that I'ma poorly written stereotipo!

ILL-FATED TOMMY O'RYAN: Faith an' begorrah, I don't even
care that I'm Oirish!

[JACK is waiting at the top of the stairs for her. ROSE and JACK kiss
and everyone applauds, because clearly the love affair of two
teenagers is more important than anything else anyone has going
on.]

OLD ROSE: Screw your grandfather, Lizzy! I didn't want to see him
again anyway!

THE GOOD PASSENGERS: Yay!

FIN.

THE MATRIX (1999)

Some Computer Screen

SOME TRACE: *runs*

TRINITY: What are we tracing?

CYPHER: I dunno. I thought that was your job.

TRINITY: Well, it's probably something important.

CYPHER: Yeah.

The Rooftop District

A passel of COPS is gathered outside a dilapidated hotel to take down one lonely computer hacker, which is our first clue that something weird is going on here. Men-In-Black-type AGENTS show up and try to take over from the local heat.

AGENT SMITH: Lieutenant, I'm afraid that . . . you and your men are morons.

SMUG COP: I think we can manage *one little girl*.

ONE LITTLE GIRL: *Judo chop! Praying-mantis kick! Patent-leather death!*

AGENTS: *facepalm*

  [Having dispatched the cops, TRINITY tries to arrange for an exit on her cell phone.]

TRINITY: The trace was intercepted! I don't know how!

CYPHER [*on phone, in the background*]: I KNOW NOTHING!

MORPHEUS [*on phone*]: We Can Get You Out Of This, But It's Going To Involve Breaking A Few Laws . . .

TRINITY: So what?

MORPHEUS: . . . Of Physics.

TRINITY: Oh, hell.

[TRINITY makes a break for it and runs across the rooftops, jumping a few gaping chasms along the way, chased by several COPS and one AGENT. SOME COP jumps but falls against the ledge of the next building –]

SOME OTHER COP: Ohhhh, right in the donut!

[– and TRINITY makes a final shiny, long-legged leap. She gazelles over the chasm –]

TRINITY: And I did it all in my Maidenform PVC corset!

[– and soars into a building through a window, rolls down the stairs and somehow manages not to break every bone in her body. After giving herself a brief pep talk, she runs outside towards a phone booth, where the phone is ringing.]

SOME GARBAGE TRUCK: NOT IF I GET THERE FIRST!

[Somehow TRINITY manages to outrun the GARBAGE TRUCK and answer the phone just as the GARBAGE TRUCK rams into the booth and smashes it into tiny, tiny pieces, which then break into even tinier pieces. The GARBAGE TRUCK backs up, revealing that TRINITY is not only not dead from smush, but is not even there at all.]

AGENT JONES: Whatever. We know their next mark.

AGENT SMITH: Neo will be MINE.

AGENT JONES: You mean 'ours'.

AGENT SMITH: That's what I . . . said.

Lonely h4ck3r Apartment

COMPUTER: GOOD MORNING, STARSHINE.

[NEO hits CTRL-X . . . the first half of the cut-and-paste command . . .]

COMPUTER: YOU MUST BE A REALLY BAD HACKER IF YOU THINK THAT'S GOING TO DO ANYTHING USEFUL.

NEO: What?

COMPUTER: FOLLOW THE WHITE RABBIT, CHUMP. ALSO, I NEED A DEFRAG.

[NEO is distracted from his COMPUTER'S insolence by a knock at the door.]

SOME HIPSTER: You got my illegal . . . minidisk . . . whatever thing?

NEO: Yeah.

[NEO takes the HIPSTER'S money and digs out a book called *Obscure Allusions to Modern Philosophy*. The tenth chapter, 'Baudrillard: We've Read Him and You Haven't', has been cut out to make a hiding place for his illegal minidisk whatever things. He pulls out one marked 'macguffin.exe' and gives it to the HIPSTER at the door.]

SOME HIPSTER: You're my savior, man. My own personal Jesus Christ, come to save me from a false reality created by artificial intelligence run amok.

NEO: Uh . . . sure.

SOME HIPSTER: You okay? You look even geekier than usual. Unplug from the slavery of your machine womb for a while, man. Come to the club with me and DuJour.

DUJOUR: Yeah, come on, baby. You might even bump into some chick and cop an accidental feel.

[DUJOUR has a white-rabbit tattoo on her shoulder. NEO stares at it, the wheels slowly grinding in his head: Follow the white rabbit. That chick has a white-rabbit tattoo. White rabbit. Follow the white rabbit. Follow the white rabbit. White rabbit. That chick has a tattoo. Tattoo. Tattoo. That chick has a white rabbit. White rabbit. Follow . . . the . . . ?]

SOME HIPSTER: Yeah, man, I can't believe her name's 'DuJour' either. You coming?

NEO: Sure, whatever.

COMPUTER: THIS DISCUSSION IS NOT OVER!

Freaky Leather Techno Club

All the extras preen and thrash to give the appropriate atmosphere of millennial decadence, while 'The System Is Down (Phat Industrial Perverzion Beats 12″ Remix)' plays on the sound system. NEO stands by his £Θή$0M€ h4x0® s3£ɾ until TRINITY approaches him.

NEO: *The* Trinity?

TRINITY: Yeah, I left the Holy Ghost in the car. Look, I know why you live alone and spend all day staring at your computer.

NEO: Because I'm a l33t h4x0r g33k who can't get laid?

TRINITY: If you didn't look like Keanu Reeves, I would say yes. But you and I know that you do, and that what keeps you up at night has nothing to do with your mythical inability to score. The ~~truth~~ answer is out there, Neo.

£0n3Ly h4cK0r 4p4rTmΣn†

Somehow, NEO wakes up in the middle of this conversation and finds that it's morning, and that he's overslept by, like, two hours. He hauls ass to work.

Evil Monolith Industries, Inc.

SOME MONOLITHIC EMPLOYER: You think that you are so special, Mr Anderson, such a unique little snowflake, and that the rules therefore do not apply to you. But this is a top software company where you are merely one tiny, insignificant flake in a faceless collective. You can bow to our authority or YOU CAN DIE.

NEO: Dude, all I did was oversleep!

The Matrix: The Text Adventure

NEO is in his cubicle. A MESSENGER arrives with a cell phone.

AGENTS are coming to get NEO. There is an exit south.

MORPHEUS [*on other end of phone*]: Do You Know Who I Am, Neo?

NEO: OMG I AM YOUR BIGGEST FAN.

MORPHEUS: That's Nice, But Agents Are Coming To Get You. Can You Play A Little Game With Me?

NEO: Sure thing!

MORPHEUS: All Right. There Is An Exit South Of Your Cubicle. Go South.

NEO: There is an empty cubicle in front of me.

MORPHEUS: Go There. Stay Low.

[NEO makes a flying-squirrel dive into the empty cubicle. AGENTS check his actual cubicle and, seeing no one there, pass by.]

NEO: There is a hall in front of me!

MORPHEUS: Go Down The Hall.

NEO: There's an office at the end of the hall!

MORPHEUS: Go There.

NEO: I am there.

MORPHEUS: Go In It.

Neo: Sorry, I don't understand that.

MORPHEUS: GO INTO THE OFFICE.

NEO: . . .

MORPHEUS: *OPEN THE DOOR* AND GO INTO THE OFFICE.

NEO: Oh, okay.

MORPHEUS: God, I Hate Text RPGs.

[The office is empty. There is a window. The only exit is through the window. The office is on the 334th floor.]

NEO: There's a window!

MORPHEUS: Climb Out Of The Window.

NEO: WHAT? No way! NO WAY! What do you think this is, a movie? Real people don't climb out on window ledges three hundred floors up and not die!

[NEO hears the AGENTS coming and tries to climb out of the window, but punks out and ends up getting captured. Woe.]

Some Interrogation Room

AGENT SMITH: My colleagues think that we are . . . wasting our time, and that we should . . . just cap you in the back of the head before you discover . . . well, never mind that.

NEO: Mind what?

AGENT SMITH: We've been following you for . . . some time, Mr Anderson. We know about your . . . double life. By day you are . . . a welder, and by night . . .

NEO: . . .

AGENT SMITH: I'm sorry, I believe I picked up . . . the wrong file. Here we are. By day, you are . . . a mere snowflake in a faceless . . . collective. By night, you 'hack' these . . . 'computers'. You have committed . . . every computer crime we . . . have a law for. And some we don't.

NEO: Hey, man, that porno site said the sheep were over eighteen!

AGENT SMITH: Let's be . . . honest, Mr Anderson—

NEO: Okay, some of them were underage.

AGENT SMITH: What we really want is a certain . . . individual, this 'Morpheus'. He is . . . the most dangerous man alive.

NEO: More dangerous than Saddam Hussein?

AGENT SMITH: Yes.

NEO: More dangerous than Osama bin Laden?

AGENT SMITH: Yes.

NEO: More dangerous than G—

AGENT SMITH: That's enough of that, Mr Anderson.

NEO: Is this conversation going to seem extremely inappropriate in two years?

AGENT SMITH: . . .

NEO: . . .

AGENT SMITH: Let's just skip straight to the torture and mind-fucking, shall we?

[THREE STRANGE MEN throw NEO down on a table and start taking off his clothes.]

NEO: THIS IS EXTREMELY NOT COOL! BAD TOUCH!

[They implant a techno shrimp in his gut and NEO'S mouth melts shut and this is a bad, bad—

£0ñ3ℓ¥ h@x0Я 4p4®7m€Й†

—nightmare?]

PHONE: *rings*

NEO: AHHHHHHHH . . . hhhhhh. Phone. It's just the phone. I love you, phone.

MORPHEUS [*on phone*]: This Line Is Tapped, So It Is Necessary That I Keep My Loquacity To A Quantity Less Than Maximum. If They Knew What I Know – That You Are The One, And Will Eventually Give Your Life To Free Mankind In A Less-Than-Satisfying Sequel To A Sequel – You Would Be Dead Right Now.

AGENTS TAPPING THE LINE: OMGWTF!

NEO: Well, they know it now, *Einstein.*

MORPHEUS: Do You Still Want To Meet?

NEO: Dude . . . are you asking me out?

MORPHEUS: If You Are Still Interested, Go To The Bridge On Adams Street, Located At Coordinates . . .

AGENTS TAPPING THE LINE: *are busy writing this down*

A Dark and Stormy Night

A car meets NEO at the bridge. The back door opens and, against his better judgment, he gets in, only to find TRINITY and some ALBINO CHICK inside. Somehow the AGENTS fail to follow him, swoop down and capture everyone. The ALBINO CHICK points a gun at him.

NEO: You're not very nice for a Holy Ghost.

ALBINO CHICK: Take off your shirt.

TRINITY: And your pants.

ALBINO CHICK: Down, girl.

[TRINITY and her sidekick ask NEO to trust them and do whatever they – two strange, aggressive women with large, scary equipment who want him to take his clothes off – say.]

NEO: WHY DOES EVERYONE WANT ME NAKED?

ALBINO CHICK: Don't answer that, Trin.

TRINITY: Now: try to relax while we rip a techno shrimp out of your gut.

NEO: WAHHHHHHH!

Some Dilapidated Hotel. No, the Other One

Whatever the hotel was before, it's apparently a techno bordello now.

MORPHEUS: We Meet At Last. Hookah?

NEO: I'm . . . good, thanks.

MORPHEUS: This Must Seem Like A Bad Dream To You. Like Alice Falling Down The Rabbit Hole. I Can See It In Your Eyes.

NEO: Dude, you have to at least give me flowers before you start with the sweet talk.

MORPHEUS: Do You Believe In Fate?

NEO: No.

MORPHEUS: Why Not?

NEO: I don't like to think that I'm not in control of my life.

MORPHEUS: So . . . You Work For A Faceless Corporate Conglomerate.

NEO: Shut up, dude.

[MORPHEUS presents NEO with two pills, one red and one blue.]

MORPHEUS: If You Take The Red Pill, I Will Show You What The Matrix Is. If You Take The Blue Pill, You Go Home And You Never Find Out. You Can Believe That We're Just A Bunch Of Techno-Fetish Weirdos –

NEO: Yeah, I'm pretty sure I don't need a pill to figure that one out.

MORPHEUS: – Or You Can Lie Awake At Night Wondering What You Would Have Found Out. I'm Sure That Won't Bother You At All. Or . . . You Can Take The Red Pill, And You Can Go Beyond The Looking Glass, Stay Here In Wonderland, See How Deep The Rabbit Hole Goes, Play The Red Queen's Croquet Of Mystery—

NEO: Damn, if I take the red pill, *will you shut up*?

MORPHEUS: *Cheshire-Cat smile*

A Different Room in the Dilapidated Hotel

MORPHEUS: Excellent Choice, Neo, Particularly Considering That I've Been Looking For You All My Life.

ALBINO CHICK: Dude, you two seriously need to get a room.

[TRINITY, ALBINO CHICK, CYPHER and SOME GUY hook NEO up to a machine next to an old cracked mirror.]

NEO: You went through all of this, too?

TRINITY: Well, he bought *me* dinner first.

CYPHER: Hold onto your slippers, Dorothy, because the tornado's on its way.

ALBINO CHICK: Wrong children's book, *genius*.

CYPHER: I hate you all so very, very much.

[While MORPHEUS and FRIENDS noodle around on their machines, NEO starts tripping, like whoa, as the mirror liquefies and all the cracks disappear and he reaches out to touch them and the mirror sticks to his fingers like a mirror taffy-pull, man, but it's a mirror, you know, like, glass and stuff, but now it's, like, flowing, man, and it's going up his arm and it's totally cold and it's going to swallow his face—]

NEO: THE RED ACID IS THE BAD ACID! WAHHHH!

The Jell-o Hive

NEO wakes up naked and hairless in a punch bowl full of strawberry Jell-O placenta with cables sticking out of his arms and legs and things that cables should really not stick out of, and some nannybot comes by and gives him a chiropractic adjustment and all the cables shoot out of his body, and he looks up and to his horror there are spillions upon spillions of Jell-o wombs all stacked up in massive electrofizzle honeycombs, and then he gets flushed out of the placenta bowl, and maybe we see NEO'S bits, but the jury is still out on that one.

Sick Bay, on the *Nebuchadnezzar*

Some time later, NEO *is laid out on a table and covered with giant acupuncture needles.*

NEO: Why can't I move?

MORPHEUS: You've Never Used Your Muscles Before.

NEO: Except when I broke out of the Jell-o womb. I can't see, either.

MORPHEUS: You've Never Used Your Eyes Before.

NEO: Except when I looked around at the Jell-o hive.

MORPHEUS: I'm Going To Leave You Here Until You Feel A Little Less Contrary, Mister.

Several Years Later, After Neo's Muscles Have Recovered From Total Atrophy

MORPHEUS: This Is My Ship, The *Nebuchadnezzar*.

NEO: The who in the whazzar?

MORPHEUS: A Very Intellectual Reference That Is Supposed To Impress You.

NEO: Oh.

MORPHEUS: I Believe You Know Most Of My Crew – Tough-Babe Love Interest, Suspicious Character Actor, Albino Chick, Vaguely Ethnic Guys, Cannon Fodder and Shut Up Mouse.

MOUSE: Oh my God Neo this is such an honour I've wanted to meet you for so long we've all heard so much about you—

MORPHEUS: Shut Up, Mouse.

The Loading Program (Diet Matrix)

REAL!MORPHEUS plugs raggedy REAL!NEO into an offline version of the Matrix so he can show him around. MATRIX!MORPHEUS is dressed all swank in leather, showing that people who are 'awake' in the Matrix can basically become the coolest, most ideal versions of themselves. He sits MATRIX!NEO down in some ratty old armchair.

MORPHEUS: Here, We Can Load Anything. Except New Furniture.

[He proceeds to give MATRIX!NEO the expositional lowdown on the post-technological apocalyptic dystopia of suck, dream-world machine back-story blah, Simulation and Simulacra blee—look, just go rent *The Animatrix*, okay?]

MORPHEUS: Hey, What Time Is It?

NEO: Half-past BORING.

MORPHEUS: Really? I Thought It Was A Quarter To Airhead, NEO.

NEO: Whatever.

MORPHEUS: Fine. I'll Give You The Short Version. What Is The 'Matrix'? The Matrix Is A Construct. What Is A 'Construct'? A Construct Is A Means Of Control Through Devices Of The Unreal. What Is 'Control'? What Is 'Real' . . . ?

NEO: OH MY GOD, I'M TRAPPED IN A WORLD RUN BY PHILOSOPHY MAJORS! I WANT OUT! LET ME OUT!

[The crew unhooks NEO, who panics, runs around in circles and horfs on the ship floor.]

CYPHER: I'm *not* cleaning that up, Chief.

Scenes from a Post-Apocalyptic Dystopia

TANK brings NEO some dystopian mush.

TANK: Me and my brother, Other Vaguely Ethnic Guy, we're old-school grade-A preservative-free human, born free-range right here in the craptastic real world. I've never gone into the Matrix and I ain't gonna start now. Zion's where it's at, baby—

NEO: Dude, all I said was, 'Could you pass the salt?'

[TANK starts flexing his muscles recreationally to kill some time.]

NEO: I can't go back, can I?

TANK: Back to the strawberry Jell-o womb? Hell no. Just relax on your hard metal bed and get some rest.

NEO: For what?

TANK: It takes a lot of training to be a Jesus.

* * *

NEO gets strapped into a chair to fulfill the dream of every pasty geek: to have awesome fighting skills uploaded straight into his brain.

TANK: We could learn some totally yawn-inducing crap, like, you know, how not to die and stuff, but I'm sure you'd much rather learn something trendy like drunken boxing.

[NEO takes to the training programs like a surfer dude to water.]

TANK: Look at him go! He's *a machine*.

MORPHEUS: THAT'S NOT FUNNY.

* * *

MOUSE [*bursting into the mess hall*]: FIGHT! FIGHT!

RAGGEDY CREW: WOOT!

[MORPHEUS and NEO are sparring in the imaginary Diet Matrix dojo. There is a lot of Wire-Fu and Intoxicated Tae Bo or whatever the kids call it these days. The crew settles in to watch and waits for Oneness to be revealed.]

MOUSE [*reading monitors*]: His midichlorians are way above normal!

NEO: Hey, this is kinda fun—

MORPHEUS: PILEDRIVER!

NEO [*crumpled upside-down*]: Ungggh.

MOUSE: Wow, he's getting his ass kicked faster than anyone I've ever seen!

CYPHER: HAHAHAHAHAHAHA.

MORPHEUS: You Are Still Thinking Instead of Being, Grasshopper.

ALBINO CHICK: Somehow, I have a hard time believing that 'thinking' is this kid's problem.

MORPHEUS introduces NEO to the jump program, where he can learn to leap tall buildings in a single bound just like TRINITY, or at least figure out that the law of gravity has been repealed for the Matrix. NEO gives it the old college try and falls five hundred stories onto his face.

MORPHEUS: The Mind Makes The Matrix Real, Even Though It Is Not. This Is Why People Die In The Matrix, Because The Body Can't Live If The Mind Thinks It Is Dead.

NEO: Hey . . . do I think I'm dead right now?

MORPHEUS: Let's Say . . . No.

* * *

MORPHEUS: Here's A Different Training Program. Don't Let The Lady In Red Distract You.

THE LADY IN RED: Hey, baby.

NEO: Hey, you can distract me all night long, baby.

THE LADY IN RED: *turns into Agent Smith and shoves a gun in Neo's face*

NEO: THAT IS SO BOGUS, MAN!

* * *

Everyone holds their breath and hides as a giant floating techno shrimp comes looking for the ship. MORPHEUS and one of the VAGUELY ETHNIC GUYS set up an electromagnetic pulse to scare the giant mechasquid away.

NEO [*wonderingly*]: I had one of those in my tummy.

TRINITY: SHUT UP, NEO.

NEO: So . . . why don't you guys get a lot of ships with a lot of EMPs, and—

MORPHEUS: You With The Earth Logic! Shut!

* * *

CYPHER: WHOA! Neo! You scared the post-apocalyptic dystopian Jesus outta me.

NEO: So . . . what are you doing?

CYPHER: Nothing! Nothing! Just . . . night shift, you know, making sure the machines don't come kill us – not that I would have anything to do with that – I mean – you know . . . HERE, HAVE SOME BOOZE.

NEO: Post-apocalyptic booze?

CYPHER: Yeah, Dozer brews it under his bed out of leftover turpentine and antifreeze.

NEO: YUM.

[The two guys drink their liquid burning for a couple of minutes in manly silence.]

NEO: So . . . the Matrix code is a bunch of katakana and backwards numbers?

CYPHER: That's about the way of it, yeah.

NEO: Wow, the machines sure have a lot of aggro for Buddhists.

CYPHER: For serious, man. You see an agent, screw Morpheus – you run. You run your ass off, like a cowardly informant who totally sold out his crew to the enemy.

NEO: . . .

CYPHER: Here! Have another shot of turpenfreeze!

My Dinner with Agent Smith

A WOMAN is playing a harp in a plush restaurant, because when faceless machine AGENTS wine and dine their rats, they really spare no expense.

160

CYPHER: I want steak and cigars and a 1982 Chateau de Weasel.

WAITRESS: And what will your earpiece be having, sir?

AGENT SMITH: The eradication of mankind. Medium-rare.

CYPHER: Don't forget the hookers and blow!

A New Day Dawns on the *Nebuchadnezzar*

MORPHEUS: Eat Up, Everyone. We're Going To Visit The Oracle.

MOUSE: Hey, Neo! I made you some Cream of Amino Acid! With extra synthetic sucrose, just the way you like it!

NEO: Hey, how did you know that's . . . ?

MOUSE: What?

NEO: . . .

MOUSE: . . .

   [NEO and MOUSE stare at each other in confused silence for a few moments.]

MOUSE: You like it? It almost tastes like Tastee Wheat – but what *is* Tastee Wheat? It's neither tastee nor wheat—

VAGUELY ETHNIC GUY: Shut up, Mouse.

MOUSE: Hey, I can also get you digital sex.

TRINITY: SHUT UP, MOUSE.

Neo Re-enters the Matrix for the First Time Since His Rescue

NEO: Whoa.

Outside the Oracle's Apartment

NEO: What did she tell you?

MORPHEUS: That I Would Find A Skinny White Boy, And He Would Be The One.

The Oracle's Apartment

NEO sits in the living room with all the little wonder kids, looking like a college student at the paediatrician's office.

BABY KRISHNA: There is no spoon.

NEO: Well, if there is no spoon, what did I eat my Tastee Wheat with, then?

BABY KRISHNA: There is no Tastee Wheat.

NEO: Damn, you're good.

The Oracle's Kitchen

THE ORACLE: Hi, Neo, come on in. Yes, it's nice to meet you, too. Well, fine, don't sit down, you just be that way. Don't worry, I've got a dozen vases like that—

NEO: *turns around and breaks her vase*

THE ORACLE: Mmmmmmm-hm.

NEO: How'd you know—

THE ORACLE: Hello, I'm an *oracle*. You didn't come to get your tyres rotated. Now come here and lemme get a good look at you.

Half an Hour Later

NEO: Wow, you're thorough. But was a prostate exam really necessary?

THE ORACLE: What is 'necessary'?

NEO: Oh, God, don't you start with the Socratic crap, too.

THE ORACLE: Fine, let's get to the point. You've got the gift, but you ain't walkin' the walk.

NEO: So I do have the gift?

THE ORACLE: Well, you're not using it.

NEO: But does having the gift make me the One?

THE ORACLE: Using the gift would make you the One. But you're not.

NEO: AM I ACTUALLY THE ONE?

THE ORACLE: Morpheus believes you are. He's going to die, by the way.

NEO: WHAT?

THE ORACLE: Well, unless you sacrifice yourself for him. You'll get to choose. But one of you will die. Well, maybe not in this movie. But you see what I'm saying. Cookie?

Outside the Oracle's Apartment

MORPHEUS: What Was Said Was For You Alone.

NEO: But she said—

MORPHEUS: For You.

NEO: She said that I'm not—

MORPHEUS: Alone.

NEO: But I think you ought to know—

MORPHEUS: Mmm, Cookies.

Some Dilapidated Hotel. (The Second One. Maybe?)

NEO: Whoa.

TRINITY: What?

NEO: Nothing, just a little . . . whaddaya call it . . . dijon . . . ?

TRINITY: OH NO.

NEO: What?

MORPHEUS: Déjà Vu, The French For 'Already Seen', Is A Phenomenon Wherein One Believes That One Is Experiencing Something That One Has Already Experienced Once Before. As It Pertains To The Matrix, Déjà Vu Is A Glitch In The Matrix That Means Something Has Been Changed.

NEO: What?

TRINITY: BAAAAAD.

NEO: Oh no!

Upstairs in the Hotel

MOUSE opens some curtains covering a window and finds only a brick wall. As a crazy superstealth SWAT team leaps down from nowhere with sudden suddenness and floods the building, he pulls out two gigantic automated self-cleaning machine shotguns and goes down in a hail of bullets. And then he gets dead.

Downstairs

ALBINO CHICK [*looking up*]: There goes a brave Mouse to the Big Shut Up in the Sky.

CANNON FODDER: *tear*

CYPHER: OH MY GOD WE'RE TRAPPED THEY KILLED MOUSE THERE'S NO WAY OUT DON'T EVEN BOTHER LOOKING!

MORPHEUS: Dude, You Must *Chill*.

164

Inside the Walls

The gang shimmies down the hotel plumbing in a narrow crawl-space.

TRINITY: I'm so glad Tank was able to find us an escape route down these pipes.

CYPHER: Well, I know I wouldn't have missed the experience of getting splinters jammed up my ass for the *world*.

[Suddenly AGENT SMITH punches through the wall and grabs NEO by the throat and there is shrieking and choking and wall-crumbling and general crew-panicking.]

MORPHEUS: *BELLYFLOP OF DOOOOM!*

TRINITY: MORPHEUS NOOOOOOOO!

MORPHEUS: NEO IS ALL THAT MATTERS!

[While everyone else escapes, AGENT SMITH breaks a toilet with MORPHEUS'S face. Then he leaves MORPHEUS to the tender mercies of the SWAT team, because the imagery of a black man getting beaten up by a dozen cops is not inflammatory at all these days.]

Some Abandoned Appliance Store

An old phone rings. Theoretically, the gang will use this connection to get back to the ship.

CYPHER [*on other end of phone*]: Hey, baby.

TRINITY: You're not Tank . . .

[CYPHER is somehow back on the ship. He has electrocuted the VAGUELY ETHNIC GUYS with some kind of lightning gun, which would be a handy thing to have around the house, really. He is currently going around and jumping on/straddling/otherwise molesting the unconscious real-world bodies of his plugged-in crewmates. The less that is said about this, the better.]

CYPHER: For a long time, I thought I was in love with you, Trinity.

[TRINITY stares at the phone in horror, because she knows that no conversation starting out that way has ever, ever turned out well.]

TRINITY: OH MY GOD YOU KILLED BOTH THE VAGUELY ETHNIC GUYS AND BETRAYED MORPHEUS.

CYPHER: Well, I don't know how you drew that conclusion so quickly, but that's about the way of it, yeah.

TRINITY: WHYYYYYY?

CYPHER: Have you looked in the mirror lately? REAL LIFE SUCKS. We eat Cream of Crap and we dress like orphans. They're gonna put me back in the Jell-o hive and make me imaginary rich and imaginary famous, so screw all y'all and the pretty boy, too.

[CYPHER pulls CANNON FODDER's plug, which means that his mind is separated from his body and, therefore, he gets dead.]

CANNON FODDER: *gets dead*

ALBINO CHICK: We can't die this way – we can't die completely unglamorized and unfetishized! EVEN MOUSE GOT TO GO DOWN SHOOTI— [gets dead]

CYPHER: Oh! Bonus! Before I kill you too, Trin, I'm going to show you that Neo's not the One! If Morpheus was right, a total miracle will stop me from killing N—

A TOTAL MIRACLE: *stops Cypher*

TANK: I WAS DEAD BUT NOW I KEEL YOU!

Back on the *Nebuchadnezzar*

Charred and blasted, half of TANK's internal organs are hanging out. The other VAGUELY ETHNIC GUY, however, has stayed dead.

TRINITY: You're hurt.

TANK: I'll . . . walk it . . . off.

TRINITY: Your brother?

TANK: *tear*

VOICE FROM THE HEADSET: Hey, guys . . . ? Guys? Could you get me out of here . . . ? Nothing matters but me . . . ?

166

Some Government-Controlled Building

The AGENTS have MORPHEUS drugged up and bound to a chair in an interrogation room that has wall-to-wall windows for better . . . interrogating. AGENT SMITH makes a big speech to the effect of, 'I'm really going to enjoy this.'

MORPHEUS: *drools*

Woe on the *Nebuchadnezzar*

TRINITY, TANK and NEO are standing over REAL!MORPHEUS'S unconscious body. If the AGENTS torture some code out of MATRIX!MORPHEUS, the refugee city of Zion will get hacked or blowed up good or something. A choice must be made.

TANK: I'm going to pull the plug. Any objections?

NEO AND TRINITY: . . .

TANK: You're sure? I mean, this will kill him.

NEO AND TRINITY: . . .

TANK: Positive?

NEO AND TRINITY: . . .

TANK: Speak now or forever hold your peace.

NEO AND TRINITY: . . .

TANK: Right then. We loved you, Morpheus, and you were like a—

NEO: STOP! I don't believe this is happening!

TANK: *facepalm*

NEO: I'm not the One.

TANK: What?

TRINITY: WHAT?

NEO: So I've got to go back in there after Morpheus, because—

TRINITY: Because he sacrificed himself to save you, so SIT YOUR ASS DOWN, PRIVATE RYAN.

NEO: But . . . but . . . I *believe* I can bring him back!

TRINITY: Fine. Whatever. I'm coming with.

NEO: But you're a *girrrrrrrrrrrl*—

TRINITY: Yeah? You wanna know what I believe? I believe that you have the mental capacity of an ice cube. A real pretty ice cube we fished out of a punch bowl *last week*. I believe that if you go in there alone, you're going to get yourself blown up before you even know what hit you. I also believe that I am currently the ranking officer aboard this shit-heap, and you can suck my nonexistent dick if you wanna make something of it.

NEO: . . .

TANK: . . .

TRINITY: Well? Clap your hands, Tinkerbell, let's get this show on the road.

NEO: Yes, ma'am.

Some Interrogation Room

AGENT SMITH and MORPHEUS have a little heart-to-heart.

AGENT SMITH: I've been here a . . . few thousand years, and I'd . . . like to share a little epiphany I . . . had. Humans are . . . theoretically mammals, but . . . despite the fact that they . . . have hair and nurse their young . . .

MORPHEUS: Short Version?

AGENT SMITH: You are the virus and we are . . . the cure.

MORPHEUS: Actually . . . You Can't Cure Viruses.

AGENT SMITH: WE ARE THE CHEMOTHERAPY FOR YOUR CANCER! WE ARE THE AMPUTATION FOR YOUR LEPROSY!

MORPHEUS: *cries*

NEO and TRINITY step into a Diet Matrix closet housing every imaginary firearm known to man.

TRINITY: No one's ever done anything like this.

NEO: That's why it's going to work.

TRINITY: You know, by that logic, inviting the agents to an ice-cream social would work just as well.

NEO: Sure, we can try that when we get back.

Some Interrogation Room

AGENT SMITH: LISTEN, YOU MAMMAL. I hate this place. I hate the stink . . . of humans. It . . . contaminates me, it saturates . . . my clothes, it goes . . . home with me. You may not know this, but . . . I have a pretty. little. machine. daughter at home. And it's even . . . infected her.

http://www.agents.gov/smith/home/livingroom.html

PRETTYPRINCESS.EXE: But Daddy, I love him!

AGENT SMITH: Once Zion is destroyed, our time is over! You belong with the other programs!

PRETTYPRINCESS.EXE: I don't care, Daddy! I love him!

AGENT SMITH: NO DAUGHTER OF MINE IS REPLICATING WITH A HUMAN!

PRETTYPRINCESS.EXE: *But Daddy!*

Some Interrogation Room

AGENT SMITH: I HAVE TO GET HER OUT OF HERE, DO YOU UNDERSTAND?

169

Lobby of Sexy Death

Slo-mo! Semi-automatic security-guard death! Flying debris! Cartwheels of doom!

TRINITY: Man, it's a good thing impressionable teens are impervious to images of glamorous, dehumanized violence.

The Rooftop of Some Government-Controlled Building

NEO and TRINITY take a flaming elevator to the top of the building in order to commandeer a helicopter. In the five seconds it takes TRINITY to call the ship and upload an Insta-Pilot course straight into her brain, NEO gets into trouble.

NEO: Help! Agent! Gun! BAD!

AGENT: *BLAM BLAM BLAM*

[NEO leaaaaans backwaaaards to dooooodge the bullllllllets, the sheer force of the special effects causing his coat to billooooow. And then he gets hit, falls over on his ass and lies there while the totally fearsome, completely invincible AGENT advances upon him.]

AGENT: FOOLISH MORTAL! YOU CANNOT DEFEAT ME! ONLY A TOUGH BABE IN BLACK LEATHER SNEAKING UP BEHIND ME COULD DO THAT!

TRINITY [*sneaking up behind him*]: HA HA!

[She blows the AGENT away at point-blank range, despite previous assertions that AGENTS cannot be killed, but he's only temporarily dead anyway, so . . . yeah.]

TRINITY: Where . . . did you learn . . . to do *that*?

NEO [*shrugging*]: Third-Age Limbo Champion.

Some Interrogation Room

NEO shoots up the whole office but manages not to purée MORPHEUS.

AGENT SMITH shoots at him with a single revolver but only hits the helicopter.

HELICOPTER: OW! SON OF A BITCH!

[Oh, and MORPHEUS'S ankle.]

MORPHEUS [*jumping*]: I LEAP TO YOU!

NEO [*jumping*]: I EMBRACE YOU TENDERLY!

MORPHEUS: UH, I HOPE YOU'RE TIED TO SOMETHING!

THE MOVIE'S INSURERS: *keel over and die*

[TRINITY drops NEO and MORPHEUS off on nearby rooftops but the helicopter is losing fuel and is going to crash. NEO gets one of his bright ideas and grabs the end of the rope he and MORPHEUS were hanging from. NEO runs and skids to the edge of the roof and finally plunges over and the helicopter explodes and NEO and TRINITY die in a flaming explosion of glass and the movie ends and there are no sequels.]

NEO: No, actually, our eventual deaths are *even lamer*.

[NEO runs and skids to the edge of the roof and magically locks his feet against a tiny concrete lip and does not plunge over, and the helicopter explodes against a windowlicious skyscraper but not until TRINITY is safely dangling from the whatever rope. NEO pulls her up and they stare at each other makingoutively.]

MORPHEUS: Do you believe now, Trinity?

TRINITY: I *believe* you are wrecking my game, man.

Some Subway Station

MORPHEUS [*picking up phone*]: Over And Out, Bitches.

[Some OLD HOBO curled up in the corner with a bottle of Mad Train watches MORPHEUS disappear.]

NEO: So . . . you know . . . now that we're not actually safe, you wanna . . . y'know . . . stand around and not confess our love for each other?

TRINITY [*shyly kicking dirt*]: Yeah . . . sure.

A TRAIN: *roars through*

NEO: . . .

TRINITY: . . . I dunno, man. I feel weird talking about this . . . you know . . . *in front of the train.*

NEO: Well, tell me when we get back to the ship, then?

TRINITY: Okay!

[TRINITY picks up the ringing phone and disappears just as the OLD HOBO sits up, turns into AGENT SMITH and shoots the phone.]

On the Ship

TRINITY: Send me back!

TANK: I would, but Agent Hobo kind of *shot the phone up*, dude!

In the Subway

NEO *and* AGENT SMITH *face each other.*

TUMBLEWEED: *rolls through the station*

On the Ship

TRINITY: WHY IS HE NOT RUNNING?

MORPHEUS [*proudly*]: He's Beginning To Believe In His Oneness.

TRINITY: I'm about to make you believe in MY FOOT UP YOUR ASS.

NEO and AGENT SMITH leap shooting at each other and manage to miss at nearly point-blank range. And then they run out of bullets. And then they throw their guns away and kick-punch-judochop the crap out of each other. And then NEO breaks AGENT SMITH'S sunglasses. OH, NOW IT'S ON.

AGENT SMITH: I'm going to enjoy avenging the death of my favourite shades . . . MR ANDERSON.

NEO: *rabbit punch!*

AGENT SMITH: *Three Stooges punch!*

NEO: *fruit punch!*

AGENT SMITH: *MEGASUPERULTRAMULTIPUNCH!*

[And then AGENT SMITH initiates internalbleeding.exe and NEO is down for the count.]

INSIDE AGENT SMITH'S HEAD: *You could choke him with your tie. (Nah, too easy.) You could smother him with your suit jacket. (Nah, too clumsy.) You could garrotte him with your earpiece. (That has a definite appeal, but . . .)* I KNOW! DEATH BY CONVENIENTLY APPROACHING SUBWAY TRAIN!

CONVENIENTLY APPROACHING SUBWAY TRAIN: RAAAAA!

NEO: *Backflip of Triumph!*

THE VILLAIN: *is dead from train*

THE MOVIE: *is over*

THE TRAIN: *stops*

THE VILLAIN: *is not dead*

THE MOVIE: *is not over*

AGENT SMITH'S NEW SHADES: PWN3D!

NEO: RUN AWAY!

Back on the *Nebuchadnezzar*

TANK: TECHNOSQUIDS COMING OH NOES!

Some Crowded Street That Probably Has a Fruit Cart

NEO [*calling ship from cell phone*]: HELP!

SOME GUY: HEY, THAT WAS MY PHONE!

TANK: HOTEL!

NEO: WHICH ONE?

TANK: THE OTHER ONE!

NEO: HOW? HELP BULLETS OW—

TANK: THE DOOR, NEO! DOORS ARE FOR GOING THROUGH!

Some Dilapidated Hotel. (No, the First One)

TANK: GO FORWARD! NO, YOUR OTHER FORWARD!

PHYLLIS: Why, Wilma, whatever is this nice young man breaking into our apartment for?

AGENT WILMA: *whips a knife at Neo's head*

NEO: WAHHH!

Room 303

PHONE: *rings*

NEO: Whee! I'm almost—

AGENT SMITH: *BLAM BLAM BLAM*

NEO: *is totally dead*

AGENT SMITH: Awww. Now I have . . . no one to play with.

AGENT JONES: This is why we can't have nice things, Smith.

Back on the *Nebuchadnezzar*

MORPHEUS'S ENTIRE WORLD: *is destroyed*

MORPHEUS'S ENTIRE SHIP: *is being destroyed*

TRINITY: You can't be dead because I love you!

[TRINITY leans down and gives REAL!NEO the Tender Tough-Babe Kiss of True Love. It actually works.]

MORPHEUS: Oh My God, That Snow-White Shit Actually Worked?

TANK: Dude, are you sure *she's* not the Jesus?

TRINITY: NOW KICK ASS AND TAKE NAMES!

Some Dilapidated Hotel Hallway

RESURRECTED NEO: Whoa.

AGENTS: *BLAM BLAM BLAM*

BULLETS: *stop mid-air and preen*

SOME BULLET: Pick me, Neo! Pick me!

SOME OTHER BULLET: No, me!

RESURRECTED NEO: [*reaching out*]: Ooo, shiny.

[AGENT SMITH charges but NEO'S so fast it's like playing patty-cake.]

AGENT SMITH: *goes boom*

OTHER AGENTS: RUN AWAY!

TRINITY: NEO! STOP FLEXING AND ANSWER THE PHONE!

REAL!NEO wakes up in the nick of time. MORPHEUS turns the EMP key and all the technosquids fall over dead.

TRINITY: You wanna make out?

NEO: ®0X0®.

Somewhere Out in the Same World Where You Live, Theoretically, Until the Next Two Movies Blow That Idea All to Hell

NEO: This is just the beginning . . . of a trilogy of expensive but ultimately unsatisfying movies, stuffed full of state-of-the-art effects, never-ending fistfights and philosophy-major rambling. I'm going to show them a world without machines – without air conditioning or hygiene or plots that make sense, where no one has anything better to do than gyrate sweatily to bad techno.

MORPHEUS: Pssst, Neo!

NEO: What?

MORPHEUS: Actually, We Have A Lot Of Machines In Zion.

NEO: We do?

MORPHEUS: Yeah. Central Heating, Air Conditioning, Water Purifiers And Giant Transformer Robots. Sometimes We Even Have Lightswitch Raves. Tuesdays Are Cosmic Bowling.

TRINITY: Also, there's sex.

NEO: Dude, for real? Sex *and* cosmic bowling? What the hell are we hanging around here for?

FIN.

GLADIATOR (2000)

Your History Lesson for the Day

At the height of its glory, the Roman Empire stretched from the boundaries of Northern England to the deserts of Africa and ruled more than one-fourth of the world's population. And all of those people, apparently, spoke English.

In the winter of AD 180, Emperor Marcus Aurelius was nearing the end of a twelve-year campaign against barbarians in Germania . . . mostly because, in real life, his son and co-emperor, Commodus, struck an ill-advised truce with them. After his father's death, the fully armed Commodus went on to fight hundreds, if not thousands, of gladiators armed only with wooden swords, assuming he wasn't booked for the day with his harem of three hundred women and boys. After twelve years of Senatorial corruption, mass murder and other lovable hijinx, Commodus was strangled to death while sleeping by the athlete and gladiatorial trainer Narcissus.

You will see none of this in the following film.

Faraway Fields of Wheat

There are fields, and they are wheaty.

Germania, Also Known As 'The Ass End of the Empire'

LITTLE BIRD: Cheep cheep?

MAXIMUS: Ah, yes, little bird. War is hell, and I am studly.

 [MAXIMUS walks through the ranks, rolling mud around in his hands. Up on a hilltop, MARCUS AURELIUS is really, really old.]

THE SOLDIERS: General! General, we love you! WOOOOO, GENERAL!

[At the front line, QUINTUS is trying to negotiate with the BARBARIANS.]

QUINTUS: Hey, you guys? You sure you don't wanna give up now? I mean, we've conquered a lot of people . . .

[The BARBARIANS send the Romans' MESSENGER back headless. And then they throw back his head.]

QUINTUS [*eyeroll*]: I *told* you letting *Braveheart* play in the boondocks was a bad idea!

VALERIUS: Done smelling your mud yet, sir?

MAXIMUS: Almost . . . wait . . . Done.

QUINTUS: Strength and honour, you guys!

MAXIMUS: Strength and honour! And stabbing things!

THE SOLDIERS: AND STABBING THINGS, WOOOO!

MAXIMUS: Oh, and by the way, unleash Hell.

[MAXIMUS and the cavalry storm down the wooded hill. The flaming arrows are loosed, the flowerpots of fire are flung, the long-distance spears are sprung, Hell is unleashed, and so on and so forth. Watching from a hilltop twenty miles away, MARCUS AURELIUS is really, really old.]

MAXIMUS: STAY WITH ME! STAY WITH ME!!

SOME SOLDIER: Stay with you? Where else are we going to— [*Rides into tree, falls over, is crushed by horse.*]

[The cavalry storms the battlefield. RIDLEY SCOTT breaks out the Dramatic Shaky Slo-Mo to show us that war is hell (and MAXIMUS is studly). MAXIMUS falls over and is nearly skewered by a GERMAN, but his pet wolf bounds through the woods, chews on the barbarian's head and saves the day.]

MAXIMUS [*petting wolf*]: Good boy! Goooood Hell.

[Eventually the ROMANS realize that there is nothing left in the forest to burn, kill or maim.]

MAXIMUS: ROMA VICTOR! STABNUS MAXIMUS!

THE SOLDIERS: WOOOOO!

Wagon of Luxurious Scheming

COMMODUS: So he wouldn't call us up here unless he was really dying, right? I mean, he might call us, but he wouldn't call the senators, too. Would he? I mean, he might call the senators but not us, or us but not the senators, but if he calls the senators *and* us it must mean . . . I MUST START PLANNING FUNERAL GAMES FIRST THING.

LUCILLA: The first thing I'm gonna do at camp is draw a *long . . . hot . . . steamy* bath and soak in it *all. night. long.*

INSIDE COMMODUS' HEAD: *Omg! Sis really* does *want my body!*

INSIDE LUCILLA'S HEAD: *Man, I hope I packed the lavender soap and the scrub brush.*

Marcus Aurelius Visits the Battlefield

MARCUS AURELIUS: Ah, Maximus, my greatest general. Everyone loves you, including me, which may actually lead to my own downfall. Good job!

MAXIMUS: Oh, no, sire, the men are honouring *you.*

MARCUS AURELIUS: Right, sure they are. Hail, Maximus!

THE SOLDIERS: WOOOOOOOOOOOOOOOOO!

  [The SOLDIERS throw flowers, confetti, underwear and other
  tokens of their appreciation at MAXIMUS.]

MAXIMUS [*pulling centurion boxers off head*]: Well, that's nice and all, but . . . since there's no one left to fight . . . can I go home now?

MARCUS AURELIUS: Yeah . . . about that . . .

COMMODUS: Oh, Daddy, Daddy! Did I miss the battle?

MARCUS AURELIUS: You missed the whole *war*, you twit.

COMMODUS: Well . . . I . . . then I'll sacrifice lots of bulls in your honour!

MARCUS AURELIUS: Save the beef. Honour Maximus.

COMMODUS: I embrace you as a brother that I really hate, Maximus.

MAXIMUS: Yeah . . . thanks.

COMMODUS: Here, let me help you, Dad—

MARCUS AURELIUS: *gives Commodus the hand, leaves with Maximus*

THE SOLDIERS: OH SNAP.

Party Time!

SENATOR GAIUS: Simply smashing battle, old chap. Ever thought about going into politics?

MAXIMUS: No. I farm.

SENATOR FALCO: He's a man of few words. But a lot of stabbing.

COMMODUS: Say, I'm going to need a good stabby guy like you after Dad's kicked the bucket. How about it?

MAXIMUS: I said, I'M GOING HOME TO FARM.

COMMODUS: Oh, well, sure. Livestock's great . . . Did I mention that my sister's here? You know, the one you used to have a thing with? She's a widow now, and you're the big dog – I'm sure I could spare her some night if, you know—

MAXIMUS: Are you actually pimping out your sister?

  [Speaking of whom . . .]

MARCUS AURELIUS: Lucilla, stop ogling Maximus and come pretend like we actually have a decent relationship.

LUCILLA: Awww, don't we? We seem to get along pretty well.

MARCUS AURELIUS: Yes, but there's apparently a lot of off-screen baggage that the audience isn't privy to.

LUCILLA: Oh, that. Right. Well, what can I do you for?

MARCUS AURELIUS: It's your brother, Lu.

LUCILLA: It's *always* my brother. Gonna need some specifics, Dad.

MARCUS AURELIUS: Well, see, it's like this: I wish you'd been born a man, because you, of all my kids, are actually pretty awesome, and I think you'd have made a good emperor.

LUCILLA: Well, you'll notice that I seem to be a good bit older than Commodus, so theoretically, couldn't I just be your heir and become *empress*?

MARCUS AURELIUS: No, because that would actually make sense and solve our problems.

LUCILLA: Oh.

MARCUS AURELIUS: Which leaves us stuck with Commodus as my heir. Now, I know that no one really likes to talk about it, but it's obvious that I'm fairly decrepit, and I'm going to keel over pretty soon, and when that happens, your brother is going to need you more than ever. Because he loves you, Lucilla. I mean, *a lot*.

LUCILLA: Dad? You have no idea.

Camp, the Next Morning

Walking through camp, MAXIMUS sees COMMODUS practising sword fighting with his GUARDS.

COMMODUS: Must stab faster! Harder! Must! Make! Daddy! *Love me!*

[MAXIMUS shakes his head and keeps going.]

The Tent of Marcus Aurelius

MARCUS AURELIUS: Why are we here, Maximus?

MAXIMUS: Uh, to kill people and take their stuff?

MARCUS AURELIUS: Oh, right. But see, that's it exactly – I'm worried about how I'll be remembered. As a philosopher? A soldier? A tyrant? Headmaster of Hogwarts? 'The guy who killed people and took their stuff'?

MAXIMUS: Well, I mean, what with the killing and the stuff-taking, some of that is inevitable.

MARCUS AURELIUS: Maximus, I once dreamed of a dream that was Rome. In a dream. Let us whisper about it together.

MAXIMUS: Sire, are you high again?

MARCUS AURELIUS: Rome – well, Rome is *my* home. Tell me about *your* home.

MAXIMUS: Well . . . I've got a hot wife and a great kid and a farm in Spain with lots of fruit trees and olives and grapevines and stuff, and I'd kind of like to get back there, if you don't mind. What's all this about, anyway?

MARCUS AURELIUS: Well, I was thinking . . . I want Rome to be a republic again when I'm dead and *someone* has to keep my son out of the way— I mean, uh, 'give power back to the people' . . .

MAXIMUS: Oh God please no.

MARCUS AURELIUS: MY SON IS NOT A MORAL MAN.

MAXIMUS: See, you keep saying this, but I've yet to hear exactly what it is he's done that's so terrible.

MARCUS AURELIUS: But you *are*! A very moral man!

MAXIMUS: It was sheep, wasn't it?

MARCUS AURELIUS: That's why you have to be the one to give Rome back to the people!

MAXIMUS: Goats?

MARCUS AURELIUS: No one who actually wanted to do it would be worthy of the job, so that's why it *has* to be you!

MAXIMUS: Camels?

MARCUS AURELIUS: Maximus, *you* are the son I should have had!

MAXIMUS: It was totally camels.

MARCUS AURELIUS: Look. You take over after I'm dead and settle things with the Senate. Commodus will accept this.

MAXIMUS: Sire, do you know your son at all? He totally, totally won't.

MARCUS AURELIUS: I CAN'T HEAR YOU LA LA LA LA LA.

The Camp Courtyard

LUCILLA: I can tell you and my father are up to something, because I'm crafty like that.

MAXIMUS: I'M JUST TIRED, ALL RIGHT?

LUCILLA: Please. You're no good at lying, being a strong, sexy, moral hero and all. Can I get you to promise that you'll serve my brother?

MAXIMUS: I will always serve . . . *Rome*.

LUCILLA: Yeah . . . you totally won't serve my brother.

MAXIMUS: Forget this – I'm going home, where I have a wife and a son.

LUCILLA: I'll be going to Rome, where I have a son and a dead husband.

  [They exchange smouldering glances.]

MAXIMUS: So, have we established that we once had a thing, but we now both have children, the ultimate bittersweet evidence of us having done it with other people?

LUCILLA: Yeah, I think so.

MAXIMUS: Awesome. See you around.

Maximus' Tent

While his SERVANT mixes up a toddy, MAXIMUS prays for his family, his future and his dignity, not realizing that the Gods of Irony are now required to screw over all of them.

MAXIMUS: Hey, Cicero . . . do you find it hard to do your duty?

CICERO: Well, I spent years being dragged hither and yon around Scotland by that crazy rebel, so I'm used to it by now.

MAXIMUS: Yeah, well . . . I don't think we're going home.

CICERO: Aww, shite.

The Tent of Marcus Aurelius

MARCUS AURELIUS: . . . So basically, not only are you not going to be emperor, there isn't even going to *be* an emperor.

COMMODUS: DADDY, WHY DON'T YOU LOVE ME?!

MARCUS AURELIUS: Aww, son, it's not that I—

COMMODUS: ALL I EVER WANTED WAS A HUG!

MARCUS AURELIUS: Aww! C'mere.

COMMODUS [*hugging him*]: I WOULD KILL EVERYONE IN THE WORLD IF YOU WOULD JUST LOVE ME!

MARCUS AURELIUS: See, Commodus, that's the whole problem right thARRRRRHGHGHGHHHHGHGHHHH!

[MARCUS AURELIUS is now dead from hug.]

The Emperor Is Dead, Long Live the Emperor

SENATOR GAIUS: Maximus! The emperor needs to see you!

THE EMPEROR: *is Commodus*

MAXIMUS: Oh *shit*.

COMMODUS: Serve me, Maximus!

MAXIMUS: *gives Commodus the hand, leaves*

SENATOR GAIUS: Oh *snap*.

[LUCILLA – who knows the score – comes in with tears in her eyes, slaps her brother stupid and then kisses his hand.]

SENATOR GAIUS: . . . And if you'll excuse me, I'll just show myself out before this gets any weirder.

Maximus' Tent

MAXIMUS: Cicero! Fetch my sword and wake the senators!

QUINTUS: Oh, Maximus, why'd you go sass Commodus like that? Now we have to kill you and your family!

MAXIMUS: AHHHHHHH!

QUINTUS: Hey, man, I'm real sorry about it, too. Nothing personal, okay?

Snowy Battlefield of Irony

MAXIMUS: So I lead you people to victory and this is the thanks I get. Well, at least give me a clean death.

PRAETORIAN [*moving behind* MAXIMUS]: Sure thing, boss.

[MAXIMUS then grabs the PRAETORIAN'S sword, flips out and kills everyone present with his hands still tied, because he is just that bad-ass.]

Somewhere in . . . Oh, Let's Say, the Pyrenees

Wounded and frantic, MAXIMUS has taken two of the Praetorian HORSES to journey from Germania back home. TO SPAIN. Wracked by visions of his wife and son, he stops to camp out for the night to give the HORSES a rest, because they've threatened to go on strike otherwise.

WHITE HORSE: And we want double oats when we get there, too!

MAXIMUS: YOU'LL GET YOUR DAMN OATS, ALL RIGHT?

Trujillo, Spain

MAXIMUS has already ridden one HORSE to death. He sees his villa smoking in the distance and spurs the other one on in a panic.

BROWN HORSE [*falling down*]: Ack! Everything . . . growing dark . . . tunnel of light . . . Snowflake, I'm coming . . . !

OUR LADY OF SOUNDTRACK SORROW: MmmmHMMM mmmHMMMmmm HMMM *wahhhhhhhhhhhhhh!*

  [MAXIMUS has not made it back in time. Woe.]

Some Desert

MAXIMUS: Man, I just had the worst dream *ever*. Commodus killed the emperor and was going to have me executed and my family was burnt and crucified, and then a bunch of Bedouin came and hauled my sobbing carcass away like yesterday's trash, and then this African guy was standing over me saying—

JUBA: Don't die. The maggots will clean your wound.

MAXIMUS: AHHHHHHHHHHHH!

Zucchabar, Morocco. Or Algeria. Somewhere Around There, Anyway

SLAVE TRADER: And so – if I give you the gay giraffe rebate – nnnghhh! – and sell you the Spaniard, the AfricaNNNGHHH – cheap! Very cheap! – you'll let go of my balls?

PROXIMO: Maybe.

SLAVE TRADER: NNNNGAHHH! I THROW IN THE HYENA FOR FREE!

PROXIMO: Sold!

Proximo's Gladiator School

PROXIMO: You will die to the sound of applause, and you will LIKE IT. Hagen! Show me what we've got!

HAGEN: Some candy-ass scribe!

SCRIBE: WAAAAA!

PROXIMO: Definitely the yellow mark. Next!

HAGEN: Some African hunter!

[HAGEN, the German trainer-gladiator, takes a swipe at JUBA. JUBA puts a dent in his skull.]

PROXIMO: Red! Excellent! Next!

[MAXIMUS steps up, but throws down his wooden practice sword because he doesn't give a shit. HAGEN smacks him in the gut, but he gets back up. HAGEN whacks him upside the head, but he gets back up.]

PROXIMO: What the hell's wrong with him?

HAGEN [*examining* MAXIMUS]: Well, it's not a TUUUMAAAAAH . . .

PROXIMO: Oh, for God's sake. Next!

The Gladiator Kennel

MAXIMUS is scraping off his Roman Legion tattoo, mostly just for spite.

JUBA: Why won't you fight? Everyone has to fight.

MAXIMUS: . . .

JUBA: Won't you piss off your gods if you scrape that off?

MAXIMUS: . . .

JUBA: Amazing how we come from two different continents, but we both speak English, isn't it?

MAXIMUS: . . .

JUBA: FINE, BE THAT WAY.

Two-Bit Arena, Zucchabar

PROXIMO: So basically, what I'm telling you is that we're all going to die, but you can weep like little girls and piss yourselves, or you can go out there and die in bone-crunching, gut-stabbing agony like heroes. And by 'heroes' I mean 'guys who actually lose'.

[All the men are chained in pairs – a red with a yellow. In the holding pen, 'yellow' MAXIMUS is rolling a handful of dirt between his palms while the SCRIBE just in front of him bawls. MAXIMUS feels something wet on his foot and looks down.]

MAXIMUS: So . . . you've made your choice, I see.

> [The gate opens, the GLADIATORS charge out and the first ones into the arena are immediately butchered. The SCRIBE dies whimpering, which is just fine with HAGEN, because he'd rather work solo anyway. JUBA and MAXIMUS clean up because they work well together. No one else survives, but we don't care, because none of the dead GLADIATORS had any lines.]

Triumph of the Shrill, Rome

COMMODUS and LUCILLA ride back into Rome in a parade of chariots and soldiers. Red rose petals fill the air, although where they're being dropped from is a mystery.

PEASANTS IN THE CROWD: Go away! You SUCK!

LUCILLA: Praetorian, these are not the happy peasants we ordered.

COMMODUS: WHY DOES EVERYONE HATE MEEEEEE?

LUCIUS: Hail, Mommy!

LUCILLA: Oh, baby, I've missed you so much! I hope it never occurs to your uncle that you would be a perfect pawn in his twisted quest to get into my pants!

LUCIUS: Look, Mommy, I brought you flowers!

[Meanwhile, the SENATORS stand around bitching about COMMODUS – except for FALCO, who is totally on his payroll.]

GRACCHUS: Look at all this – you'd think he conquered all the barbarians by his precious self. Heil *Caesar*.

FALCO: Real funny, smartass.

GRACCHUS: Oh, *rock me*, Amadeus. [*To* COMMODUS:] Sire! We have many important matters of business to ask you about . . .

The Senatorial Chamber

COMMODUS: Oh, blah blah blah, with your 'book-learning' and your 'health hazards' and your 'people' dying of 'plagues'. I *know* the people—

GRACCHUS: The ones who sleep with their sisters, anyway.

COMMODUS: I HEARD THAT.

FALCO: Sire, you were saying? About the people?

COMMODUS: Oh, yes! The people! I feel a great love for them, as if they were my children, my actual blood relations, and I will embrace them to my bosom and hug them and kiss them and—

FALCO: Sire? Even I'm getting a little creeped out here.

COMMODUS: WHY DOES NOBODY UNDERSTAAAAND MEEEE?

LUCILLA: Excuse us, my brother is tired and WE HAVE TO GO.

Hissyfit Chamber, Imperial Palace

COMMODUS: WHY DO THEY VEX ME SO? WHO ARE THEY TO TELL ME WHAT TO DO? IT SHOULD BE JUST YOU AND ME AND YOUR FORTY-NINE PAIRS OF DANGLY GOLD EARRINGS.

LUCILLA: Fifty-three. I hit Marcus Spenserius this morning.

COMMODUS: I'll show them! I'll show them all! I know what the people want! They don't care about what's really going on in the world – they just want a *vision* of greatness! They want to be entertained! Entertained in a gruesome, pandering way that will distract them from the real problems of the world! And I will give them exactly what they want. I call it . . . *reality television*.

LUCILLA: Um, brother? Television isn't going to exist for another two thousand years or so.

COMMODUS: Really? *Dammit*. Well, let's boil it down to the basic principles and call it . . . *fun death*.

[He kisses LUCILLA's hand, and she lets him, because he hasn't seen the bill from Marcus Spenserius yet.]

Later That Evening

FALCO: Is Caesar all right? He seemed a little ticked off back there.

LUCILLA: He'll be fine, he's just—

COMMODUS: LUCILLAAAAA! THE CHEESE TOAST IS VEXING ME AGAIN!

LUCILLA: I have to go now.

The Senators Take a Three-Goblet Lunch

GRACCHUS is reading a flier left on his table:

GAIUS: A HUNDRED AND FIFTY DAYS OF GAMES?

GRACCHUS: Yeah, he's a smart one, that Commodus. Bread and circuses and all that.

GAIUS: Oh, do you *really* think the people will fall for that?

THE PEOPLE: Gladiatores AND violentia? Sign me up!

Two-Bit Arena, Zucchabar

THE CROWD: PSEUDO-BRITISH SPANIARD GUY! PSEUDO-BRITISH SPANIARD GUY!

[MAXIMUS is sent out by himself to fight five guys in totally gnarly helmets. It's still a pretty low-rent operation, though, because establishment can only afford pink rose petals to dump on his head. It takes MAXIMUS thirty seconds to kill everyone, and this includes the pre-fight dirt-holding. The crowd sits there and stares at him.]

MAXIMUS: WAS THAT DEATH NOT *FUN* ENOUGH FOR YOU?

[He hurls his sword into a pavilion full of noble spectators.]

191

SOME LADY: Goodness me, they really *are* cranky up there in Pseudo-British Spain, aren't they?

Proximo's Digs

PROXIMO: Look, Spartacus, what exactly do you want? You want a girl? We got 'em. You want a boy? We got this Antoninus kid, he's good with poetry—

MAXIMUS: You wanted something?

PROXIMO: Yeah, I did. The new emperor's commemorating his father's death with lots of fun death, so I'm taking you lot up to Rome, and if you carry on like this up there, we're not going to last a week. If you get over yourself for five minutes, you could become the greatest gladiator ever, and maybe the emperor will even free you, the way he did me. Which was awesome, by the way.

[The wheels turn in MAXIMUS' head.]

MAXIMUS: What do I want? Well, I want to stand in front of the emperor, too, and totally kill him.

PROXIMO: That's the spirit! Here's some armour – try it on while I ramble on about thunder gods and suckling the great whore Rome over here.

Juba and Maximus Have a Heart-to-Heart

JUBA: My wife and daughters are out there somewhere. I don't know that I'll ever see them again. They'll probably never give us free. Even if I die, it will be many years before they do, and I'll have to wait a long, long time.

MAXIMUS: My wife and son are already dead.

JUBA: Man . . . that really does suck.

The Great Whore, Rome

PROXIMO'S band of newly arrived GLADIATORS gape at the vast Coliseum.

JUBA: I never knew that CGI could build such things.

Meanwhile, Back at the Palace . . .

LUCILLA finds COMMODUS staring at LUCIUS while he sleeps.

COMMODUS: Look at him, so happy and loved. Remember when I used to stand over your bed and watch you sleep, Lucilla?

LUCILLA: What, you mean like this morning?

[LUCILLA moves the conversation to COMMODUS' room rather than let her brother get any new ideas.]

COMMODUS [holding head]: ALL MY DESIRES ARE DRIVING ME CRAZY!

LUCILLA: Commodus, please drink this tasty beverage I have concocted, which is not at all intended to knock you out so I can get a decent night's sleep.

COMMODUS [drinking]: I KNOW! LET'S DISSOLVE THE SENATE!

LUCILLA: Time for bed!

COMMODUS: STAY WITH ME!

LUCILLA: No, but I'll leave the night light on.

COMMODUS: KISS ME!

[LUCILLA very gingerly takes his head in her hands, kisses her brother's forehead and then walks out of the room with small, careful steps.]

LUCILLA: Ew. Ew ew ew. Ew ew ew *ew*!

The Coliseum

While the bookies take down bets and PROXIMO haggles over rates and billing with an MC in a Bozo wig, MAXIMUS meets a YOUNG FAN:

SOME KID: Your armour is neato. I like the horses on it.

MAXIMUS: They were my horses, but they're in Elysium now.

SNOWFLAKE [*in Elysium*]: NO THANKS TO YOU, MAN!

SOME KID: I like you, Pseudo-British Spaniard Guy. Will you be my father figure, as my own father, Lucius Verus, is dead and my uncle the emperor is crazy?

MAXIMUS: Oh my G— I mean, uh . . . sure! That sounds great!

The 'Battle' of 'Carthage'

JUBA: I kept meaning to ask you – why do you always pick up a handful of earth like that? Does it tell you something deep and meaningful about the land upon which you are about shed blood, or . . . ?

MAXIMUS: Nah. My palms sweat.

MC BOZO: . . . So put your hands together for . . . *the Barbarian Hooooooooorde*!

  [Ignoring the irony for the moment, MAXIMUS calls his fellow GLADIATORS into a huddle:]

MAXIMUS: Okay, look: they've set this up so that we all get mowed down. You wanna get out of this alive, you listen to me. And *stay together*.

MC BOZO: . . . Ladies and gentlemen! SCIPIO AFRICANUS' CHARIOTS OF DOOOOOM!

THE CROWD: WOOO!

  [Golden chariots with bladed wheels and CRAZY ARCHER CHICKS roar out and start racing around the arena killing people. Two GLADIATORS who do not understand the concept of 'staying together' immediately get speared. HAGEN understands but just

194

doesn't care, and gets arrowed in the leg for his trouble.]

MAXIMUS: SHIELDS IN DIAMOND FORMATION!

Proximo's Box

ALL THE OTHER TRAINERS: HA HA! All your guys are about to get *smoked*!

PROXIMO: Oh, really?

The 'Battle' of 'Carthage'

There's a three-chariot pile-up and CRAZY ARCHER CHICKS go flying, because MAXIMUS is just that smart. MAXIMUS saves HAGEN from a wheel blade, thereby earning his eternal trust and respect blah blah brotherhood blee. JUBA and MAXIMUS kill some CRAZY ARCHER CHICKS, and one of them just gets cut in half by her own chariot wheel. Then MAXIMUS seizes the prettiest white horse and starts commanding his new army:

MAXIMUS: Some of you kill people on the LEFT, and some of you kill people on the RIGHT!

CHARIOTS: *go flying*

THE CROWD: This is the best history lesson EVER!

[HAGEN and JUBA finish off the drivers after MAXIMUS does the CRAZY-ARCHER-CHICK-beheading honours. MAXIMUS prances around the arena on SNOWFLAKE JR., armed with a spear, but decides that he doesn't have a clear shot at COMMODUS.]

MC BOZO: And . . . somehow . . . Carthage . . . wins?

THE CROWD: YAY!

COMMODUS: Huh. I should be vexed, but I find myself mildly entertained. Bozo, who is that cheeky fellow on the pretty horse?

MC BOZO: They call him Pseudo-British Spaniard Guy, sire.

COMMODUS: How quaint! Introduce me.

[Down in the arena, the PRAETORIANS come out and surround the GLADIATORS.]

PRAETORIANS: Drop your weapons and make way for the emperor!

[MAXIMUS drops his spear, but when he kneels, he picks up an arrow and hides it behind his arm. You would think that this would be some great piece of foreshadowing, but since LUCIUS comes down with his uncle, we never see the arrow again.]

COMMODUS: What's your name, Pseudo-British Spaniard Guy?

MAXIMUS: My name . . . is Gladiator.

COMMODUS: Oh, stop being modest and just *tell me*.

MAXIMUS: My name . . . is Rumplestiltskin.

COMMODUS: OH, IT IS *NOT*.

MAXIMUS: . . .

COMMODUS: QUINTUS, HE IS *VEXING ME*!

MAXIMUS [*removing helmet*]: Fine. My name . . . is Maximus Decimus Meridius, commander of the northern armies, husband and father to a crispy family and FUTURE KICKER OF YOUR ASS.

LUCIUS: Omg!

LUCILLA [*in the stands*]: OMG!

COMMODUS: OMGWTF!

QUINTUS: *Awkward.*

THE CROWD: LIVE! LIVE! LIVE!

COMMODUS: Nnnrghh! Must! Kill! Maximus! Can't! Piss off! Crowd! NAAARRRRGHHHH!

[Finally, COMMODUS surrenders to the inevitable and gives the thumbs-up.]

THE CROWD: WOOOOO! MAXIMUS! MAXIMUS!

COMMODUS: ARRRRRRRRGGGGHHHH!

196

Hissyfit Chamber, Imperial Palace

COMMODUS: WHAT THE HELL, LUCILLA?

LUCILLA: Hey, that whole 'kill him and his family' thing was all you, brother.

COMMODUS: I AM MUCHLY VEXED! MY VEXATION IS COLOSSAL, LUCILLA!

LUCILLA: No, seriously, tell me how you *really* feel.

COMMODUS: How did you feel when you saw him?

LUCILLA: I . . . I felt exactly what you would expect a recently widowed single mother who has just realized that her first love is not, in fact, dead to feel: nothing. Absolutely nothing. Yes. Nothing.

COMMODUS: GOOD.

The Gladiator Kennel

LUCILLA: So I thought I'd come say hi.

MAXIMUS: IF I WEREN'T CHAINED TO THIS WALL I WOULD KILL YOU RIGHT NOW.

LUCILLA: So . . . that means you *don't* want to make out?

The Coliseum

This time, MAXIMUS is pitted by himself against a guy in a giant silver tiger helmet. Named TIGRIS. Somehow, this does not tip him off to . . . well, you'll see.

MAXIMUS: Hey! You have two swords, and I only have one! That's not fair—

TIGRIS: *kicks sand in his eye*

MAXIMUS: HEY! THAT'S NOT FAI—

TIGERS: *jump out and chew on his head*

MAXIMUS: MMF! MMGH'F MGH MMHF!!

[MAXIMUS defeats TIGER GUY anyway, because he is just. that. bad. ass.]

THE CROWD: KILL! KILL! KILL! KILL!

[MAXIMUS looks to COMMODUS, who's kind of pissed that TIGER GUY let him down.]

COMMODUS: Nnnnrgh . . . well . . . eh. Thumbs down!

MAXIMUS: *does not kill Tiger Guy*

THE CROWD: Wow! He disobeyed the emperor? This is even more fun than death! MAXIMUS THE MERCIFUL! MAXIMUS THE MERCIFUL!

COMMODUS: GAHHHHHHHHHHHHHH!

Down in the Arena

COMMODUS: You just won't die, will you?

MAXIMUS: Not until I've kicked your ass, no.

COMMODUS: Here – come and get it!

[MAXIMUS knows that would be stupid because COMMODUS has umpteen hundred PRAETORIANS with him.]

COMMODUS: What are you . . . CHICKEN?

MAXIMUS: . . .

COMMODUS: Your son squealed like a girl and your wife moaned like a whore!

[Even the PRAETORIANS know he's gone too far; they all back away with murmurs of, 'Say whaaaaaat?', 'That ain't right!', 'Oh no he di-in't,' etc.]

MAXIMUS: *gives him the hand, turns away*

THE PRAETORIANS: OH SNAP.

COMMODUS: STOP SAYING THAT!!

In the Crowd Outside the Coliseum

CICERO: General! We're camped at Ostia!

MAXIMUS: Cicero! How are the men?

CICERO: Fat and lazy from not fighting!

MAXIMUS: Oh. Well, I don't so much want them then.

CICERO: Oh.

MAXIMUS: I'm kidding! Go find the emperor's sister and arrange some kind of intrigue with her!

CICERO: Awesome! Oh, and I brought your voodoo family prayer dolls!

MAXIMUS: *sniffle*

Hissyfit Chamber, Imperial Palace

COMMODUS: I can't let him live because he sasses me but I can't kill him because it makes me look bad! IT'S LIKE THIS NIGHTMARE I CAN'T WAKE UP FROM!

FALCO: Patience, sire.

COMMODUS: PATIENCE? That's the best you can come up with?!

FALCO: Well, I mean . . . I'm the oily second-in-command. I'm contractually obligated to do the whole 'bide your time while we concoct evil plans' thing.

COMMODUS: *pouts*

Lucilla's Litter, the Market Square

CICERO [*running along*]: My lady! I served your father at Vindebona!

LUCILLA: So? *Everyone* served my father at Vindebona.

CICERO: I served General Maximus!

LUCILLA: Aww . . . but, again, your point is . . . ?

CICERO: *And I serve him still.*

LUCILLA: STOP, STOP, EVERYBODY STOP!

The Gladiator Kennel

LUCILLA: So you said you'd meet our one good politician, Maximus. Here he is.

GRACCHUS: I hope my actually setting foot in this hellhole is evidence that you can trust me.

MAXIMUS: Well, here's the plan: get me outside the city, take me to my army at Ostia, and in two days I'll return with five thousand men.

GRACCHUS: So, basically, you're going to take over Rome.

MAXIMUS: Yes.

GRACCHUS: And then just . . . magically . . . give it back to the Senate.

MAXIMUS: That's about the way of it, yeah.

GRACCHUS: BULLSHIT.

MAXIMUS: Look, you give me Commodus, you can have the rest.

GRACCHUS: I have no idea why I'm going to trust you, except that there's pretty much nothing you can do that would be worse than what we've got going right now, so . . . sure.

MAXIMUS: Sweet.

Proximo's Digs

MAXIMUS: What do you mean, 'No'?!

PROXIMO: I mean, *No*, I *won't* be a party to this insanity. I'm not so much into the whole dying thing, you know.

MAXIMUS: YOU MAKE A LIVING OFF DEATH!

PROXIMO: Off *other people's* deaths, Maximus. *Duh.*

Commodus' Chamber, Imperial Palace

COMMODUS: I had Gracchus arrested for looking at me funny. Does that upset you?

LUCILLA: No . . . Of *course* not. Not at *all*.

COMMODUS: Actually, I'm going to make the whole Senate bleed. It'll be so much fun!

LUCILLA: But not tonight, right?

COMMODUS: Not if you come sit on the bed with me.

INSIDE LUCILLA'S HEAD: *Ack! Lie back and think of Rome! Lie back and think of Rome!*

COMMODUS: Do you remember what our father said once?

LUCILLA: 'Hey, kids, don't get it on'?

COMMODUS: He said that life is a terrible dream, and I have only you to share it with.

LUCILLA: Oh, it's a nightmare, all right.

   [COMMODUS begins putting his fingers in her mouth and starts up with the 'I love you' routine, but before it gets really ugly, he passes out on her shoulder.]

LUCILLA: THANK GOD FOR SLEEPY-TIME TEA.

Maximus' Cell

LUCILLA: Shit's going down – my brother had Gracchus arrested and then he put the moves on me and we have to leave NOW.

MAXIMUS: We?

LUCILLA: I mean . . . you. *You* have to leave. Of course. That's what I meant.

MAXIMUS: Okay, because that's what I thought the plan was – just *me* leaving—

LUCILLA: OH MY GOD PLEASE TAKE ME WITH YOU!

MAXIMUS: Lucilla! You're strong! You can do this! Think of your son!

LUCILLA: I know! But I'm tired of being strong, and I'm tired of *being groped by my brother*!

MAXIMUS: Yeah . . . that . . . that's rough.

LUCILLA: Seriously, can we make out now?

MAXIMUS: Sure – you've had a hard night, treat yourself.

The Imperial Palace

COMMODUS wakes up to find LUCIUS having play swordfights with the SERVANTS in the hall.

COMMODUS: Ah, yes – conqueror of the living room. I used to play that myself.

LUCIUS: I'm not conquering anything! I'm *gladiating*!

COMMODUS [*twitching*]: Say what?

LUCIUS: Mom says gladiation is the best! And that the Pseudo-British Spaniard Guy is awesome! She may have said something about killing you and saving Rome, I can't remember.

COMMODUS: Kid? We need to have a talk.

Dinner with the Imperial Family

COMMODUS: . . . And that's the story of Caligula and his three sisters who all loved him very, very much.

LUCIUS: Whee!

COMMODUS: And if you're a very good boy, tomorrow I'll tell you the story of Emperor Claudius, whose slutty traitor sister sold him out to the Senate for a gladiator she had the hots for. Lucilla, could you pass me the salt?

LUCILLA: *cries*

The Gladiator Kennel

MAXIMUS escapes in the middle of the night, but everyone else is left up a creek when the PRAETORIANS show up.

PROXIMO: Aww, hell. First decent thing I do, and— [Dies.]

HAGEN: You will never take us alive! Oh, crap, I'm dead. [Dies.]

　[Everyone else is taken prisoner.]

JUBA: Well, shit. Now we're given even less free than we had before.

Some Misty Glade

MAXIMUS sees CICERO waiting for him with the horses.

CICERO: Maximus! It's a trap!

　[The trap is that if CICERO warns MAXIMUS, his horse will bolt away and leave him hanged from a tree. Oh, and then he'll be arrowed.]

MAXIMUS: NOOOOOO!

SNOWFLAKE [in Elysium]: VENGEANCE IS MINE!

Hissyfit Chamber, Imperial Palace

COMMODUS: You tell Lucilla that Lucius stays with *me* now, and that if she so much as looks at me cross-eyed, I will kill him –

FALCO [writing on tablet]: . . . so much as . . . cross-eyed . . .

COMMODUS: – and if she kills *herself*, I will kill him, and she will sleep with me, and she will LIKE IT, or I will KILL HIM!

THE AUDIENCE: OMG Lucilla is right there hearing all this!

LUCILLA: *cries*

Maximus' Cell

COMMODUS: So you're going to fight me in the arena, and I'm going to kill you, and then this will ALL BE OVER.

MAXIMUS [*chained to wall*]: Yeah, I'd like to see you try.

COMMODUS: You think you're such hot stuff because you loved my father, but I loved him too! So that means we're brothers!

MAXIMUS: Are you going to hit on me now?

COMMODUS: *stabs him in the heart*

MAXIMUS: Nnngh! Well . . . given the . . . alternative . . .

The Coliseum

A haggard LUCILLA watches as her brother bounces into the arena, punching the air, while QUINTUS and the PRAETORIANS form a circle for the fight. MAXIMUS staggers out, nearly falls over and . . . still manages to kick COMMODUS' ass. He knocks COMMODUS' sword out of his hand, and it goes . . . somewhere COMMODUS can't get it. We don't know where. Maybe a fifth dimension invisible to the human eye. The point is, now he's unarmed. MAXIMUS could probably snap his neck like a twig, but he's too busy hallucinating that he's back home on the farm to finish him off.

COMMODUS: Give me a sword!

QUINTUS: . . .

COMMODUS: GIVE ME A SWORD!

QUINTUS: . . .

COMMODUS: *SWORRRRRD!!!*

QUINTUS [*to* PRAETORIANS]: Don't even think about it.

PRAETORIANS: *sheathe swords*

COMMODUS: QUINTUS!!

[Running out of options, COMMODUS pulls a secret dagger out of his sleeve and charges. Wounded and dying, MAXIMUS still manages to beat his ass into the dirt and stab him in the throat. Everyone in the Coliseum stares in shock.]

Faraway Blue Fields of Wheat

There are fields, and they are wheaty, and they are blue.

The Coliseum

MAXIMUS: Free my men, and Senator Gracchus, and Rome. Strength and honour and all that jazz. [*Falls over.*]

[They free GRACCHUS, and the other GLADIATORS, and Rome. LUCILLA runs down from the stands and cradles MAXIMUS and tells him to go to his wife and child, which, judging by the intermittent wheaty flashbacks, he's already doing a pretty good job of. He dies.]

OUR LADY OF SOUNDTRACK SORROW [*softly*]: *Wahhhhhhhhhhh.*

LUCILLA: Noooo! *Now* who's going to make out with me? [*Turning to others:*] Gracchus, this whole Roman Republic thing BETTER be worth it, or you'll be hearing from ME. Now – who will carry his body?

[GRACCHUS, LUCIUS, JUBA, *freed* GLADIATORS, etc. all approach the *fallen* MAXIMUS.]

LESS-DEAD-THAN-PREVIOUSLY-SUSPECTED COMMODUS: HEY! Who's going to carry *my* body?

GRACCHUS: . . .

LUCIUS: . . .

JUBA: . . .

LUCILLA: . . .

OUR LADY OF SOUNDTRACK SORROW: . . .

LESS-DEAD-THAN-PREVIOUSLY-SUSPECTED COMMODUS:
Man, I hate you ALL. [*Dies.*]

The Empty Coliseum, Later That Night

JUBA: Rest in peace, tiny people. Now we are given free. I will see
you again, Maximus . . . but I'm not in all that big a hurry, if you
get what I'm saying. I have my own wife and children to get back
to. So . . . from Italy to Africa . . . that ought to take about . . .
three horses, you think? I'll get the kind that can swim.

FIN.

HARRY POTTER AND THE ~~PHILOSOPHER'S SORCERER'S~~ PHILOSOPHER'S STONE (2001)

- - - - - - - - - - - - - - - - - -

MOVIE EXECUTIVE 1: Why do we keep changing the name, again?

MOVIE EXECUTIVE 2: Well, because they changed the name of the book for American readers.

MOVIE EXECUTIVE 1: And why did they change the name of the book?

MOVIE EXECUTIVE 2: What, you think Americans know what philosophers are? *Shpffffff.*

MOVIE EXECUTIVE 1: Hey, what is a philosopher?

MOVIE EXECUTIVE 2: I . . . I don't know.

Some Dark Street

A greatly aged WIZARD rendezvous with a CAT in front of a suburban house. Or a CAT who's really a WITCH. Or maybe a WITCH who's really a CAT . . .

DUMBLEDORE: What's new, pussycat?

McGONAGALL: That really never gets old for you, does it?

[. . . but we can hash that out later. They have more important things on their minds right now:]

McGONAGALL: Are you sure we should leave this to Hagrid?

DUMBLEDORE: I would trust him with my life.

McGONAGALL: I saw him drinking Aristocrat behind the garden shed two hours ago.

DUMBLEDORE: Well . . . I would trust him with the subject of this movie, at the very least.

[An ENORMOUS MAN with a bundle arrives on a flying motorcycle, as one does.]

DUMBLEDORE: We have to leave the baby with his only remaining blood relative – his aunt – in order for him to be safe.

McGONAGALL: But Albus – I've been watching them, and these people are total asshats!

DUMBLEDORE: Yes, but it's really the best thing for the boy – subjection to asshaberdashery builds character, you'll see.

McGONAGALL: But he's so helpless! And adorable! With his little lightning-shaped scar . . . ! [*Batting lashes*] You know, we could always take the baby and set up that love nest we've always talked about . . .

DUMBLEDORE: Hagrid? Put the baby on the doorstep.

The Sad Tale of Cinderharry

AUNT PETUNIA: Cook the breakfast, boy!

COUSIN DUDLEY: Count my birthday presents, boy!

UNCLE VERNON: Wax my chest hair, boy!

HARRY: *shudder*

UNCLE VERNON: Listen up, boy! We're taking Wudleykins to the zoo for his birthday, and you're coming only because I don't trust you not to burn down the house while we're gone. BUT YOU HAD BEST BEHAVE.

Two Hours Later

UNCLE VERNON: All right. Let's try this one more time. *What*, exactly, HAPPENED?

HARRY: Well, you see, I was chatting up this nice snake and we were getting along really well, you know, both of us bred in captivity and no one ever asks a snake if he's got anything to say so he was quite glad to have some company, you know, and then suddenly Dudley came along and started being . . . uh . . . his usual delightful self, and then the glass just disappeared and the talking snake slithered away and . . . I should quit while I'm ahead, shouldn't I?

UNCLE VERNON: INDUBITABLY.

You've Got Mail, Day 1

DUDLEY: Look! Some owl brought Harry a letter! WHY DON'T BIRDS BRING ME MAIL?

AUNT PETUNIA: There, there, Wookums, we'll get you a carrier pigeon . . . condor! A carrier CONDOR! With a . . .

[Suddenly, the DURSLEYS all begin to stare at the envelope, but particularly the coat of arms on the back.]

HARRY: It's mine! Give it back! What is it, anyway?

UNCLE VERNON: Nothing, nothing! Just . . . an invitation . . . TO A SCHOOL FOR JUVENILE DELINQUENTS. YES. Back in the cupboard with you, boy, or I'll take them up on it!

You've Got Mail, Day 2

AUNT PETUNIA: Vernon! There's more owls outside! With LETTERS! Why are there owls? Why are they doing this? [*Turning on* HARRY] We NEVER had problems with avian mail delivery until YOU came along! I think YOU'RE the cause of all this! You're evil! EVIL!

UNCLE VERNON [*barricading door*]: Woman, shut your piehole and find me some more nails!

You've Got Mail, Day 3

UNCLE VERNON stands before the fireplace burning letters one by one from a giant pile.

UNCLE VERNON [*with evil smile*]: You know, boy . . . there was a time when we burnt more than letters.

HARRY: *gulp*

You've Got Mail, Day 4

UNCLE VERNON [*singing*]:

> *Oh how I love the Sabbath day*
> *Sabbath day, Sabbath day*
> *Oh how I love the Sabbath day*
> *'Cos we don't get no mail!*

[Five thousand OWLS OF IRONY chuck an avalanche of letters down the chimney. Rather than picking up the nearest one on the floor and running like the Dickens, HARRY gives UNCLE VERNON ample time to tackle him and confiscate it.]

UNCLE VERNON: THAT'S IT! WE'RE GOING INTO THE WITNESS PROTECTION PROGRAMME!

AUNT PETUNIA: But Vernon, isn't that something only Americans have?

UNCLE VERNON: THEN WE'LL GO *THERE*, FIND A MOB HIT TO WITNESS AND GET IN IT THAT WAY!

Hut-on-a-Rock, the Sea

A GIANT MAN with a pink umbrella breaks down the door. As one does.

HAGRID [*to* DUDLEY]: Wow, Harry, I ain't seen you since I carried you away from the smoking ruins of your home and family! Don't look like I'd be able to do that *now*, though . . .

DUDLEY: I'm not Harry! Eat *him*! Eat *him*!

HAGRID: Oh! Well, then, Harry, [*turning to actual* HARRY] I have a charmingly misspelled birthday cake for you!

DUDLEY: Cake? I'M HARRY! I'M HARRY!

HARRY: Who are you?

HAGRID: I'm Rubeus Hagrid, the groundskeeper of Hogwarts!

HARRY: What in the warts now?

HAGRID: You know, where your parents learned everything!

HARRY: Huh?

HAGRID: You know, wizardry! You're a wizard!

HARRY: Whazzat?

HAGRID: You know! That's why weird things happen when you're around! Because you're a born wizard! Here's your acceptance letter to the school!

HARRY: Say what?

AUNT PETUNIA: HE'S NOT GOING THERE! I SWORE AFTER MY SISTER GOT BLOWN UP THAT WE'D NEVER HAVE ANYTHING MORE TO DO WITH THOSE FREAKS!

HARRY: *WHAT?*

HAGRID: Yes, and no Muggle's gonna stop you from studyin' under Albus Dumbledore, the best headmaster in the history of ever!

HARRY: Wossname?

HAGRID: Dumbledore!

HARRY: No, the other.

HAGRID: Oh, that – *muggle*. Non-wizard people, like your 'family' here. Asshattery is usually optional. USUALLY.

UNCLE VERNON: HE'S NOT GOING TO ANY SCHOOL RUN BY THIS CRACKPOT CRUMBLESNORE OR BUMBLEWHORE OR WHATEVER HIS NAME IS—

HAGRID [*drawing duelling umbrella*]: I DEMAND THE
SATISFACTION OF A VERY LARGE GENTLEMAN!

[Cake-snorfling DUDLEY ends up with a pig's tail.]

THE DURSLEYS: WAHHHHHHH!

HAGRID: So, Harry? You comin' or not?

HARRY: Hagrid? You had me at 'cake'.

First Stop: The Leaky Cauldron!

BARKEEPER: Flaming Wallbanger for you, Hagrid?

HAGRID: Oh, no, no time to booze, Tom. I'm just helpin' THE
FAMOUS HARRY POTTER buy his first-year school supplies
today.

[The tavern breaks out in fannish cries of 'OMG YOUNG
MR POTTER SQUEEEEE!' and an enthusiastic flurry of
undergarments.]

HARRY [*pulling underwear off head*]: Ewww, wizard panties!

SOME GUY IN A TURBAN: H-H-H-H-Hello, H-H-H-H-Harry!
I'm P-P-P-P-P-P-Professor Q-Q-Q-Q-Q-Quirrell—

HAGRID: Look, I'm gonna sum up, or we're gonna be here all day:
he's the new Defence Against the Dark Arts teacher at Hogwarts
and he's happy to meet you and he'll see you in class, blah blah
blah. NO TIME TO SHAKE HANDS, HARRY, COME ON!

[In the back of the tavern, HAGRID starts poking at things with
seeming purpose. Emphasis on 'seeming'.]

HARRY: Hagrid? I got the distinct impression back there that . . .
I'm sort of famous.

HAGRID: Sort of? Why, Harry, you're the famousest eleven year
old there ever was, and that's sayin' a lot!

HARRY: But . . . why? What'd I do?

HAGRID: I'm not sure I'm the right person to tell you that, Harry.
But I might be five scenes from now, so we'll get back to that later.

We're off to Diagon Alley now!

HARRY: How do you get there?

HAGRID: Well, you'd think that, often as I go there, I'd know exactly what to do, but . . . boozing takes its toll, you know. Maybe it's in this here coat closet—

SOME FAUN: OI! YOU PEOPLE AGAIN?

HAGRID: Crap, that's how you get to Narnia. Wait, I remember!

[HAGRID goes to a brick wall out behind the tavern and starts tapping at the bricks with his umbrella. They rearrange themselves into an opening and—]

SOME YOUNG BRUNETTE: Do you know the way to the Goblin King's castle?

SOME CATERPILLAR [*in the distance*]: I TOLD YOU NOT TO GO THAT WAY!

HAGRID [*closing bricks*]: Let's try that again, shall we?

Diagon Alley, the Land of Wish Fulfillment!

HAGRID: Here we are, Harry! Here's where you buy all your school supplies, except instead of boring old pencils and notebooks, you get quills and ink and parchment! And every day's like dress-up in crazy robes! And you get to mix stuff up in cauldrons and, if you're anything like me, blow it up! And look, racing brooms!

HARRY: But . . . I don't have the money to buy this. I don't have any money, really, except a bus token Aunt Petunia gave me once for sterilizing the garage.

HAGRID: Sure you've got money, Harry! And plenty of it! It's a sad sort of orphan who don't turn out to have an amazing fortune waiting for him!

Gringotts, the Wizard Bank

HAGRID: Mr Potter would like to withdraw some of his parents' treasure hoard so that he can go to wizard school and buy all the sweets he wants. Also, I need the thing.

SOME OFFICIOUS GOBLIN: The thing?

HAGRID: You know. *The thingummer's thing.*

SOME OFFICIOUS GOBLIN: You mean the thingamajig's thing?

HAGRID: No, the *thingummer's* thing, because Americans don't know what thinga-majigs are.

SOME OFFICIOUS GOBLIN: Ahhhhh, of course. Right this way!

Ollivander's Wand Shop

HAGRID has important business to go screw up, so he leaves HARRY to manoeuvre the spooky, heavily ~~fore~~shadowed wand shop by himself.

MR OLLIVANDER: Ahhhh, young Mr Potter! Here, try this one!

HARRY: Wouldn't you like to . . . uh . . . take some measurements? Like . . . the width of my nostrils, or something?

MR OLLIVANDER: No, no, just go ahead and start breaking things!

THE FIRST WAND: *blows up the back storeroom*

MR OLLIVANDER: Here, try this one. And aim it at the street this time.

HARRY: You don't think it's the right one, then?

MR OLLIVANDER: Oh, good heavens, no. The right one is always the third one, but we can't get to the third one without the first and second, now, can we?

THE SECOND WAND: *blows a crater in the street*

MR OLLIVANDER: Excellent, excellent! I never liked Doris Crockford anyway. Now, what should I give you now that it actually counts? Oh, WAIT. I bet there's a highly significant and poetically ironic selection in the back that might be just the ticket.

[From the smoking ruins of the storeroom, MR OLLIVANDER brings forth . . .]

THE THIRD WAND: *blows back Harry's hair with a halo of wonder and mystery*

MR OLLIVANDER: This wand contains one of two phoenix tail feathers drenched in danger and irony and foreshadowing. The wand containing the other killed your parents and blew up your house and gave you that scar. You see now why this wand had to be the third choice.

HARRY: . . .

MR OLLIVANDER: Will that be cash or credit?

Five Minutes Later

HARRY: So, now I've got spell books, a magic wand, a crapload of money and—

HAGRID: Look, a pet owl of your very own! Happy birthday!

HARRY: Wow, this is so much better than the fungy toenail clippings Dudley gave me last year.

Back at the Leaky Cauldron: The Tale of the Boy Who Lived

HAGRID: Well, Hare, now that I've got a few Wallbangers in me, lemme tell you why you're famous.

HARRY: Shoot.

HAGRID: Well, Harry, most wizards are good but some are very, very bad, and there was one who was so bad we don't even say his name no more, but for the purposes of exposition it's Voldemort—

HARRY: VOLDEMORT?

HAGRID: SHHHHHHH! Anyway, he went around in a big black hood killin' folks as what got in his way, and by the time it occurred to anyone important that he needed to be stopped he was too powerful for anything to be done about it, so your parents got toasted as well. Thing was, he was all set up to kill you, too – liked killin' babies, he did – and something happened. We don't know what it was, but apparently you pulled some kinda infant hoodoo on him, because he ended up disembodied and such, and you didn't get no more harm than that there evil curse scar. And that's why everyone knows your name, because you're The Boy Who Lived™.

HARRY: . . .

HAGRID: Well . . . ?

HARRY: Really, I just thought you were going to say that my picture was on jars of baby food or something.

The Train Station

SOME PORTER: Can I help you, lad?

HARRY: Well, this giant with a pink umbrella just dropped me off here at the station and told me to go to Platform Nine and Three-Quarters, but I can't seem to find it. He left with the thingummer's thing on his flying motorcycle before I could get anything else out of him. Do you know the way?

SOME PORTER: God, I hate this time of year.

The Hogwarts Express

SOME REDHEAD KID: Can I sit with you?

HARRY: Sure thing! If it weren't for your mum shoving me through that pillar, I wouldn't be here at all!

SOME REDHEAD KID: Wicked! I'm Ron Weasley!

HARRY: I'm Harry Potter.

RON: With the—

HARRY: Yes, with the scar.

RON: And the—

HARRY: Yes, and the dead parents.

RON: My sister wants to know if you really have green eyes, too.

HARRY: Huh . . . I've never heard anything about green eyes before. Mine are blue.

RON: Well, I guess you can't believe everything you hear.

[Just then, the SWEETS LADY arrives with her trolley.]

RON: No thanks . . . I'm poor.

HARRY: Two of everything, my good woman!

SWEETS LADY: Don't forget, you can really buy all these magical confections and more at fine book stores and theatre concession stands near you! Look for the Harry Potter display – free Snitch keychain with every fourth bag of jellybeans!

HARRY POTTER: Yum!

RON: Oh, and this is my plot point, Scabbers.

HARRY: Wow, I've never seen a real live plot point before.

RON: Well, he's not a very good one – he's not even any use until the third movie. My brothers taught me a spell to use on him—

[A GIRL with ~~frizzy~~ attractively tousled hair flounces into their compartment:]

SOME GIRL: I bet it doesn't work, though. [*Turning to* HARRY] *I* can already do rudimentary spells like fixing your glasses, resoling your hand-me-down shoes and giving you a proper haircut, *and* I know words like 'rudimentary' besides. Hey! You're Harry Potter! *I'm* Hermione Granger.

RON: And I'm—

HERMIONE: Dirty, did you know that? And poor.

RON: THANKS.

Welcome to Hogwarts!

HAGRID: All first years in the boats! I saved a good spot for you, Harry.

RON: Wow!

HARRY [*beaming*]: Yeah, I have connections.

SOME WEASELLY BLOND KID: Ah, you're just my sort, then. These are my henchmen, Crabbe and Goyle, and I'm Draco Malfoy, son of the richest, purest-blooded family in Wizardom.

HARRY: I'm . . . happy for you?

DRACO: Seriously, that doesn't mean anything to you?

HARRY: Besides 'spoiled and inbred'? Not really, Casper.

THE OTHER KIDS: OH SNAP.

PROFESSOR McGONAGALL: That's enough recruiting for one night, Malfoy! Now come on, they're ready to sort you first years!

The Sorting Hat

McGONAGALL: Any and all Weasleys please proceed to the Gryffindor table.

RON: So . . . you don't want me to come up there?

McGONAGALL: NEXT!

[HERMIONE is immediately sorted by the TALKING HAT into Gryffindor, as is anyone who's had a speaking part so far. Well, with the exception of . . .]

McGONAGALL: Draco M—

THE SORTING HAT: SLYTHERIN!

McGONAGALL: Malf—

THE SORTING HAT: SLYTHERIN!

McGONAGALL: Could you let me say the kid's name?

THE SORTING HAT: SLYTHERIN!

DRACO: WOOT!

McGONAGALL: Harry Potter!

THE SORTING HAT: Ooooo, the famous Harry Potter! I could put you in Ravenclaw or Hufflepuff, except that the movies ignore those two houses almost completely, so forget that!

HARRY: Could we not have this conversation out loud? Everyone's *staring at me*.

THE SORTING HAT: Shpffff, get used to it. So: Slytherin or Gryffindor? Yeah, this one's a real nail-biter.

HARRY: Not! Slytherin! Not! Slytherin!

THE SORTING HAT: Kid, I was being sarcastic. Of course you're in Gryffindor, *duh*.

THE SLYTHERINS: But – but there are many reasons why Harry might be in Slytherin, including but not limited to the transfer of some of Voldemort's powers when—

THE SORTING HAT: I SAID GRYFFINDOR!

THE GRYFFINDORS: YAY!

Dinner in the Great Hall

DUMBLEDORE: I would like to announce that I am absentmindedly beneficent.

NEARLY HEADLESS NICK: I'm a ghost!

HERMIONE: I know everything, because I read it in *Hogwarts: A History*!

NEVILLE: I'm completely hapless— OW! MY FORK IS IN MY EYE!

NEARLY HEADLESS NICK: I'm a headless ghost!

SEAMUS: I'm a half-blood! Has my water turned to rum yet?

RON: Dude, and possibly a burgeoning alcoholic.

SEAMUS: Yeah? Well, you're POOR.

RON: SHUT UP, I KNOW.

NEARLY HEADLESS NICK: I'm a *disgruntled* headless ghost!

PERCY: I'm overweeningly officious, which will be important four books from now.

THE FAT LADY: I'm a painting!

THE STAIRCASES: We're fickle bitches!

NEARLY HEADLESS NICK: PAY ATTENTION TO MEEEEEEEEE!

Harry's First Night at Hogwarts

HARRY: I'm all alone in this dormitory windowsill, in a new school, away from everything I know.

HARRY'S WHITE OWL: And this is a problem because . . . ?

HARRY: Touché.

The First Day of Class

McGONAGALL: I'm cranky. And sometimes a cat. But mostly cranky.

SNAPE: I hate all of you. BUT PARTICULARLY *YOU*, POTTER.

DRACO: *perks up*

SNAPE [*to* DRACO]: Perhaps I hate *you* a little less.

DRACO: *beams*

SNAPE: Don't push it, Malfoy.

MADAM HOOCH: All right, call your brooms!

HARRY: Hey, I'm actually good at this!

HERMIONE: HEY, I'M ACTUALLY BAD AT THIS!

RON: OW!

HARRY: Hey, where's Neville going?

NEVILLE: Heeeeeeeeeelp!

RON: Ah, good old Neville, always making sure someone screws up worse than me.

[As soon as MADAM HOOCH has borne NEVILLE and his broken wrist away to the infirmary –]

MADAM HOOCH: EVERYONE STAY ON THE GROUND!

[– DRACO decides to take NEVILLE's ~~MacGuffin~~ Remembrall and throw it on the roof or up in a tree or something.]

RON: God, Malfoy, you're such a bastard.

DRACO: I'LL HAVE YOU KNOW I CAN TRACE MY FAMILY BACK TO THE NORMAN CONQUEST!

[Only HARRY is brave – or stupid – enough to defy MADAM HOOCH and chase after DRACO, who decides to go long. No one expects HARRY to actually catch the Remembrall, least of all—]

McGONAGALL: POTTER, COME WITH ME.

HARRY: *wibbles*

McGONAGALL: Now, for your disobedience and complete disregard for safety . . . I've decided to put you on the Quidditch team as the youngest Seeker in a hundred years!

HERMIONE: Look at this trophy, Harry! Your father was a champion Seeker!

HARRY: And I would be thrilled, if I had any clue what you people are talking about!

Hogwarts Gets a New Pet

McGONAGALL: Albus, are you sure this is a good idea? I mean, those fickle stairs could randomly dump the children right on the third floor at any moment!

DUMBLEDORE: Oh, pish, Minerva, I told them that the third floor held only death and dismemberment. I'm sure none of our hormone-addled adolescents will find their curiosity piqued or their decisions reckless at all.

McGONAGALL: Albus? This is why *I* teach and you *don't*.

DUMBLEDORE: Woman, don't sass me in front of our co-workers!

SNAPE: Really, Albus, she's right. You put a giant three-headed dog up there where students could randomly stumble upon him, and you're flirting – nay, running away for the *weekend* – with disaster.

DUMBLEDORE: So you do think—

SNAPE: But then, I'd be more than happy for some of those little brats to get eaten, so . . . let the good times roll.

The Third Floor, Two Days Later

HARRY, HERMIONE AND RON: WAHHHHHHHHHHH!

Harry's First Quidditch Lesson

QUIDDITCH CAPTAIN OLIVER WOOD: All right, Potter, this should be easy. You've got seven players on two teams, for a total of fourteen, plus three balls and six hoops. The two Chasers, which are actually four Chasers by the time you factor in both teams, try to score goals with the Quaffle through one of six hoops, although of course each team uses only the three hoops on the other team's side and has a Keeper to defend their own hoops. Meanwhile, the two Beaters, which are actually four Beaters, beat the two Bludgers off their teammates, and sometimes *onto* the other team's players if they feel like being right bastards. And then there's a Seeker, one for each team, which means that there are actually two Seekers, who ignore the Quaffles and dodge the Bludgers and basically sit on their asses waiting for the Golden Snitch to show up, at which point catching it generally – but not always – renders the entire rest of the game moot, because it's worth one hundred and fifty points and is basically an immediate game-ender. For the purposes of this lesson, we will not consider the Golden Snitch a ball, because then there would really be *four* balls, what with the one Quaffle and the two Bludgers, and I would have to start all over again. Or maybe it's really three *kinds* of balls. Yeah. We could say that. So: piece of cake. Got it?

HARRY: . . . Yeah?

QUIDDITCH CAPTAIN OLIVER WOOD: And now I must leave, lest my Scottish jailbait charms overpower the audience completely.

ALL THE GIRLS IN THE AUDIENCE: *swoon*

Charm Class, Not to be Confused with Charm School

PROFESSOR FLITWICK: All right, students! Today we're going to learn levitation. Mr Weasley, I would ask that you particularly pay attention, as you're going to need this spell in about ten minutes.

[RON makes a valiant attempt at levitating a feather, but fails.]

HERMIONE: No, no, NO, it's '*Wingardium LeviOOOOOsa*', not '*LeviosAAAAH*', as you would *know* if you had *read*—

RON: *Hogwarts: A History*, I KNOW, I KNOW!

HERMIONE: Actually, I was going to say 'last night's assigned reading', but if you'd like to make an even bigger fool of yourself, go right on ahead.

RON: Gah, no *wonder* everyone hates you.

HARRY: Where's Hermione?

NEVILLE: Still crying in the girls' lavatory, RON.

RON: Look, how was I to know she'd take something as simple as a declaration of universal hate so *personally*?

[PROFESSOR QUIRRELL races in at this moment, shrieks something about a TROLL in the dungeon and passes out flat on his face, inciting the general student body of Hogwarts to panic and hysteria.]

ALL THE STUDENTS: WAHHHHHHHHHHHHHHHHHH—

DUMBLEDORE: SIT DOWWWWWN!

ALL THE STUDENTS: . . . ahhhh?

DUMBLEDORE: If the troll is in the *dungeon*, why would you run screaming from the *hall*, where you're safe? What are we teaching you people here anyway, underwater basket-weaving? Ten points from each house, for rampant stupidity! Now all of you, go to your rooms! QUIETLY!

McGONAGALL: What on earth was Quirrell doing in the dungeon, anyway? And where's Snape gone off to?

CARETAKER FILCH: Really, I wouldn't ask, if I were you. Mmm-hmmmm.

McGONAGALL: . . .

[En route to the dormitory, HARRY and RON have realized that HERMIONE is still in the lavatory and doesn't know about the TROLL. Normally this wouldn't be a problem, as the TROLL is (1) in the dungeon and (2) male, but somehow the one TROLL with a taste for little girls has found its way into Hogwarts.]

HERMIONE: Heeeeeeelp!

RON AND HARRY: We'll save you!

[Five minutes later, HERMIONE is hiding under a half-crushed sink and the TROLL'S got HARRY by the feet.]

HARRY: RON, THINK OF SOMETHING!

HERMIONE: Oh, we're going to be here all night, then!

RON: SHUT UP!

[RON desperately searches his memory for anything that might help:]

RON: *Trollus . . . deadus! Trollus . . . droppus! Trollus . . . letgous!*

HERMIONE [*helpfully*]: *Wingardium . . . !*

RON: *Wingardium trollus?*

HARRY [*swinging from warty* TROLL *fist*]: OH FOR THE LOVE OF GOD, RON, IT'S *WINGARDIUM LEVIOSA—*

RON: No it's not, it's '*Wingardium Leviooosa*'—

[The TROLL's club is levitated long enough to bop the TROLL on the head coming down. Thus ends the tale of the one spell RON is allowed to use successfully in these movies. The PROFESSORS rush in to find HARRY and HERMIONE cheering for RON over a stunned heap of wartflesh.]

McGONAGALL: EXPLAIN YOURSELVES!

HERMIONE: Professor, it's nobody's fault, because Ron and Harry knew I was in the lavatory and that I didn't know the troll was on the loose, so they came to warn me and then the troll found us and we had to defend ourselves.

McGONAGALL: A LIKELY STORY, MISS GRANGER!

HERMIONE: Well, then, it's . . . my fault, because I *did* somehow know about the troll, and I thought I could take it on by myself, because I'm a complete know-it-all . . . ?

SNAPE: All right, *that* I believe.

[HARRY notices that SNAPE's leg is ever-so-slightly chewed. SNAPE glares at him.]

McGONAGALL: All right, I'm taking points from each of you fools for reckless endangerment. And then I'm giving them right back, because you're the stars of the movie, in such a way that you actually come out on top. But understand that I am VERY, VERY DISAPPOINTED IN YOU!

The Seeker's Last Meal

HARRY: . . . and so that's why I believe Snape let the troll in, because clearly the three-headed dog is guarding Very Very Secret Hogwarts Business and he wanted the troll as a diversion while he tried to get past the dog.

HERMIONE: Wow.

RON: Are you going to eat your bacon?

[Just then, HARRY'S WHITE OWL delivers a . . . brand-new racing broom!]

HARRY: Thanks, H—

HERMIONE: Gee, it sure is lucky that someone sent you a decent broom just before the game!

RON: Not just decent – a Nimbus 2000, top of the line!

HERMIONE: What *were* you going to fly on, Harry?

HARRY: A mop Filch threw out and a whooooole lotta hope.

RON: Who could possibly have sent this to you, Harry?

McGONAGALL [*passing by*]: You better win this, Potter, or my bookie's going to want to have a chat with you.

The First Game of Quidditch

MADAM HOOCH: Now, I want a clean, civil game, but I'm not going to do anything about it if you decide to kill each other. GO!

[Our dashing friend OLIVER WOOD is the captain of the Gryffindor team. The Slytherin captain is an ill-favoured young man named MARCUS FLINT, which is pretty ironic considering that he doesn't look like he's even discovered fire yet. After a few promising goals by the Gryffindors, FLINT decides to play dirty and knock out some of the Gryffindor players—]

HAGRID [*yelling from Gryiffindor stands*]: OI, HOOCH! CALL SOME FOULS ALREADY!

HOOCH: You're absolutely right! Foul on Gryffindor for messing up my nice sand with its Keeper's crumpled body!

[After about an hour of sitting on his broom watching Slytherin score goals on Gryffindor's unguarded hoops –]

HARRY: What, you think I understood a word of that little Quidditch 'lesson'? I'm not going out there!

[– the Golden Snitch finally starts parading before HARRY'S face. Unfortunately, it is at this precise moment that his new broom decides to kill him.]

SOME WIZARD: I'm staring intently at young Potter's imminent demise!

QUIRRELL: I'm staring intently at young Potter's imminent demise!

SNAPE: I'm staring intently at young Potter's imminent demise, *and* I'm moving my lips right where anyone can see!

RON: CLEARLY SNAPE IS BEHIND THIS! WE MUST DO SOMETHING!

[Fortunately, HERMIONE knows the spell for Gothic Hotfoot, and SNAPE'S robes going up in flames distracts him and, indeed, everyone in a fifty-foot radius. HARRY recovers, hops back on his broom, wins a game of chicken with the Slytherin SEEKER and successfully catches the Snitch with his face. Never has a crowd cheered so loudly for such golden vomit.]

Fluffy?

HAGRID: Oh, why would Professor Snape try to kill Harry?

RON: Because he hates everyone, but particularly Harry?

HARRY: Because he's trying to get past the three-headed dog on the third floor and steal whatever's hidden up there?

HERMIONE: Also, he looks weirdly like Michael Jackson from certain angles.

THE KIDS: *shudder*

HAGRID: Snape would do no such thing, since he's one of the teachers protecting it, and even if he *would*, he'd never get past my Fluffy to the Thingummer's Th— [*Clapping hands over mouth*] OMG I NEARLY TOLD YOU WHAT IT WAS. You ought not to meddle in these things!

HARRY: But we're the stars of the movie! That's what we *do*!

HAGRID: Well, you three can stop that right now! We've gotten along just fine without a plot so far, hain't we? Just lots of nice episodes about young Harry's adventures at wizard school! Don't see no reason why we've got to go introducing a plot *now*, of all things, so you just keep to yourselves and don't ask no questions about Nicholas Flamel, hear?

Christmas at Hogwarts

HERMIONE: And *that* is why I'm sending you to infiltrate the Restricted Section to read up on Nicholas Flamel while everyone else is home for the holidays, Harry.

HAPPY CAROLLERS:

> *Merry Christmas, Merry Christmas!*
> *Ring the Hogwarts bell!*
> *Merry Christmas, Merry Christmas!*
> *Cast a Christmas spell!*
> *Never mind that Christian fundies*
> *think you'll all go to hell!*

RON: Plot point to E-5!

[RON'S queen smashes HARRY'S knight, rapes his village and sows his fields with salt.]

HARRY: Whoa.

RON: And *that* is how you play wizard chess. I'm going to have a *lot* of fun beating you over and over for the next two weeks.

HERMIONE: Awww, Ron! Not going home because your parents are poor?

RON: NO, I'm not going home because they love my brother

Charlie better, and they've gone to Romania to visit him and his dragons there! HA!

Christmas Morning

RON: Wake up, Harry! You've got presents! I know it's only a hand-knitted sweater and a box of my mum's homemade fudge, a wooden flute that Hagrid whittled himself and a case of your favourite chocolate frogs from Hermione, but . . .

HARRY [*awed*]: This is the best Christmas *ever*.

RON: Wow, really?

HARRY: Actually, it's my *only* Christmas ever. Unless you count the year Uncle Vernon used me to clean out the chimney.

RON: Aww, he used you instead of a real chimney sweep?

HARRY: No, he used me instead of a real broom. Oh, wow, some-one's sent me my father's invisible cloak! But there's no name on the card! And why did my father give this away anyway? Why didn't he use it to hide me and Mum? Oh, there are so many mysteries attached to this anonymous gift!

RON: . . . Instead of a *broom*?

The Restricted Section

HARRY'S invisicloaked foray into the forbidden zone ends abruptly when the books start shouting at him.

FILCH: WHO'S THERE?

[HARRY drops and breaks his lantern, but manages to escape before the CARETAKER finds him. All the librarians in the audience fall over dead at the thought of live flames being anywhere near a bookshelf. Meanwhile, SNAPE is giving QUIRRELL what-for at the other end of the hall:]

SNAPE: . . . and that is why you should stop doing the thing that you were doing, or I will be VERY, VERY CROSS WITH YOU—

229

SNAPE: Quirrell, did you just feel hot air at approximately the mouth level of an eleven-year-old boy? Someone's here! I KNOW YOU'RE HERE!

[While SNAPE paws at the air, both HARRY and QUIRRELL take the opportunity to flee in opposite directions.]

The Mirror of Erised

HARRY [*dragging in* RON]: Ron! Ron! You've got to see this! I randomly found this extremely magical mirror while running away from Snape! It shows me with my parents! Look!

RON: Wow! I'm head boy and Quidditch captain and my parents are actually paying attention to me and Hermione likes me!

HARRY: What?

RON: I mean, uh, GIRLS HAVE COOTIES AND WE DON'T WANT ANY. Also, there are no girls in the future. At all. None. It does show the future, right?

HARRY: No, because my parents are DEAD, stupid.

RON: Oh.

[A week later, and HARRY is still sitting in front of the mirror.]

DUMBLEDORE: Harry? I'm going to have to take the mirror away now. That's it. There you— Let it go now, all right? 'Letting go' involves loosening your fingers, Harry. Theeeeeere we go.

HARRY [*sobbing*]: But it's the only glimpse I've ever even had of my parents! I grew up in a cupboard under the stairs without even a cockroach for company!

DUMBLEDORE: And that's why you see your parents in the mirror, for the Mirror of Erised shows us the deepest desires of our hearts. And that's why I must take it away, before you forget to live in the present and waste away to nothing, as others before you have actually done.

HARRY: Really? That's what the mirror does?

DUMBLEDORE: Yes. You don't even want to know what Professor McGonagall saw in there.

A Random Scene in a Snowy Courtyard to Show the Passage of Time

HARRY'S WHITE OWL: Can't you just say my name *once*? I mean, you *did* give me one, right?

HARRY: Sure thing, H—

A New Season, A New Semester

HERMIONE [*slamming down giant book*]: I can't *believe* I had you in the wrong section of the library when all this time the answer was in a book I'd checked out *months* ago. Look! 'Nicholas Flamel, only known maker of the ~~Philosopher's~~ ~~Sorcerer's~~ Philosopher's Stone'! It must be what Fluffy's guarding, since it's the title of this movie!

HARRY: What does the ~~Philosopher's~~ ~~Sorcerer's~~ Philosopher's Stone do?

HERMIONE: Let's see . . . 'Turns any metal into gold and produces an Elixir of Life that grants the drinker immortality.' Which is fortunate, because it would really suck to live for ever but in poverty, like Ron.

RON: HEY!

Hagrid's Hut, The Dead of Night

THE KIDS: We know about the ~~Philosopher's~~ ~~Sorcerer's~~ Philosopher's Stone!

HAGRID: Can't let you in right now, illegal dragon egg I won off some guy at the pub is hatching!

DRACO [*peering in through window*]: BUSTED!

[The KIDS return to the castle to find MCGONAGALL waiting for them, because DRACO is a filthy SNITCH.]

McGONAGALL: I'm deducting fifty points from Gryffindor to ensure that there will be no nocturnal gallivanting in future movies!

RON: Shpfffff, like that's going to happen.

McGONAGALL: EACH.

RON AND HARRY: WAHHHH!

McGONAGALL: AND DETENTION.

The Forbidden Forest

Which apparently starts NOW.

FILCH: And if I had my way, you'd all have a taste of the thumb-screws! My iron maiden does get lonely down there in the dungeons with no one to hold all these years!

HAGRID: Ugh, Filch. Just when I go thinkin' nothing can give me the heebs, here comes *you*.

DRACO: Why do *I* have to gooooo?

HAGRID: Because you're a no-good ratfink, Malfoy. Now go on, before I start thinking about poor little Norbert . . . all by his lonesome . . . in Romania . . . [*sobs*]

RON: There, there, Hagrid. My brother Charlie says that Norwegian Plotpoints like Norbert can live a good three hundred years – there's plenty of time to go visit him later!

HARRY: What's our detention again, Hagrid?

HAGRID: Something's out there in the Dark Forest killin' unicorns, the rarest and most powerful of mythical beasts, so I'm takin' you four wee sprats out there with me to look for it.

DRACO: We can't go in there! There's . . . death in there, and stuff!

FILCH: Ohhhhhh, it's worse than *that*.

DRACO: THIS IS WHAT I'M SAYING! Just you wait until MY FATHER hears about this! HIS PIMP CANE SHOWS NO MERCY!

HAGRID: Oh, suck it up, Malfoy. I'll take Ron and Hermione this way, and you and Harry can take my dog Fang that way. I'd tell you not to get killed too hard, but knowin' my luck, there's nothin' out there as would want *you* anyway.

[HAGRID is at least partly right, because when the BOYS eventually stumble across a HOODED FIGURE vampirizing a UNICORN, it's only interested in HARRY. Nonetheless, DRACO and FANG run away screaming.]

HARRY: Wow, I didn't even know a dog *could* scream like that . . .

SOME HOODED WRAITH: *Shiiiiire . . . Baaaaaaggins . . .*

HARRY: *falls down*

[Suddenly, a badly CGI'd CENTAUR leaps out of nowhere to administer a two-hoof beatdown. The WRAITH disappears into the loving arms of its PUPPETEER.]

HARRY: Wow, thanks for saving me. What *was* that?

FIRENZE THE CENTAUR: Only the most terrible of monsters could kill a unicorn thus – its blood will keep even the most deeply wounded alive, but at the price of a cursed half-life ever after.

HARRY: But who would be evil enough to do that?

FIRENZE: Duh?

HARRY: OMG.

FIRENZE: Just one more thing—

HARRY: Yes?

FIRENZE: Can I have your autograph?

The Gryffindor Common Room

HARRY: Snape doesn't want the Stone for himself! He wants it to bring back Voldemort . . .

HERMIONE: . . . who's out in the Dark Forest right now. [*Shudders.*]

RON: You don't think he'll try to kill you . . . ?

HARRY: No, he'll probably just invite me to tea. OF COURSE HE'LL TRY TO KILL ME.

Hagrid's Hut, Exam Week

HARRY: Waaaait a minute . . . why did some stranger just *happen* to have an illegal dragon egg right when Hagrid wanted one? Why didn't I see it before?!

HERMIONE: Uh, because you're eleven?

HARRY: Hagrid! That dragon egg! Who gave it to you?

HAGRID: I dunno . . . some hooded wraithy guy, I guess. I was kinda drunk at the time, y'understand. I said to him, I says, 'Sure I can handle a dragon – I've got a giant three-headed dog back at Hogwarts that rolls right over if you play him some music,' I says!

THE KIDS: *facepalm*

Professor McGonagall's Classroom

HERMIONE: Don't worry, Harry. Everything'll be all right as long as Dumbledore's here to protect us. He'll stop Snape from getting the Stone!

HARRY: Yes. Professor McGonagall – where is Professor Dumbledore?

McGONAGALL: Oh, he was called away by a conveniently inconvenient owlgram.

234

The Halls of Hogwarts

RON: What're we going to do?

HARRY: Snape obviously knows how to get past Fluffy now!

[SNAPE just happens to be passing by at that moment and busts all three of them. A well-deployed eyebrow leaves RON and HERMIONE speechless, but HARRY just glares at him until SNAPE is like, 'Are you actually giving me the hairy eyeball? I'll be damned, I think you really are,' and he's so taken aback by a kid with that much nerve that he just turns around and storms off.]

HARRY: We go down the trap door – TONIGHT.

HERMIONE: But . . . what good is that really going to do? We're just kids, and we've already alerted the proper authorities, however ineffectual, that something's going to happen . . .

HARRY: Don't argue with hero logic, Hermione.

The Gryffindor Common Room

NEVILLE: Stop! I can't let you guys sneak out again!

RON: Neville, we're the stars of the movie. It's okay when *we* do it!

NEVILLE: No! You've already cost us a hundred and fifty house points! We're behind *Hufflepuff* now!

HARRY: Well, it doesn't really matter if we lose any more, then, does it?

NEVILLE: I'll fight you! All of you!

HERMIONE: I'm really sorry you're making me do this, Neville.

[HERMIONE whips out her wand and petrifies the kid. He goes down like a sack of rocks.]

RON: Don't lie, you *enjoyed* that.

Fluffy's Room

The KIDS creep on up to the third floor under HARRY'S cloak. The door can be opened with 'Alohomora', a spell so simple that even RON can do it. Good job there, teachers.

HARRY: Wow, it's a good thing Snape already got here and set up a magical harp to lull Fluffy to sleep, because we really came up here without a plan of our own to handle that. We'd better come up with some kind of plan now, so . . . I'll go first, and you two wait for a sign, and if anything should happen, you go get help and I'll . . . Hey, what's that giant wad of drool on your shoulder, Ron?

RON: EWWWW!

FLUFFY: RAAAAAAAAAAAAAA!

HARRY: JUMP!

Three Kids, Three Puzzles

HERMIONE: Wow, it really is fortunate that I pay attention in Herbology, isn't it? The Devil's Snare was *thisclose* to totally strangling Ron.

HARRY: Yeah, and I guess it's a good thing the next barrier was totally based around my Quidditch Seeking skills, because Ron's 'Alohomora' wasn't getting us anywhere.

HERMIONE: Really, I'm just glad there weren't any potions to figure out, or we'd have been here all night.

RON: Look, there's *got* to be something here I can do, right? RIGHT?

[The next room is a giant game of wizard chess.]

RON: SWEET.

HERMIONE: But . . . but . . . I don't wanna be pillaged!

[Despite RON'S l33t chess skillz, he still ends up having to sacrifice himself to win the game:]

RON: Harry, it's you that's got to go on! It's you that's in the title

of the movie! It's not *Ron and the ~~Philosopher's~~ ~~Sorcerer's~~
Philosopher's Stone*, now, is it? Although that would be a totally
awesome movie, with lots of Quidditch and explosions and—

HARRY: MOVE, RON.

RON: OKAY, OKAY! KNIGHT TO H-3!

[Once the game is over and HERMIONE has administered first aid
(as explained in *Medical Magic and You*) to RON, HARRY prepares
to meet the final challenge alone.]

HERMIONE: You really are a great wizard, Harry, despite not really having done anything in the way of spells or . . . wizardry, really,
over the course of this movie . . .

HARRY: Me? I'm just good at sports, and occasionally telling people what to do.

HERMIONE: Harry, I'm trying to give you a pep talk. Shut up and
take a compliment, okay?

The Final Puzzle

HARRY discovers PROFESSOR QUIRRELL staring into the Mirror of
Erised.

QUIRRELL: Unfortunately I can't figure out the riddle of the
mirror – I see what I want, but I can't get to it – so maybe if I
reveal the whole of my dastardly plan to you, you'll think of a way
to help! Yes, that's right! I, Professor Quirrell, have been in league
with Voldemort the whole time! I was the one who loosed the troll
on unsuspecting students! I was the one who enchanted your
broom! I've been faking my st-st-st-*stutter* the whole time! And I
would have gotten away with it entirely if it weren't for Snape
dogging my steps, for no one – NO ONE! – would have suspected
their beloved Professor Quirrell!

HARRY: Did I even have a class with you?

QUIRRELL: TELL ME WHAT YOU SEE IN THE MIRROR!

[HARRY sees a MIRROR HARRY reach into a mirror pocket and pull
out the ~~Philosopher's~~ ~~Sorcerer's~~ Philosopher's Stone, and then . . .

wink at himself. The real Stone is heavy in his real pocket.]

HARRY: I – I'm head boy and Quidditch captain and I've won the house cup and girls like me and . . . I think I just hit on myself.

QUIRRELL: LIAH!

[At the request of a strange, disembodied voice, QUIRRELL unwinds his turban and unleashes *figurative expressions made terrifyingly literal!*]

QUIRRELL: That's right! I have eyes in the back of my head! I'm TWO-FACED!

HARRY: Ack! Overpowered . . . by . . . awful puns!

VOLDEMORT [*from the back of* QUIRRELL'S *head*]: MINION! UNLEASH THE FINGERSNAPS OF FLAME!

[QUIRRELL snaps his fingers and the chamber bursts into flame. HARRY is really starting to wish about now that he'd made a run for it during the five minutes QUIRRELL took to unwrap his turban.]

VOLDEMORT: JOIN MEEEEE, POTTER! COME TO THE DARK SIIIIDE!

HARRY: NEVER!

VOLDEMORT: HARRYYYY, I AM YOUR FA— WAIT, SORRY. WRONG DARK-SIDE SPEECH. [*Cough.*] HARRYYYY, I CAN BRING YOUR FATHER BAAAACK! AND YOUR MOTHER, TOO!

HARRY: NO!

VOLDEMORT: DOESN'T THAT TEMPT YOU AT ALL? YOU'RE SUPPOSED TO BE TEMPTED, DAMMIT!

[VOLDEQUIRRELL springs forward like a two-faced flying squirrel and starts throttling HARRY. Fortunately for HARRY, his hands burn QUIRRELL'S skin at the slightest touch, and HARRY POTTER, BABY ACTION HERO! attacks QUIRRELL with his newfound power rather than let VOLDEMORT get the Stone. QUIRRELL ends up as a small pile of dust on the floor.]

HARRY: Oh, I am so gonna get detention for this.

[And then VOLDEWRAITH floats through HARRY for spite and knocks him out. Or something.]

Dumbledore Explains It All

DUMBLEDORE comes to visit HARRY in the infirmary.

HARRY: How are my friends? Are they okay?

DUMBLEDORE: Oh, they're fine.

HARRY: Where is the Stone?

DUMBLEDORE: The Stone has been destroyed. I had a little . . . uh . . . chat with my friend Nicholas.

HARRY: But without the Stone, he'll die now, won't he?

DUMBLEDORE: Yes, but he was about to turn 666 years old. Can't have the Christian groups protesting, now, can we?

HARRY: How did the mirror keep the Stone from Quirrell but give it to me?

DUMBLEDORE: Deep irony.

HARRY: So Voldemort can't come back now?

DUMBLEDORE: No, he can totally come back, and will proceed to try for at least six more movies.

HARRY: Why did my hands burn Quirrell?

DUMBLEDORE: Your mother's love lives in your skin, Harry.

HARRY: But . . . then why did he have no problem strangling my bare neck?

DUMBLEDORE: I think it's time for you to rest, Harry.

HARRY: Did my mother love my neck less, or something?

DUMBLEDORE [*waving wand*]: *SOMNIUS!*

The House Cup!

DUMBLEDORE: Slytherin wins! But wait! Let's invent reasons to give the main characters points and hand the cup to *their* house! I know, we could have stolen the cup from Slytherin *before* we hung the banners and served the feast and at least let them save some face, but hey! They're not people like you and me – they're *Slytherins*!

THE GRYFFINDORS: YAY!

The Hogwarts Train Station

HARRY: I'm not really going home, for Hogwarts is my real home. Everything else is a pale imitation at best, and at worst, actual torture.

RON: Harry, that's . . . just kind of sad.

HARRY: I know, dude.

FIN.

So You Want a Superhero Movie . . .

It's a tough choice for your summer movie season, but it can be a rewarding one: nothing appeals to all demographics and rakes in the dough quite like a guy in tights. But moviegoers already have the two great superheroes – the Man of Steel and the Dark Knight. How are you ever going to compete with them?

SPIDER-MAN (2002)

What You Need Is Some Teenage Angst.

PETER PARKER: This is a story about a girl. Well, actually, it's a story about tragic father-figure death and the betrayal of friendship and the great responsibility that comes with great power, but . . .

[MARY JANE'S flame-red hair ripples in the slo-mo wind.]

PETER PARKER: . . . there's this girl, and I have loved her since I was a kid.

THE AUDIENCE HEARS: WAH WAH WAH WAHWAHWAH Kirsten Dunst is really hot WAHWAHWAHWAH WAH WAH.

KIRSTEN DUNST'S SMILE: *ding!*

As For Your Hero, You Need: (1) A Bespectacled Geek or (2) A Rich Kid With Daddy Issues.

PETER PARKER [*huffing, puffing*]: Hey, guys! Stop the bus! Please!

[PETER trips over his own shoelaces, falls flat on his Harry Potter glasses and gets knocked in the head by his backpack full of science journals.]

MARY JANE [*to* BUS DRIVER]: Look, wouldja *stop* already?

BUS DRIVER: Hey, we're on a schedule here!

[You can make up a city if you want . . . but since every comic is basically set in New York, you may as well just use the real thing.]

MARY JANE: *Whatever.* You circled Queens three times just to screw with him!

As For the Best Friend, You Need: (1) A Rich Kid With Daddy Issues or (2) A Bespectacled Geek.

HARRY: Daaaaaaaaaad, why'd you have to take me to school in the Rooooolls?

NORMAN: You know, when you went to private school, your friend Bruce Wayne never whined to *his* dad about how he got to school.

HARRY: That's because his dad was MURDERED.

NORMAN: Aren't you going to introduce me to your friend?

HARRY: Peter, Dad. Dad, Peter. Whatever.

NORMAN: Nice to meet you, Peter. Harry says you like the science. You might say I dabble in it a bit myself.

PETER: Why, Mr Osborn, you're only the most goshdarn awesome nanotechnologist on the East Coast! [*Digging through bag*] Will you sign my copy of *Abstracts of the General Meeting of the American Society for Microbiology*?

NORMAN: Sure thing! Wow, you're way smarter than my son. Why don't *you* ever ask me for autographs, Harry?

HARRY: *seethes*

It's Time for the Origin Story!

The Midtown High seniors are on a field trip to view science people doing sciency things.

TOUR GUIDE: Here at the Columbia University Genetic Research Institute, we don't use tiny white mice for our experiments –

TINY WHITE MICE: DAMN STRAIGHT, BITCHES!

TOUR GUIDE: – we use spiders. There are some 32,000 known species of spider, and we keep all of them right here, in extremely shoddy and easily escaped cages. The spiders have a wide variety of skills – the Delena spider jumps great distances to catch its prey, while this one, the net web spider, spins webs strong enough to dangle cable cars of screaming children from bridges!

THE KIDS: Oooooooo!

TOUR GUIDE: And this one has sculpted abs and the ability to break box-office records!

THE KIDS: Aaaaaaaaaah!

TOUR GUIDE: This spider here hunts with such finely attuned reflexes that it borders on precognition. If it could talk, maybe it would tell us some good lottery numbers! Ha ha!

THE KIDS: . . .

[Meanwhile, in the back . . .]

PETER: You know, many spiders camouflage themselves as a defence mechanism.

HARRY: Sure, Poindexter. Are you gonna talk to Mary Jane or what?

PETER: *wets himself in terror*

[PETER is supposed to be taking pictures for the school newspaper, but FLASH THOMPSON and his NEANDERTHUGS are too busy thumping him upside the head and giggling for him to get very far.]

HARRY [*sidling up to* MARY JANE]: You know, many spiders wear camo to their self-defence classes.

MARY JANE: Wow! That's so cool.

HARRY: I know. I read it in *Abstracts of the Meeting of American Generals for Microwave Biology.*

TOUR GUIDE: . . . and we use them all to create hand-painted, genetically designed superspiders, which we will then use to take over the Earth. I mean . . . 'cure diseases'.

MARY JANE: Hey, one of them's missing.

TOUR GUIDE: I guess . . . uh . . . they're giving that one a tune-up. COME ON, KIDS, LET'S GO.

PETER: Hey! Uh! M-M-Mary J-J-Jane! Can I take a picture of you for the school paper?

MARY JANE: *strikes her best Vargas Girl pose*

THE MISSING SPIDER: *CHOMP!*

MARY JANE: *wanders off*

PETER: DAMMIT! Even invertebrates are cockblocking me!

Everybody Loves Science and Technology!

DR STROMM: So we have this glider and this extremely weird biomechanical suit.

GENERAL SLOCUM: Yes, yes, we've *seen* that, and it *is* weird. What about the biological performance enhancers? Because if they suck, we're giving all your funding to your rival, Quest Aerospace.

NORMAN: They're fabulous, and—

DR STROMM: Cause insanity and death.

NORMAN: I hate you so very, very much.

Someone, Somewhere in Your Movie Has a Loving Family.

UNCLE BEN: I'm down on my luck but still optimistic!

AUNT MAY: I'm supportive but spunky!

UNCLE BEN: But how will we get by?

AUNT MAY: I love you, and Peter loves you, and you love us, and that's all that matters!

[PETER comes home looking a bit green around the mandibles.]

AUNT MAY: What's wrong, sweetheart?

PETER: Well, see . . . there was this spider in red and blue camo and Mary Jane was pinned to a calendar and the spider learned cockblocking in self-defence class and I . . . I don't feel so good.

AUNT MAY: Ben? I think it's time to break out the castor oil.

The Transformation!

PETER is pasty and emaciated. And that was before he was bitten. While he drools on the floor of his room, CGI dramatizations show his DNA spontaneously splicing and recombining with spider-venom RNA.

THREE GENETICISTS IN THE AUDIENCE: *fall over dead*

Your Villain Transforms As Well, Because Science Changes Everyone!

Having decided to try the serum on himself in an extremely risky procedure, NORMAN starts taking off his shirt and tie.

DR STROMM: You don't want to change your pants or your shoes . . . ?

NORMAN: No, science usually affects only the torso.

[After tossing back a very scientific-looking potion, NORMAN is seized by clouds of green mist and fits of violent scenery chewing.]

DR STROMM: Noooooo! Norman! Speak to me, NormaNNNNNNNNNNNGH!

SLIGHTLY-LESS-DEAD-THAN-SUSPECTED NORMAN [*strangling* DR STROMM]: I'll teach you to care about the safety of test subjects! HEH HEH HEHHHHHHH!

Your Hero Wakes to New Possibilities!

PETER wakes up on the floor of his room the next morning, only to discover that he has perfect vision and surprisingly unnerdy musculature.

AUNT MAY: Peter? Are you all right in there?

PETER: Damn, I'm *fine*.

AUNT MAY: Well, that sounds like a big change from yesterday!

PETER [*looking crotchwards*]: Ohhhhh yeah.

She's Not Just 'The Girl' – She's a Damsel in Distress!

MARY JANE'S DAD: You're trash, with your miniskirts and go-go boots! Nothing but retro trash!

[MARY JANE trudges off crying to the bus stop, and PETER follows at a respectfully worshipful distance:]

PETER: Hey . . . remember me? I'm the kid next door, and I've loved you since I was knee-high to a genetically enhanced frog, and I don't think you're trash. I would always treat you right, and I would hug you and kiss you and pet you and call you MJ . . .

[But of course he's twenty feet away, so she doesn't hear any of this. And then he misses the bus. Again.]

The Plot Thickens . . . Even Though We All Know Who Did It.

After his night of murderous debauchery, NORMAN was still able to put his shirt and tie back on, because even villains have to keep up appearances.

HARRY: Dad! Are you okay? What are you doing on the floor?

NORMAN: I just . . . I . . .

[NORMAN remembers an extremely stylish flashback of the night before.]

NORMAN: . . . uh . . . got ripped off by a hooker and left for

246

dead, Harry, it's fine, don't worry about it—

NORMAN'S ASSISTANT [*running in*]: Dr Stromm is dead! In the lab! With the candlestick! And the flight suit and glider have been stolen!

NORMAN: I WONDER HOW THAT COULD HAVE HAPPENED.

Everyone Notices That Your Hero Is . . . *Different*.

MARY JANE saunters by with her lunch tray in bodacious slo-mo, only to slip – and be caught by PETER.

MARY JANE: Wow, Peter, you have great reflexes! And nice eyes! And unusually sculpted abs!

PETER: *drools*

MARY JANE: So . . . uh . . . yeah, I'll be going now.

[Still thrilled by his brush with MARY JANE, PETER experiences that most embarrassing phenomenon of male adolescence: premature web emission.]

FLASH: OW! SON OF A BITCH!

MARY JANE: Flash, no! I'm sure Peter just lassoed that tray and slammed it into the back of your head by accident!

FLASH: I'm gonna give you what-for, Parker! Put up your dukes!

PETER: And *I'm* the dork, somehow . . . ?

[PETER is able to elude FLASH'S assault with a careful combination of spontaneous gymnastics and Spider-Fu. And then somehow he knocks the class jock into next semester.]

MARY JANE: Peter, I . . .

HARRY: . . . that was . . .

EVERYONE ELSE: TOTALLY UNCOOL! YOU SUCK!

PETER: ARGHHH! EVEN WHEN I WIN THEY HATE ME!

PETER flees the school into a nearby alley, where he sees a spider web and does the math:

PETER: Hey . . . I got bit by a spider. That spider had ESP, and I have ESP . . . That spider could shoot really strong webs, and I can shoot really strong webs . . . That spider had really good abs . . . I HAVE REALLY GOOD ABS! OMG!

[PETER instinctually starts climbing up the wall and discovers that he has spider Velcro on his hands. (As with any young superhero, feel free to get a good close-up of your star's ass if it's convenient.) With the help of his new spider genes, PETER realizes he can also ~~leap buildings in a single bound~~ jump from roof to roof.]

PETER: All of these super abilities, and somehow I'm still dumb enough to try all of this! Whee!

[But now the distance is too great! How will he jump across the street?]

PETER: Go web!

PETER'S WEB: . . .

PETER: Go go gadget web-shooter!

PETER'S WEB: . . .

PETER: Open sesame!

PETER'S WEB: . . .

PETER: SHOOT, DAMN YOU!

PETER'S WEB: . . .

PETER: What was I doing the first time it happened?

[MARY JANE saunters by with her lunch tray in bodacious slo-mo . . .]

PETER'S WEB: *shoots across the street and punches through three windows*

PETER: Ohhhhhhh.

PETER: Oh, crap – I was so busy flinging myself around New York that I forgot to come home and help paint the kitchen! I'm such a terrible, terrible kid, what with making my good grades and never getting into any trouble, ever, except for this one particular day!

UNCLE BEN'S NOTE: 'MEATLOAF AND RICE IN OVEN, SLACKER.'

PETER: Why is it always rice?

[Unfortunately, MARY JANE next door has no such idyllic life.]

MARY JANE'S DAD: You're trash! Trash, you hear me!

PETER: Hey, I knew I forgot something.

[While taking out the garbage, PETER runs into a fleeing MARY JANE.]

MARY JANE: You know, you really freaked us out the other day when you just randomly laid the ninja smackdown on Flash. We were all totally wondering what was up with that, so . . . what are you doing after graduation?

PETER: I'm thinking about moving into the city, building a web of my own. You know, stuff.

MARY JANE: Yeah. Stuff is good.

FLASH [*out front*]: HEY, MARY JANE! COME SEE MY NEW CAR OR I'LL BELT YOU ONE!

MARY JANE: SoIgottagobye!

PETER [*calling after her*]: You sure you don't want to stay? Because . . . BIG CHANGES, MARY JANE . . . !

[MARY JANE does not want to stay.]

PETER: So . . . girls don't want guys who are nice, or smart, or actually interested in anything they have to say, or are even big in the crotchwards department. They want . . . cars. That they couldn't possibly get for themselves. Cars.

ALL THE GUYS IN THE AUDIENCE [*taking notes*]: *Kirsten . . . Dunst . . . likes . . . cars.*

Now Your Hero Has a Dream.

ASSORTED NEWSPAPER ADS:

- **PORSCHE: $39,990**

- **JAGUAR: $25,990**

- **BUSTED HOOPTY: $2,598**

- **WANTED: AMATEUR WRESTLERS! WANNABE SUPERHEROES A MUST! $3,000 FOR THREE MINUTES IN THE RING!**

PETER: Hoopty it is!

Show Your Hero Learning to Use His New Skills. Again.

After ~~a Marvel Comics artist~~ PETER sketches several costume ideas, he practises web-slinging on a can of Dr Product Placement and wrecks his room in the process.

AUNT MAY: Peter! What's going on in there?

PETER: Uh . . . nothing, Aunt May! Don't come in, I'm not dressed!

AUNT MAY: Your room isn't covered in sticky white emissions, is it?

PETER: . . . No.

AUNT MAY: Yeah. I'm washing his sheets the red-hot second he leaves this house.

But Your Hero Is Not the Only One Leading a Double Life!

A dizzy, sweating NORMAN sees in the paper that Quest Aerospace is totally kicking Oscorp's financial ass.

NORMAN: Oh, if only I were evil enough to do something about this!

DISTANTLY FAMILIAR LAUGHTER: HEH HEH HEHHHHHH-HH!

The Time Has Come to Tell the Audience the Moral of Your Story.

UNCLE BEN: So, uh . . . Peter.

PETER: Uncle Ben.

UNCLE BEN: I wanted to drive you to the library so that . . . uh . . . we could . . . Look, Peter – I understand what you're going through. Becoming a man. I went through exactly the same changes—

PETER: No, you didn't. You totally, totally didn't. Trust me on this.

UNCLE BEN: That's what every boy says! Look, on the sticky emissions front – and this is important – I don't think it's advisable to do it in the shower. It wastes water and electricity and we all expect you to be doing it there in any case. And not, uh . . . in your room for your Aunt May to see—

PETER: I had this exact conversation with Dad years ago! So stop trying to be my father!

UNCLE BEN: With great power comes great responsibility, Peter!

251

PETER: Uncle Ben, I'm in HIGH SCHOOL. Now, if you will excuse me, I am going to the LIBRARY, because I am in HIGH SCHOOL, and that is what NORMAL kids DO.

UNCLE BEN: Someday you'll see that I'm right! I'll be dead from a carjacker's bullet and you'll see!

PETER [*slamming car door*]: *Whatever*, Uncle Ben.

Your Hero's Costumed Debut!

Now your hero needs to choose a name.

PETER: I'm the Homo-Arachnid-Sapien!

ANNOUNCER: Too . . . many jokes . . . please . . . send help . . .

[Give BRUCE CAMPBELL some work, won't you?]

ANNOUNCER: LADIES AND GENTLEMEN! THE REIGNING TERROR! SKULLCRUSH McSMUUUUUUUSH!!

THE SMUSHETTES: HE'S GONNA SUCK THE MARROW FROM YOUR BROKEN BONES AND RAPE YOUR SHATTERED SKUUUUULL!

PETER: Hey, guys? I didn't sign up for skull-raping—guys? Hey – why are you lowering that cage—!

WRESTLING FANS: FUN! DEATH!! FUN! DEATH!!

PETER [*clinging spiderily to cage bars*]: Help? Somebody?

SKULLCRUSH McSMUSH: COME DOWN HERE AND LEMME SNAP YOU LIKE A SLIM JIM!

[After a brief display of spiderly acrobatics, SKULLCRUSH McSMUSH goes after PETER with a folding chair. PETER'S spine is snapped and his skull is, in fact, crushed, causing permanent brain damage and a persistent vegetative state. The end.]

THE AUDIENCE: Jigga *what*?

[After a brief display of spiderly acrobatics, SKULLCRUSH McSMUSH goes after PETER with a folding chair. PETER, unhurt except for some general wooziness, fends off an additional golf-club attack to kick SKULLCRUSH McSMUSH into the cage wall.]

ANNOUNCER: THE WINNER! AND NEW CHAMPEEN!
SPIDER-MAN!!

Your Hero Is Faced with a Moral Choice . . .

PETER: I want my money!

IMPRESARIO: Whatever, kid.

SOME ROBBER: I want *all* the money!

IMPRESARIO AND ROBBER: *look at Peter*

PETER: Eh, fuck it, take the bastard's money, see if I care.

. . . Which Bites Your Hero in the Ass.

SOME COP: . . . and after he shot this responsible old guy waiting
responsibly for his nephew, he fled in the old guy's responsible car!

PETER: Uncle Ben! Noooooo!

UNCLE BEN: *death nod*

Now Your Hero Is Forced to Learn the Ropes –
The Hard Way.

No, literally, as PETER haplessly flings himself from block to block on
random shots of spider web. He follows the fleeing carjacker to the
Abandoned Warehouse District. There is also some shooting and
swerving and car-punching, but we all know that real showdowns
only happen in empty warehouses.

PETER: Oh my God – it was YOU! You took the money AND
killed my uncle!

SOME ROBBER: And I'd have gotten away with it, too, if it
weren't for you meddling—

[The ROBBER trips and falls out of the warehouse window to his death in a way that does not actually morally implicate PETER, because your hero, unlike SOME PEOPLE, GREEN GOBLIN, is not a murderer. See also: all Disney villain deaths.]

[Unfortunately, not everyone may grasp this.]

SOME COP: Oh my God! That spider kid pushed him!

SOME OTHER COP: How dare he indirectly take the life of that armed, murdering thief! Put out an APB for Spider-Kid!

Meanwhile, Your Villain Begins His Reign of Terror!

GENERAL SLOCUM: So, how's the giant bubble suit coming?

QUEST AEROSPACE GUY: Not as good as Oscorp's weird green muscle suit, but at least there's no death or insanity, right?

GENERAL SLOCUM: Hey, what's that weird green muscly thing coming right for us?

THE GREEN GOBLIN: HEH HEH HEHHHHHHHHH!

QUEST AEROSPACE: *BOOOOOM!*

Your Young Hero Must Transition Into Adulthood . . .

Graduation day, whee!

NORMAN: Wow, you sure proved me wrong by not screwing up, son!

HARRY: . . . Thanks?

NORMAN: And I know this is a terrible time for you, Peter, so please try to enjoy this day, a day you, unlike my actual son, have worked so hard for. Call me if you ever need anything, and I'll take it from Harry and give it to you, okay?

HARRY: *pouts*

. . . Which Will Be Full of Angst.

PETER: *sob*

AUNT MAY: Peter, your uncle would be so proud of you. He knows that you would never let, say, a robber get away, thereby causing death and massive destruction of property. He never doubted that you would become a great hero and that you would never, ever disappoint him or cause his death.

PETER: Thanks, Aunt May. You're the best.

[Clearly, PETER must use his new +3 Embroidery Skills to upgrade his costume and take up the superhero mantle. Later that night, at a Joann's Fabric downtown:]

PETER: So I'm gonna need several yards of extremely durable, stretchable, form-fitting cloth with a black spiderweb pattern, probably synthetic fiber, and biosymbiotic if you've got it.

STORE CLERK: I'll . . . see what we have in the back . . . ?

PETER [*yelling after her*]: And it's gotta be *red* and *blue*!

Everyone Loves a Montage!

So, how do you feel about your Friendly Neighborhood Spider-Man?

SOME THUG: In my completely unbiased opinion, I HATE HIM and he is BAD.

SOME COP: Hey, more time for donuts, you know what I'm sayin'?

SOME FOLK SINGER: *points to sign*

SOME FOLK SINGER'S SIGN:

> *Spidey is great*
> *Spidey is good*
> *I am so poor*
> *I will sing for food*

SOME FOLK SINGER: *holds out change cup*

SOME CHICK: OMG HE IS SO HAWT SQUEEEEE!

SOME PUNK CHICK: Really, I was always more into Wonder Woman. Mmm, warrior princesses.

Every Superhero Movie Needs a Colourful Supporting Character!

J. JONAH JAMESON: I'll pay cash! Cash money! For a picture of this Spider-Man! Good money! Well, maybe not good money, but definitely bad money! He's a menace! And probably not even a real spider! Didn't he kill that carjacker?

HOFFMAN: . . .

J. JONAH JAMESON: Of course he did! Vigilante! Striking fear into the hearts of God-fearing criminals! Can't have that! No, I don't want to talk to my wife! Or my son the space cadet either! Get me Spider-Man!

It's All About the Girl, Remember?

MARY JANE: Uh . . . Peter! Hi! How's it going!

PETER: Well, I'm begging for a job I can keep with my extremely weird crime-fighting hours – how about you?

MARY JANE: Uh . . . I'm auditioning! For a role as . . . a waitress! At . . . a diner.

PETER: Ah, method acting.

MARY JANE [*whispering*]: Please don't tell Harry! We're going out and he'll think it's totally plebeian.

PETER: Oh . . . okay.

A PIECE OF PETER'S SOUL: *dies*

256

How's Your Hero Doing in the Big City?

NORMAN [*on phone*]: Quest Aerospace was blown up? That's AWESOME!

HARRY: Hey, Pete, can you help me with my homework? I swiped your girl, now I need to pick your brain!

PETER: Sorry, I gotta hit the wanted ads. Got fired today for being late.

HARRY: Again? Where do you go all the time?

PETER: Not out with MARY JANE WATSON, that's for sure.

HARRY: *hangs head*

NORMAN: Aww, that's too bad, Parker. You want me to set you up with a cushy junior executive gig?

PETER: Thanks, Mr Osborn, but I like to earn what I get.

NORMAN: You want to make it on your own, unlike my worthless son. I dig that. Can I designate you as my heir?

HARRY: *cries*

[But PETER doesn't notice, because he's just seen the front page of the *Bugle*: CASH FOR SPIDEY.]

Say Cheese!

PETER'S Spidey sense is so advanced that he can set up cameras before crimes even start to get committed. But once they are, he's front and centre fighting crime and striking poses! Meanwhile, back at the Bugle offices:

J. JONAH JAMESON [*flipping through* PETER'S *photos*]: . . . Mondo crap, super crap, übercrap! Take 'em somewhere else! No, I'll give you two hundred! No, I'll give you three hundred! Okay! Okay? Okay. But you don't have a job here! In fact, don't show your face here again! And bring me more pictures!

PETER: . . .

Finally, Your Villain Is Pushed Over the Edge.

NORMAN: Gentlemen! Costs are down, revenues are up, our stock is second only to Hudsucker Industries and, generally speaking, we rule.

FARGAS: That's why we're selling the company to what's left of Quest Aerospace while the getting is good. An unfortunate side effect is that you will be out of a job.

NORMAN: WHAT? But this is *my* company! I built it! IT'S NAMED AFTER ME!

FARGAS: Hey, sorry about that. See you at the World Unity Festival!

The Oscorp World Unity Festival

ANNOUNCER: Let's hear it for Squeaky Pop Star of the Moment!

THE CROWD: WOOOOO!

[All the Oscorp suits are gathered for the festival, in anticipation of announcing the company's takeover . . .]

BALKAN: You know, 'Quest Aerospace World Unity Festival' just doesn't have the same ring to it.

FARGAS: What, are you on Osborn's side now?

[. . . which means that HARRY and his date are also there.]

HARRY: MJ, whyyyyy didn't you wear the blaaaaaack dress?

MARY JANE: Because you don't OWN ME, Harry.

HARRY: . . . Yet.

MARY JANE: Uh, you think you can kiss me after *that*? You are totally on the metaphorical couch, mister.

[HARRY slinks off in search of his father:]

HARRY: Have you seen my dad?

FARGAS: I'm not sure he's coming, what with our complete

takeover and destruction of his life's work and all.

BALKAN: Hey! What's that?

Make Sure Your Villain Has a Cool Costume . . .

FARGAS: What the hell is that green thing?

BALKAN: Wow, it looks really lame on our stolen glider.

. . . And Awesome Weapons.

Everyone, including HARRY and MARY JANE, stand around gaping on the balcony rather than running inside.

THE GREEN GOBLIN: HEH HEH HEHHHHHHHH! TASTE MY PUMPKIN BOMBS!

FARGAS: *Pumpkin* bombs?

THE BOARD OF DIRECTORS: *blows up*

THE GREEN GOBLIN: Now that's what I call 'Smashing Pumpkins'!

   [THE GREEN GOBLIN's pun flies out of control, takes out three
   parade balloons and threatens to crush a small boy.]

BILLY'S MOM: Billy! Get out of the way of the falling pun!

BILLY: Hee hee. 'Smashing Pumpkins.'

BILLY'S DAD: BILLY!

BILLY'S MOM: SOMEBODY HELP HIM!

THE CROWD: WE'RE ALL TOO BUSY STANDING HERE!

SPIDER-MAN: MOVE, BILLY!

   [Rather than let natural selection take its course, SPIDER-MAN saves
   BILLY and delivers him into the arms of his ineffectual PARENTS.
   Meanwhile, HARRY is down for the count and MARY JANE is
   hanging from half a balcony-gone-boom.]

SPIDER-MAN: Mary Jane! I'll save you!

MARY JANE: Hey, how did you know my . . . SPIDER-MAN, LOOK OUUUUUT!

[THE GREEN GOBLIN comes after SPIDER-MAN with bullets and general fisticuffs, but SPIDER-MAN eventually disables his glider and blinds THE GREEN GOBLIN with science. While THE GREEN GOBLIN fizzles away like a deflated balloon, SPIDER-MAN saves the imperiled MARY JANE at the last moment and bungees her to safety. When costuming your superhero's best girl, wardrobe should make sure that her dress is constructed as carefully as possible to expose maximum leg while preventing her from flashing all of New York. Unless that's what you're aiming for.]

Inevitably, the Girl Will Fall for Your Hero's Alter Ego.

MASSIVE HEADWOUND HARRY [*on phone*]: And then he dropped you off at . . . a rooftop *garden*? Do we even *have* those in New York? . . . Oh, so *romantic*. La-di-*da* . . . What do you mean, he's 'amazing'? Well, yes, I know, the whole 'Amazing Spider-Man' thing, but . . . Look, let me come over, okay? I want to— Yes, well, I have amazing purchasing powers! Go Visa go! I'll buy you a— Hello?

PETER: Hee hee hee.

Can Your Villain Come to Terms With His Dual Nature? Of Course Not!

NORMAN: I don't understand! The World Unity Festival is ruined and the board of directors is slaughtered in cold blood – why, this is *awesome*! How is everything suddenly going so well for me?

DISTANTLY FAMILIAR VOICE: HEH HEH HEHHHHHHH!

NORMAN: What? Who's that? Who's there?!

DISTANTLY FAMILIAR VOICE: Damn, Sméagol, what do I have

to do – spell it out? YOU ARE THE GREEN GOBLIN, AND YOU ARE TALKING TO YOURSELF.

NORMAN: Oh . . . *ohhhhhh*.

Now the Fur Will Really Start to Fly. Or the Webs. Or Something.

J. JONAH JAMESON: So, I used your photographs in a context totally opposed to that in which you shot them. You're cool with that, right? Of course you are! Pay the kid! But not much! I need that money for Johnny's astronaut school!

PETER: But . . . Spider-Man totally saved that little old blind lady from falling off the bridge!

J. JONAH JAMESON: Shpffff, he was probably in her will! I bet he pushed her off! Only the watchful eyes of New York stopped his nefarious plans! And he's totally in cahoots with that shady Green Goblin (™ me, all rights reserved) character! Don't lie, you know it's true! Why else was he at the World Unity Festival?

PETER: Uh, because *everyone* was there?

J. JONAH JAMESON: Gotta hone your journalistic instincts, kid! Go take a class or something! Say hi to Johnny if you see him!

A NEARBY FAMILIAR VOICE: HEH HEH HEHHHHHHHH!

J. JONAH JAMESON: What the—

THE GREEN GOBLIN: TELL ME WHO PHOTOGRAPHS SPIDER-MAN!

J. JONAH JAMESON: Totally not the kid I was talking to about photographs just now, why do you ask?

[SPIDER-MAN suddenly appears, because apparently no one noticed some college kid tearing off his clothes in the ensuing hysteria.]

SPIDER-MAN: Unhand that motor-mouth editor, you—

[THE GREEN GOBLIN hits SPIDER-MAN with a blast of Raid and carries him off.]

J. JONAH JAMESON [*yelling out window*]: And YOU! Go with Parker to the Learning Annex and take some hero classes!

Your Hero Is Tempted.

SPIDEY wakes up on a ~~romantic~~ secluded rooftop, where THE GREEN GOBLIN is waiting with his offer:

THE GREEN GOBLIN: Join me, Spider-Man!

SPIDER-MAN: To do . . . what?

THE GREEN GOBLIN: Create amazing things – or destroy amazing things!

SPIDER-MAN: Like . . . what kind of things?

THE GREEN GOBLIN: You know . . . things. And stuff.

SPIDER-MAN: Uh . . . I think I'm good with the specific crime-fighting programme I currently have going, thanks.

THE GREEN GOBLIN: NO ONE SAYS NO TO ME!

SPIDER-MAN: Except me, right now.

THE GREEN GOBLIN [*gliding away*]: SHUT UP!

Your Hero Should Get at Least a *Little* Sumpin'-Sumpin'.

PETER: Hey, MJ! I was just in the neighbourhood! In the neighbourhood of your neighbourhood, which is not really anywhere near your neighbourhood at all, but – uh – HOW DID YOUR AUDITION GO?

MARY JANE: It went really . . . crap.

PETER: Awww. Can I buy you a burger of consolation?

MARY JANE: Sorry, I'm going out with Harry tonight to a really romantic, expensive restaurant – why don't you come with us? I'm sure he'd love that!

PETER: Rrrrrright. Awkward, table for three.

[While PETER and MARY JANE are discussing her strange, passive-aggressive attempt at relationship sabotage, the lovely would-be actress is not going unnoticed:]

HOODLUM 1: Why, look there, comrade! What an attractive specimen of the fairer sex!

HOODLUM 2: Do you think she would deign to give us an audience?

HOODLUM 1: I am sure that we could win her favour with animal noises and rough treatment!

HOODLUM 3: Soft! She parts now from her swain!

HOODLUM 1: What ho!

HOODLUM 2: *That* ho!

HOODLUM 3: O ho!

[The HOODLUMS chase MARY JANE through a sudden rainstorm into an alley, where they rip off her coat to reveal her Cling-Film top, because no superhero movie is complete without attempted gang rape and visible nipples.]

SPIDER-MAN: Mary Jane! I'll save you!

HOODLUM 2: What ho, fair spider! Do you shoot your web at me?

[MARY JANE dodges flying rapists with glee.]

MARY JANE: Oh, Spider-Man! My hero!

[SPIDER-MAN'S mask has come off, so he pirouettes away to put it back on before MARY JANE can see his face. Then he drops down to hang upside down behind her, because he is a total show-off.]

SPIDER-MAN: I was just in the neighbourhood. Please ignore the fact that this was the first thing that Peter Parker, whose voice is extremely similar to mine, said to you five minutes ago.

MARY JANE: Ignore what?

SPIDER-MAN: Exactly.

[MARY JANE, soaking wet in her chiffon tank top, leans over and kisses SPIDER-MAN upside-down, and a million preteen boys spontaneously enter puberty.]

SPIDER-MAN: Ack . . . blood rushing to . . . mmmmmmmmf.

MARY JANE [*running off*]: Thanks again, Spider-Man!

SPIDER-MAN: Does this mean I'm not a virgin any more?

Good Spidey Always Helps!

Half of Queens is gathered around watching a building burn.

SOME BLONDE WOMAN: MY BABY'S IN THERE GET MY BABY MY BABY'S IN THERE MY BAAABYYY! SAVE MY BAAAABYYYY!

SOME FIREMAN: Can't . . . save baby . . . brain leaking out . . . through ears . . .

SPIDER-MAN: I'll save your baby!

SOME COP: Stop! We're here to arrest you, Spider-Man, for heroism without a licence!

SOME BLONDE WOMAN: NOOOOOO MY BABY'S IN THERE MY BAAABYYY! SAAAAAAAVE MY BAAAABYYYY!

SOME COP [*clutching ears*]: Damn, woman! Go, Spidey, go!

   [After the building explodes in a fireball and the BLONDE WOMAN levels half the neighbourhood with her shrieking, SPIDER-MAN emerges with a small bundle.]

SOME BLONDE WOMAN: NOOOOOOOOOOOOO! MY BAAAABYYYY!

SPIDER-MAN: YOUR BABY'S FINE, WOMAN!

SOME BRUNETTE CHICK: Oh my God, there's a Wilhelm Scream still up there!

WILHELM SCREAM: AHHNOOOOOO!

SOME FIREMAN: More of a Wilhelmina Scream, don't you think . . . ?

SPIDER-MAN: I'm on it!

264

SOME COP: And . . . uh . . . we'll be down here to arrest you when you get back! So . . . try not to die, and stuff!

[Back inside the inferno, SPIDER-MAN finally locates some beshawled biddy tottering around – who is actually THE GREEN GOBLIN with an afghan over his head, playing the Wilhelmina Scream on a summer squash or an Apple peaPod or something.]

THE GREEN GOBLIN: What about my proposal?

SPIDER-MAN: You mean, to do 'stuff'? Yeah, it still kinda sucks.

THE GREEN GOBLIN: I CUT YOU, BITCH!

[THE GREEN GOBLIN throws several ninja pumpkin stars at SPIDER-MAN, who dodges them, and they have a fistfight and then THE GREEN GOBLIN throws the stars again and SPIDEY gets cut and blah blah blah burning fire smoke-inhalation blee and then—]

SPIDER-MAN: Why do I feel like I've forgotten something?

THE GREEN GOBLIN: Oh shit, me too!

Holidays Are a Great Excuse to Get All Your Issues Around One Table.

NORMAN: Hi, Aunt May! Sorry I'm late!

AUNT MAY: And on Thanksgiving, too! But that's all right – Peter hasn't come back with the cranberry sauce yet.

HARRY: Dad, this is MJ, my lovely working-class actress girlfriend.

MARY JANE: I'm so very pleased to meet you, sir.

NORMAN: Now that? Is a stone fox.

HARRY: Dad? She's hot, not deaf.

[PETER slips back into the boys' apartment through his window, but everyone downstairs hears him and goes upstairs to investigate, but PETER is hiding on the ceiling like a clever spider, except that his ninja pumpkin wound drips blood and NORMAN magically hears it fall, but by the time he turns around with a suspicious look in is eye, PETER is hiding outside under the balcony, but NOR-

MAN does not yet know that PETER is SPIDEY and PETER does not yet know that NORMAN is THE GREEN GOBLIN, so this scene . . . kind of does not make sense.]

PETER [*at the front door*]: Hey, guys! I had to beat up an old lady for the sauce, but I got it!

NORMAN [*alarmed*]: Peter . . . why are you bleeding?

PETER: Hey, even the bluehairs . . . carry switchblades nowadays . . . ?

NORMAN [*making epiphany face*]: I HAVE TO GO NOW.

HARRY: But Dad—!

[HARRY follows NORMAN outside, where NORMAN impugns MARY JANE'S character, virtue, intentions and hair colour. Loudly.]

HARRY: So . . . Dad had to go.

MARY JANE: Thanks a lot for defending my honour, *Lancelot*.

HARRY: You heard what he said?

MARY JANE: EVERYONE IN QUEENS HEARD HIM.

HARRY: Thanks, Dad, for ensuring that I will never get laid again.

It's Time for a New Approach to Villainy.

NORMAN sits cowering in his mansion, talking to his GOBLIN MASK. It's as weird as it sounds.

THE GOBLIN MASK: YOU MORON! This kid's 'like a son' to you and you didn't even notice he was kicking your ass? IT NEVER OCCURRED TO YOU TO TAKE OFF HIS MASK?

NORMAN: Look, I'm *sorry*, okay?

THE GOBLIN MASK: Well, at least we know where to hit him now!

NORMAN: Where?

THE GOBLIN MASK: Where he lives, duh!

NORMAN: But Harry lives with him, I don't want to hurt—

THE GOBLIN MASK: METAPHORICALLY SPEAKING, YOU IDIOT.

[That evening:]

THE PARKER HOUSE: *BOOM!*

[In the hospital:]

AUNT MAY: Those eeeeeyes! Those horrible yellow eyes, and those awful zucchini grenaaaaades!

PETER: My God, he knows who I am!

Girls Are Pretty, But They Aren't Very Smart.

MARY JANE: How's Aunt May?

PETER: Well, she's terrified of vegetables now, but other than that, I think she'll make it out all right.

MARY JANE: Well, now that the pleasantries are out of the way, can I tell you about my crush on Spider-Man?

PETER: Hey, sure thing.

MARY JANE: Wow, you sure are supportive of this! Harry HATES it.

PETER: Well, I mean . . . you're supposed to be going out with him.

MARY JANE: Yeah . . . not so much after the whole 'Your girl-friend's a gold-digging whore' speech.

PETER: Well, you can talk about Spider-Man all you want when you're with me. I mean, he is a close and personal friend of mine.

MARY JANE: Wow!

PETER: In fact, he told me the other day that you kissed him, and that it was awesome, and for you to please feel free to do that again any time you want. Day or night. Seriously, I can go get him right now, if you want.

MARY JANE: Did he say anything else?

PETER: Well, we were talking, and I said to him, I said, 'Spider-Man, you are totally right about Mary Jane. When you look in MJ's eyes you feel big and strong and yet weak and pitiful, because the bodacious power of her beauty is such that it both excites and terrifies you and shows you everything that a man is capable of achieving and yet also everything he can fail at, because she inspires him to such great things and yet he is so afraid that she will not love him back.'

[MARY JANE takes his hand earnestly.]

MARY JANE: Peter? I don't care what *you* said.

Your Villain Finally Figures Out Your Hero's Greatest Weakness!

HARRY: You were right, Dad. Mary Jane was totally after me for my money, which I infer from the fact that she didn't actually want me to buy her things and preferred to work for a living.

NORMAN: What?

HARRY: I caught her *holding hands* with Peter!

NORMAN: THAT SLUT! Wait – does he love her?

HARRY: I knew he loved her ever since he was a fetus, but I poached his girl anyway.

NORMAN: That rotten bastard. Here, son, let me give you an actual hug.

HARRY: omg daddy loves me!

[Back at the hospital:]

PETER: How are you feeling, Aunt May?

AUNT MAY: Well, I'd feel a lot better if you'd just tell Mary Jane you love her. *Damn.*

PETER: *Aunt May!*

AUNT MAY: Oh, please – everyone *knows*. 'The bodacious power of her beauty.' *Please.* Would it really be so terrible for you to come out and *say* that Mary Jane is the most important thing in the world to you and is completely your Achilles heel, were anyone wanting to find out what that was?

PETER: Well, actually . . . OH SHIT!

[Out in the hall, PETER calls MARY JANE'S apartment on a pay phone, and gets—]

SOME WOEFULLY FAMILIAR VOICE: HEH HEH HEHHHHH-HHH!

Your Hero Must Face the Ultimate Choice.

SPIDER-MAN finds THE GREEN GOBLIN dangling MARY JANE and a cable car full of INNOCENT CHILDREN off the Queensboro Bridge.

THE GREEN GOBLIN: THE GIRL OR THE KIDS!

MARY JANE: Oh my God, I'm too hot to diiiiiie! Save meeeee!

SCREAMING KIDS: Noooooo! Save us! Let her die, Spider-Man! Girls have cooties, Spider-Man!

THE GREEN GOBLIN: MAKE YOUR CHOICE!

[THE GREEN GOBLIN drops MARY JANE and the car's cable at the same time. SPIDER-MAN stands there for a good thirty seconds gaping, before finally deciding to grab MARY JANE –]

THE GREEN GOBLIN: I KNEW IT!

[– and then grabbing the car's cable and shooting up a web to hang from.]

THE GREEN GOBLIN: HEY! THAT'S NOT FAIR! HE CAN'T DO THAT!

SPIDER-MAN: Okay, Mary Jane? I'm gonna need you to climb down to the cable car so I can drop you both down onto that barge.

MARY JANE [*sobbing*]: I-I-I can't dooooo iiiit!

SPIDER-MAN: BITCH, I'M THE ONE DANGLING THREE TONS OF STEEL FROM MY PINKY! *CLIMB DOWN!*

BARGE GUY 1: Five bucks says he totally drops them both.

BARGE GUY 2: You're on.

[Pissed that his plan to discredit and/or kill SPIDER-MAN isn't working, THE GREEN GOBLIN starts buzzing SPIDEY in his glider in hopes of making him lose his grip.]

NEW YORKERS ON THE BRIDGE: HEY!

THE GREEN GOBLIN: Wha— OW!

NEW YORKERS [throwing bricks and pipes and bullets]: YOU WANT THAT CABLE CAR UP YOUR ASS?

SKULLCRUSH McSMUSH [in neckbrace]: I'LL EAT YOUR SPLEEN FOR BREAKFAAAAAST!

THE SMUSHETTES: SKULLCRUSH WILL TASTE YOUR PAAAAAIN!

THE GREEN GOBLIN: Uh . . . I think I will let our friend finish up here before I engage him again.

NEW YORKERS: YEAH, THAT'S RIGHT!

[SPIDER-MAN successfully lowers the cable car to the bridge. Everyone cheers.]

MARY JANE: Watch out, Spider-Man! The Green Goblin's coming back! He might use one of his skeletonizer bombs on you!

THE GREEN GOBLIN: Crap! I ran out of those!

SOME KID: Or some of his knock-out gas! I read about that in the Bugle!

THE GREEN GOBLIN: SHIT, I KNEW I FORGOT SOMETHING!

NEW YORKERS: HA HA!

THE GREEN GOBLIN: Well, I'll just have to use my old-fashioned LASSO, THEN! Didn't think about THAT, DID YOU?

It's Time for the Thrilling Final Battle!

THE GREEN GOBLIN carries SPIDEY away to some crumbly building attractively overgrown with vines and hits him with a pumpkin bomb. Then, while he's down, he pulverizes SPIDER-MAN (and Spidey's costume) until he makes the mistake of threatening MARY JANE with slow torture and death. Now unmasked, PETER wastes no time in dropping a brick wall on him . . . and punching him fifty-six times in the face for good measure.

THE GREEN GOBLIN: Ack! Help! Peter! Stop! It's me! Norman Osborn! Your best friend's father! I had nothing to do with it, except for the part where I did all of it!

PETER: Whaaaaat?

NORMAN: Have mercy, Peter! I've been like a father to you for the last hour and a half!

PETER: Yeah, what was up with that, anyw—

[PETER'S Spidey sense warns him that NORMAN is totally fronting and about to kill him with the remote-controlled glider, so PETER spider-flips out of the way at the last moment. Of course, this leaves NORMAN to get gored.]

PETER: Ohhhhh, right in the tenderloin.

NORMAN [dying]: Please – Peter – don't tell Harry that I was a terrible, cheesy villain who tried to kill him and his girlfriend!

PETER: Well, maybe you should have THOUGHT OF THAT BEFORE YOU—

NORMAN: *death flop*

PETER: Awww, hell.

Villains Never Really Die . . . They Just Leave Vengeful Relatives.

HARRY: Spider-Man! What have you DONE?

SPIDER-MAN: Well, I cleaned up your father's body and brought it home and removed all evidence of his horrifying crimes and—

HARRY [grabbing nearby gun]: I'LL KILL YOU!

SPIDER-MAN: CAN I NOT DO *ANYTHING* RIGHT FOR YOU PEOPLE?

Bring It All Back to the Moral of the Story . . .

PETER tries to comfort HARRY at his father's funeral. HARRY is having none of it.

HARRY: I didn't lose my father. He was STOLEN FROM ME.

PETER: Uh, yeah, because *my* father figure wasn't carjacked or anything, Jimmy Dean—

HARRY: And I'm going to kill Spider-Man if it's the last thing I do. Thank God for you, Peter. You're the only person left in this world who would never, ever betray me.

PETER: *Awkward.*

. . . And Above All, The Girl.

MARY JANE: I love you so much, Peter!

  [Tearfully, she kisses him.]

PETER: Yeah . . . I gotta go.

MARY JANE: WHAT? YOU JUST HIT THE JACKPOT AND YOU'RE GONNA THROW IT AWAY?

PETER [*voiceover*]: And I knew then that, no matter how much I loved her, she would never be safe so long as I was Spider-Man, and I could never be with her. Well, not until the sequel, anyway.

MARY JANE: Hey, wait a minute . . . I know that spidery after-taste! COME BAAAACK, TIGERRRR!

[Underscore the noble sorrow of PETER'S sacrifice with some angst rock. We hear it sells lots of soundtrack albums.]

FIN.

STAR WARS: EPISODE II –
ATTACK OF THE CLONES (2002)

The Traditional Crawl from the Department of Back Story

A long time ago in a galaxy so far away it seems like it exists in the future and is peopled with humans just like us, there's a lot of political strife that sounds a lot like the stuff they run on C-SPAN every day, and God knows you hate watching that crap as it is. So, to sum up: some guy named Count Dookula is riling people up and making things tough for the Jedi, and Queen Amidala (now Senator Amidala) is totally not down with that shit.

Coruscant Landing Strip

A giant fancy robe (containing an important young woman who is totally PADMÉ AMIDALA, why do you ask?) walks down a cruiser gangplank surrounded by bodyguards. CAPTAIN TYPHO and a LIEU-TENANT GUARD who is shaped suspiciously like Natalie Portman climb out of fighter ships and survey the landing strip.

CAPTAIN TYPHO: I don't know what I was so worried about, everything seems f—

THE ROYAL CRUISER: BOOM!

BODYGUARDS: *go flying*

THE AUDIENCE: OMG PADMÉ IS DEAD EVEN THOUGH SHE WAS CLEARLY IN THE PREVIEW WEARING EIGHT DIFFER-ENT OUTFITS!

[The LIEUTENANT GUARD rips off her helmet and of course it's PADMÉ.]

PADMÉ: NOOOOO! I had no idea an attempt would be made on my life! How could this have HAPPENED?

CAPTAIN TYPHO: You . . . you didn't know? Then why were you in that fighter dressed as a soldier?

PADMÉ: I just wanted to wear *pants* for once!

[PADMÉ and TYPHO kneel by the wounded DECOY!PADMÉ. You can tell the handmaiden is dying because there's a dab of blood at the corner of her mouth.]

PADMÉ: Oh, Tragedé! You can't die! *Nooooo!*

TRAGEDÉ: My lady . . . I have failed you . . . [*flops over dead*].

CAPTAIN TYPHO: Well, actually, considering that you died *instead* of the Senator, I think you did your job pretty well . . .

PADMÉ: Woe! I shouldn't have come back!

CAPTAIN TYPHO: You're absolutely right, Senator. You should totally have stayed home curled up in bed while the bill you oppose gets approved without you there to lead the resistance.

PADMÉ: Don't make me cancel your pension, Typho.

Palpatine's Office

Gathered in CHANCELLOR PALPATINE's office are YODA, JAR JAR, MACE L. WINDU, some BLUE ALIENS and JIMMY SMITS. (Sure, he has a character name, but don't lie. You don't remember what it is, either.)

PALPATINE: As previously stated, we have put off the vote on forming an army for the Republic. Lots of solar systems are joining the separatists, however, and if they break away, this thousand-year-old Republic will be split in two and . . .

EVERYONE ELSE: *glazes over*

PALPATINE: . . . and that cannot happen because then it will be . . . harder . . . for me . . . to take over . . . ?

EVERYONE ELSE: Zzzzzzzz . . .

PALPATINE [*rubbing hands*]: Excellent.

[The Loyalist committee, consisting of CAPTAIN TYPHO, PADMÉ and PADMÉ's spare handmaiden ROSÉ, arrive.]

YODA [*shaking self*]: Doze off a moment I did. Senator Amidala, seeing you alive my heart the warm fuzzies gives. Think do you who was behind the assassination attempt?

PADMÉ: It was totally . . .

MACE WINDU: Spice miners?

SOME BLUE ALIEN: Disgruntled Wookiees?

JIMMY SMITS: Rogue Jawas?

PADMÉ: . . . COUNT DOOKULA!

MACE WINDU: Milady, he used to be a Jedi. Jedi are incapable of feeling anything but love and light, even if he's the leader of the separatists who oppose you.

PADMÉ: Dookula. His name is DOOKULA. And we don't even HAVE counts in space.

MACE WINDU: Oh. Well, when you put it that way...

PALPATINE: Well, whoever was responsible for the attack, I suggest that we put the Senator under tighter security . . .

PADMÉ: Awww, *man*! Do you know how hard it is to go clubbing with forty guards on your ass?

PALPATINE: . . . such as her old Jedi friends.

PADMÉ: SWEET.

Some Elevator

Speaking of whom, OBI-WAN and ANAKIN are riding up in an elevator to PADMÉ'S Coruscant apartment. ANAKIN is using his reflection in the glass to comb his hair.

OBI-WAN: Dude, seriously? You've got to dial it down a notch.

ANAKIN: I haven't seen her in ten years! I want to look good!

OBI-WAN: Desperation isn't attractive, young padawan. Besides, the time for Clearasil was yesterday.

ANAKIN: WHY ARE YOU ALWAYS SO MEEEEEEAN TO ME?

OBI-WAN: I've tried to be a father to you, Anakin. I came to all your lightsaber recitals, we did the whole Take Your Padawan to Work Day thing, I gave you The Talk—

ANAKIN: Talk? There was no talk.

OBI-WAN: There wasn't? Well, birds and bees love each other very much, and then they do the sex. I did the best I could do for you, Anakin—

ELEVATOR: *ding!*

OBI-WAN: Here we are. Now tuck in your robe and stand up straight.

Padmé's Apartment

JAR JAR: Obiobiobiobi meesa gonna dien of happy to seein yousa! And yousa padawan – ANNIE? EESA ANNIE SO BIGGEN? AYIYIYIYIYIYIYIYIYIYI—

THE AUDIENCE: *goes rigid with horror*

OBI-WAN [*with Jedi wave*]: You want to chill the hell out, Jar Jar.

JAR JAR: Meesa wanna chill the hell out . . . ?

OBI-WAN: You want to go tell the Senator we're here.

JAR JAR: Meesa wanna tell the Senator yousa here. Be right backen!

ANAKIN: I owe you one, man.

OBI-WAN: You? That was for *my* sanity.

PADMÉ: Obi-Wan! It's so good to see you again! They told me I was going to need more bodyguards and I was totally against it until they said *you* might be the one guarding my body, as it were . . . heh . . . Annie? Is that you?

ANAKIN: Again, thank you for choosing the most emasculating nickname possible.

PADMÉ: Oh, Annie, you've learned such big words! Widdle Annie has grown so big, yes he has!

ANAKIN: And you've grown . . . uh . . . more beautiful. Not that you weren't beautiful before. Because you were. Now you're beautiful for . . . a senator. Not that senators can't be beautiful. Well, female senators can be beautiful, male senators are probably more 'handsome' . . .

OBI-WAN [*kicking Anakin in shin*]: You're *babbling*!

PADMÉ: Oh, Annie. You'll always be that snot-nosed little boy who ran around yelling 'Yippee!' to me.

ANAKIN: *pouts*

[In the background, handmaiden ROSÉ is discussing her duties with the DIRECTOR.]

ROSÉ: But Mr Lucas, this is such a small part – I mean, all I do is follow Padmé around and make condescending faces at Anakin, and most of those won't even show up in the finished cut.

GEORGE LUCAS: If you do this for me, I will get you a totally sweet gig with lots of big names in man-skirts.

ROSÉ: I don't know about this . . .

GEORGE LUCAS: And a naked Brad Pitt.

ROSÉ: Reporting for duty, *sir*!

[Meanwhile, ANAKIN and OBI-WAN are arguing again.]

ANAKIN: . . . I mean, we're Jedi! 'Protect the Senator' *clearly* means 'run around looking for the assassin'!

OBI-WAN: ARE YOU BACK-TALKING ME, PADAWAN?

PADMÉ: Come, Rosé, let's retire before this gets AWKWARD. If anyone, particularly a hot Jedi master, should need us, we will be in our bedroom. Alone.

ANAKIN: Sigh.

JAR JAR: No worry, Annie. Love no eesa love which alteren when it alteration finden. O, no! Eesa muy muy fixèd mark.

ANAKIN: . . .

JAR JAR: . . .

ANAKIN: That's deep, man.

OBI-WAN: Whatever. I'm going to go check out security. Go play with your Jedi Joe dolls, Anakin.

ANAKIN: But I don't *waaaaanna*—

OBI-WAN: Run off and play or you won't get any dessert.

ANAKIN: They're *action figures*.

Some Skyscraper Ledge, Coruscant

SOME BOUNTY HUNTER: There can be no mistakes –

STAR WARS FANS: OMG HE LOOKS JUST LIKE BOBA FETT!

SOME BOUNTY HUNTER: – so I'm contracting this out to someone else who's already screwed it up once.

ZAM WESELL: Look, you said, 'Blow up the Kabuki chick,' and I *did*.

SOME BOUNTY HUNTER: Yes, well. This time, we're going to use—

ZAM WESELL: Blasters?

SOME BOUNTY HUNTER: No.

ZAM WESELL: Poison?

SOME BOUNTY HUNTER: No.

ZAM WESELL: Angry space badgers?

SOME BOUNTY HUNTER: No.

ZAM WESELL: *Incontinent* space badgers?

SOME BOUNTY HUNTER: No.

ZAM WESELL: WHAT, THEN?

SOME BOUNTY HUNTER: Giant centipedes. Dropped off by a window-cutting droid.

ZAM WESELL: Is it too late to back out of this?

Padmé's Apartment

ANAKIN: Padmé covered the security cameras! I was just watching her undress, *gah*. But that's okay. I can still sense EVERYTHING GOING ON IN THAT ROOM.

OBI-WAN: You are such a *freakshow*. Also, please clean up your thoughts, because I can sense them from here, and they skeeve me out.

ANAKIN: I'd rather dream about Padmé!

OBI-WAN: I'd rather not have to wash your sheets again, kid.

Padmé's Bedroom

While PADMÉ sleeps, the window-cutting droid drops off the giant centipedes.

R2-D2: Bee-boo-bip!!

Padmé's Apartment

ANAKIN: . . . and that is why I think Palpatine is awesome.

OBI-WAN: Politicians suck.

ANAKIN: Do not!

OBI-WAN: Do too!

ANAKIN: OMG!

OBI-WAN: I SENSE IT TOO!

Padmé's Bedroom

ANAKIN takes out the centipedes with a flying ninja leap onto PADMÉ's bed.

PADMÉ: OH MY GOD WHY ARE YOU IN MY BED?

[Before anyone can explain anything, OBI-WAN leaps through the window, shattering the glass, grabs the window-cutting droid and gets dragged off into the night. ANAKIN runs out the way he came, passing TYPHO and ROSÉ on their way in.]

ROSÉ: What the hell was all that about?

PADMÉ: I have no idea, man.

ROSÉ: *Damn.*

PADMÉ: We got anything to drink around here?

ROSÉ: I'll go get the bottle of Red Dwarf.

The 'Streets' of Coruscant

OBI-WAN: WAHHHHH!

ZAM WESELL: Oh, here comes my droid. I guess it . . . Hey, what's that hanging . . . ?

OBI-WAN: WAHHHHH!

[ZAM WESELL picks up her rifle, shoots the droid and sends OBI-WAN plummeting fifty storeys through eight lanes of traffic, after which she makes her escape.]

OBI-WAN: *WAHHHHH!*

[In the nick of time, ANAKIN flies up in a pimpin' yellow speeder to catch him.]

OBI-WAN: WHERE THE HELL WERE YOU?

ANAKIN: Well, I couldn't find the right speeder, you know? With bucket seats, and really sweet rims, and a bitchin' performance intake—

OBI-WAN: Could you stop ricing out for a moment and let's FIND THE ASSASSIN, PLEASE?

ANAKIN: Sure thing! VERTICAL PLUNGE WHEE!

OBI-WAN: YOU STOP THIS RIGHT NOW, DO YOU HEAR? YOU'RE GOING TO HAVE A WRECK – YOU'RE GOING TO

KILL US BOTH! I AM *NOT* TAKING YOU TO GET YOUR
LICENCE IF YOU KEEP DRIVING LIKE THIS—

ANAKIN: Oh, that's right, you hate flying.

OBI-WAN: No, I hate DYING . . . WAHHHHH! POWER
COUPLINGS! MISTER, YOU WILL TURN THIS SPEEDER
AROUND RIGHT NOW—

[ANAKIN does not, and they totally get electrocuted but somehow
they don't die, and they keep chasing ZAM WESELL. Then ANAKIN
decides to take a 'short cut' by going in completely the opposite
direction, and OBI-WAN bitches at him some more, and ANAKIN
jumps out of the speeder to show off and/or get away from
OBI-NAG KENOBI.]

OBI-WAN: ANAKIN SKYWALKER! YOU COME BACK HERE
RIGHT NOW! YOU ARE GOING TO BED WITHOUT SUPPER,
YOUNG PADAWAN!

Some Nightclub, Ten Minutes Later

ANAKIN: So I fell on her speeder, and then she shot at me, and
then she crashed, and then she ran in here!

OBI-WAN: Fabulous. Go find her. Here's your lightsaber – don't
lose it again.

ANAKIN: Yes, Master. Sorry, Master. Won't do it again, Master
[*eyeroll*].

OBI-WAN: I SAW THAT. I swear, you're going to be the death of
me two movies from now.

ANAKIN: WHY ARE YOU ALWAYS NAGGING ME?

[OBI-WAN bellies up to the bar while ANAKIN goes assassin-
hunting.]

OBI-WAN: I NEED BOOZE.

BARTENDER: Teenage padawan? Drink's on the house.

MOUSE SLEAZEBAGGANO: Want some deathsticks?

OBI-WAN [*with little Jedi wave*]: You don't want to sell me any deathsticks.

MOUSE SLEAZEBAGGANO: I don't want to sell you any deathsticks . . . ?

OBI-WAN: You want to go back to your ship and think about your life.

MOUSE SLEAZEBAGGANO: I want to go back to my ship and think about my life.

OBI-WAN: You want to make Neo some Cream of Amino Acid.

MOUSE SLEAZEBAGGANO: I want to make Neo some Cream of Amino Acid.

OBI-WAN: With extra synthetic sucrose, the way he likes it.

MOUSE SLEAZEBAGGANO: With extra synthetic sucrose . . .

ZAM WESELL: I KEEL Y—

[OBI-WAN and his Spidey-sense slice off ZAM WESELL's hand before she can shoot. Unfortunately, because this is a PG movie, you can barely see the flying severed limb, so at first glance it looks as if ZAM WESELL falls over because the meannastybad Jedi knocked a gun from her hand. ANAKIN completes his general uselessness by sulking out of the club after them.]

Outside the Club

OBI-WAN: Who hired you?

ANAKIN: WHO HIRED YOU?

SOME BOUNTY HUNTER: *zing!*

ZAM WESELL: *flops over dead*

OBI-WAN: A toxic dart!

ANAKIN: Well, yes, I gathered that from the fact that something stuck her in the neck and SHE DIED, Sherlock.

OBI-WAN: GO TO YOUR ROOM!

The Jedi Council

MACE WINDU: So . . . that's all you were able to figure out? That the dart was toxic?

OBI-WAN: Yeah . . . that's pretty much the whole story as we know it.

MACE WINDU: *GAH*. Look, you go find some answers and *you*, Anakin, take the Senator home to Naboo.

ANAKIN: But . . . but I've never worked alone, and . . . she won't want to go, and . . . she'll yell at me.

YODA: Suck it up you must, young padawan.

Palpatine's Office

PALPATINE: I alone amongst all beings in the known universe think that you are mature and capable and generally awesome, Anakin.

ANAKIN: *snuggles*

Some Jedi Temple

MACE WINDU: So, there's a prophecy that says your padawan will bring the Force back into balance, or something.

OBI-WAN: *Shpfff*, whatever. He can't even balance a chequebook, much less the Force. If I had a nickel for every time that kid gave me sass . . .

YODA [*in floating La-Z-Boy*]: Damn kids these days! When a padawan I was, levitate uphill both ways we did! If lose our lightsaber we did, make new one from rocks, we had to! No temples we had! Only dark caves! [*Shaking cane*] And liked it, we did!

MACE WINDU: Word, yo.

PADMÉ: Jar Jar, I designate you my stand-in for any important Senate votes, particularly ones that might start civil wars and result in the deaths of millions, seeing as how you are clearly an intelligent and well-spoken individual –

JAR JAR: Whee! Meesa muy muy honoured to be fake senator with biggen biggen doody—

PADMÉ: – but only if you LEAVE NOW.

JAR JAR: Hmph.

[Once JAR JAR has left, PADMÉ returns to packing and bitching.]

PADMÉ: HIDING VEXES ME MUCHLY.

ANAKIN: I'm going to try to lecture you on maturity and humility, because I have any idea what either of those are like.

PADMÉ: BWAHAHAHA.

ANAKIN: SHUT UP! IT'S ALL OBI-WAN'S FAULT! HE'S HOLDING ME BACK! HE NEVER LETS ME STAY UP LATE! IT'S NOT FAAAAAAIR!

PADMÉ: Hon, I don't think there's enough cheese on this planet for that whine. P.S. Don't stare at me like that.

ANAKIN: Why not?

PADMÉ: Because it skeeves me out, WEIRDO.

ANAKIN [*leering*]: Sorry, milady.

PADMÉ: I SAID STOP IT.

ANAKIN: . . .

PADMÉ: . . .

ANAKIN: I'm not touching you! I'm not touching you!

PADMÉ: ROSÉ, MAKE HIM STOP!

ROSÉ: Only one more scene before I get to leave, only one more scene before I get to leave . . .

284

Some Space Bus

ROSÉ and CAPTAIN TYPHO watch OBI-WAN nag his padawan one last time before ANAKIN and PADMÉ set off.

TYPHO: I bet you're relieved to get away from the Senator for a while. I mean, handmaidens have a high mortality rate, you know.

ROSÉ: Yeah, but if you make it through your tour of duty, the benefits are *sweet*. Did you see what happened with Keiré? She's beating off the cute co-stars with a stick now!

[PADMÉ and ANAKIN leave for the freighter with R2-D2 in tow.]

PADMÉ: I'm scared.

ANAKIN: Yeah, me too.

PADMÉ: Well, at least we've got R2 to protect us.

ANAKIN AND PADMÉ TOGETHER: BWAHAHAHAHA!

R2-D2: BEE BOO BIP.

[Back on the bus . . .]

OBI-WAN: I hope he doesn't try anything stupid.

TYPHO: I'd be more concerned about her pulling something.

OBI-WAN: Really?

TYPHO: . . . No, it's totally all your kid.

OBI-WAN: Sigh.

Some . . . Diner?

OBI-WAN: I'm going to ask a short-order cook about the provenance of an exotic dart!

SOME CREEPY GECKO-TOAD THING: And I'm going to know the answer, because Small Projectile Identification 101 is mandatory in cooking school!

SOME ROBOWAITRESS: Hey, honey, can I get you another malted anachronism?

OBI-WAN: Ooo, thanks.

The Jedi Library

OBI-WAN: Can you help me find a planet?

SNIPPY JEDI LIBRARIAN: Sorry, I didn't go to cooking school.

Third-Class Mess Hall, Freighter

SOME CAFETERIA DROID: NO DROIDS!

R2-D2: BOO-BEE-BIP!

SOME CAFETERIA DROID: DO YOU BEEP AT YOUR MOTHER WITH THAT MOUTH?

PADMÉ: So . . . being a Jedi kind of sucks, huh? Go here, do that, wear that stupid ponytail, can't go out on dates . . . I mean, look at Obi-Wan. That's just a *tragedy*, right there . . .

ANAKIN: But, see, if you think about it, we're supposed to have compassion, which the Concise Oxford defines as 'sympathetic consciousness of others' distress together with a desire to alleviate it', which is sort of like 'caring', and if you care for someone you love them, so you could actually say that Jedi are *supposed* to love people.

PADMÉ: Okay, Annie? Love for all mankind is not the same as doing the nasty.

ANAKIN: Dammit.

Jedi Preschool

BABY JEDI: Hello, Master Obi-Wan!

OBI-WAN: What up, shorties. Hey, Yoda, could you help me find a planet?

286

YODA: Who could have erased it? Only a Jedi, but who?

OBI-WAN: I dunno, the guy who used to be a Jedi but for some reason isn't anymore? You know, the one Padmé thought was all suspicious?

YODA: Nahhhh.

Naboo Palace

SOME ADVISOR: So we all agree that Nute Gunray is *still* an ethnically offensive stereotype?

PADMÉ: Well, I would say yes, but I can't figure out which ethnicity he's offending.

SOME ADVISOR: Something Asian, maybe?

QUEEN JAMILLIA: Hmm. Form a committee and look into it. What about the Senator's safety?

SOME ADVISOR [*turning to* ANAKIN]: Any ideas, Master Jedi?

PADMÉ: Oh, he's not a real Jedi yet, so we don't really care what he thinks. I thought that the royal lake house might be a good idea—

ANAKIN: HEY!

PADMÉ: As I was SAYING—

ANAKIN: Excuse me—

PADMÉ: EXCUSE ME. What's the address of the lake house, again?

QUEEN JAMILLIA: Oh, it's on the left shore of Lake Awkward, first house on Uncomfortable Street.

The Planet ~~Seattle~~ Kamino

Clearly, OBI-WAN has no idea what he's doing here. He just plays along with everything the Kaminoans say, and they totally buy it, because they just really, really love Jedi.

TAUN WE: We love Jedi!

LAMA SU: Come on, do that thing for us! The thing with the mind-control!

OBI-WAN: 'You will believe anything I say, no matter how ridiculous or sketchy'?

LAMA SU: That's the one!

TAUN WE: We cloned a huge army for you!

OBI-WAN: Army?

LAMA SU: Yes, the army. If you're not here about the army, then . . . why are you here?

OBI-WAN: No, no! Of course! That's why I'm here, Llama Sutra!

The Royal Lake House

To discourage any advances from ANAKIN, PADMÉ wears her favourite backless halter-neck chiffon number.

PADMÉ: I have such pleasant childhood memories of swimming here and then lying out on the sand.

ANAKIN: I hate sand. Probably because I grew up on a planet made of nothing but sand. It's rough and coarse and itchy and it gets everywhere and you can't ever get it out. Do you *know* the places it gets stuck? At least here you've got a fighting chance of not getting it stuck up your ass. No, here everything's soft . . . and smooth . . . and *sexy*.

[ANAKIN stuns PADMÉ with the badness of his dialogue, allowing him the opportunity to kiss her. Silently, PADMÉ notes that, for a twenty-year-old virgin, ANAKIN kisses pretty good. And then she comes to her senses.]

PADMÉ: I can't believe I just fell for a pick-up line about sand up your ass.

Inspecting the Clones on Kamino

OBI-WAN: So . . . that's a *lot* of clones.

Some Naboovian Meadow

PADMÉ puts on her best Leia buns and takes ANAKIN on a picnic in a local meadow where they discuss her first kiss with some poli-sci wunderkind and ANAKIN gets jealous and talks about how he will someday rule the universe with a bioengineered fist. Tragedy is then narrowly averted when ANAKIN is thrown from a giant tickalo. Then he and PADMÉ roll over and over and over and over in the grass and this scene is not lame at all.

Jango Fett's Apartment

BOBA FETT: Dad! Taun We and some weird guy are here to see you!

JANGO FETT: WOMAN! Go make me a sandwich! And hide all the incriminating evidence!

TAUN WE: Yes, dear.

OBI-WAN: You let him treat you like that?

TAUN WE: Well, our people once were warriors. Now we just clone things. But we are still a people with spirit, and I figure, if I can survive waiting on this guy, I can survive anything.

JANGO FETT: WOMAN!!

TAUN WE: I have to go now.

A Romantic Dinner

To show ANAKIN that she's serious about not wanting to go out with him, PADMÉ puts on her best black leather corset. ANAKIN flirts with her anyway by floating her fruit. Somehow, this is not a euphemism for anything dirty.

By the Sexy, Sexy Fire

ANAKIN: I love you very much. Can we do the sex now?

PADMÉ: We would be living a lie!

ANAKIN: And . . . ?

PADMÉ: ANAKIN!

ANAKIN: It's not myyyyy faaaaaault I'm in love with youuuuu! Your kiss, which you shouldn't have given me, even though it was technically my kiss since I made the first move, but it's still your kiss, is a wound on my heart that leaves a scar on my spleen and a bruise on my—

PADMÉ: I'm wearing my anti-bullshit headband tonight, so don't even try.

ANAKIN: Sigh.

Obi-Wan Sends In His Report

OBI-WAN [*via hologram*]: Hey, there's this guy here? I think he's the assassin.

MACE WINDU: Why?

OBI-WAN: I . . . don't know?

MACE WINDU: That's cool.

Anakin Has a Bad Dream

PADMÉ: So . . . I heard you moaning in your sleep last night . . . OH GOD PLEASE TELL ME THAT WAS A NIGHTMARE.

ANAKIN: I dreamed that my mother was suffering. I have to disobey Obi-Nag's orders and leave you unguarded, Padmé.

PADMÉ: See, this is why we would never work out, Mama's Boy.

ANAKIN: What?

PADMÉ: I said, 'Don't worry, I'll take you with me as a ploy.'

Landing Platform, Kamino

The FETTS see OBI-WAN coming and make a run for it. There is a lot of blasting and leaping and head-butting and jet-packing. This scene is best watched with a joystick in one hand. After getting thrown off a landing platform and climbing back up, OBI-WAN runs back through the building –

TAUN WE: Hey, you're back!

LAMA SU: Yay! We love Jedi!

TAUN WE: Stay a while, have some tea!

[– and outside to the landing strip, but JANGO FETT'S ship is already leaving.]

OBI-WAN: Well, it's a good thing I have a handy tracking device to throw at his ship, or else this plot thread might just unravel entirely!

R4: Bo bee bop!

OBI-WAN: Thanks, man, but . . . it's just not the same.

Junk Shop, Tatooine

WATTO: Eyyyy! Annie! You a Jedi now!

ANAKIN: Where's my mom?

WATTO: I dunno, I sold her.

ANAKIN: Where's my mom?

WATTO: I dunno, she married some guy.

ANAKIN: WHERE'S MY MOM?

WATTO: . . . I'll go look it up.

PADMÉ: Guys, do I need to be here? Can I go sit in the rickshaw or something?

Obi-Wan Chases the Fetts Through an Asteroid Field

BOBA FETT: Dad! I think we're being tracked!

JANGO FETT: He must have put a homing device on our hull.

BOBA FETT: Or, you know, just followed us from the launch pad.

JANGO FETT: Shut up, son.

The Lars Homestead

ANAKIN: Hey, Threepio, I'm here to see Mom.

C-3PO: Yeah . . . about that . . .

ANAKIN: So you're my stepbrother? Huh. Where's my mother?

OWEN LARS: Yeah . . . about that . . .

ANAKIN: Hey, thanks for freeing my mom, man. Where is she, anyway?

CLIEGG LARS: Yeah . . . about that . . .

ANAKIN: WILL SOMEONE TELL ME WHERE MY MOTHER IS?

CLIEGG LARS: Yourmotherwasoutpickingmushroomsandthe tuskenraidersgother andmyleggotwhackedoffandshesbeengone amonth.

ANAKIN: Mushrooms? In the desert?

CLIEGG LARS: Focus, son. Your mother's dead.

PADMÉ: *facepalm*

The Lars Homestead, Ten Minutes Later

ANAKIN: So, Pad, I'm gonna leave you here with these nice farmers who couldn't even protect their own wife and stepmother, much less a senator.

PADMÉ: Have . . . fun?

The Deserts of Tatooine

ANAKIN speeds through the desert with vengeance in his eyes.

SOUNDTRACK: DUH-DUH-DAA DUN DUN DUN DUH-DA-DA!

   [ANAKIN asks some JAWA for directions.]

SOUNDTRACK: DUH-DUH-DAA DUN DUN DUN DUH-DA-DAAA!

   [ANAKIN stops for gas and a Slurpee.]

SOUNDTRACK: DUN DAAA! DUNNNNN DAAAAA!

Secret Conference, Geonosis

COUNT DOOKULA: As I explained to you earlier, rendering this speech somewhat redundant, I'm sure that thousands of systems will join us if those of you present support the cause, which is to gather an army big enough to ensure capitalist exploitation and profit for all!

NUTE GUNRAY: Can we have Amidala's head, too?

COUNT DOOKULA: Sure, whatever.

OBI-WAN [*eavesdropping*]: OMG!

Tusken Raider Camp

ANAKIN: Mom? Mom!

SHMI: Annie? Is that you?

ANAKIN: Mom!

SHMI: You look . . . good . . . have you been . . . working out . . . ?

ANAKIN: Mom, everything's gonna be okay now—

SHMI: Oh, Annie . . . I fear . . . these cuts on my face are . . . mortal . . .

ANAKIN: Mom, nooooo!

SHMI: *flops over dead*

ANAKIN: RAAAAAAAAA!

Yoda's Pad, Jedi Temple

YODA and MACE WINDU are sacked out on Jedi beanbag chairs.

YODA: Great pain and suffering and hey-hey-ow-it-hurts I feel.

MACE WINDU: Yeah . . . too bad you can't sense, you know, THE BAD GUYS.

YODA: Up, you shut.

Lars Homestead

ANAKIN: WHY'D SHE HAVE TO DIE?

PADMÉ: Well, I'm thinking being strung up and starved for a month in a Tusken raider camp had something to do w—

ANAKIN: I WILL LEARN TO STOP DEATH. I WILL BE THE MOST POWERFUL JEDI EVER! I WON'T HAVE TO CLEAN UP MY ROOM AND I WILL STAY UP ALL NIGHT LONG AND I WILL NEVER EAT MY VEGETABLES! NEVER!!

PADMÉ: Anakin, I think—

ANAKIN: IT'S ALL OBI-WAN'S FAULT! HE'S JUST HOLDING ME BACK 'CUZ HE'S JELLUS!

PADMÉ: I . . . wow.

ANAKIN: And the Tusken raiders? I killed them all!

PADMÉ: You killed them *all*?

ANAKIN: All of them! The mama Tuskens and the daddy Tuskens

and the grandma Tuskens . . . even the littlest Tusken!

PADMÉ: *Not the littlest Tusken!*

ANAKIN: *weeps*

PADMÉ: There, there. Everyone commits a little mass murder now and then. It's what makes us human.

Shmi's Funeral

CLIEGG LARS: Dear Shmi: You were the best slave-turned-wife a man could have ever had. I know that wherever you are, it's better than this broke-ass moisture farm. Please enjoy this grave in our front yard.

ANAKIN: I wasn't strong enough to turn back time and unraid the farm, Mom, but I promise that someday I'll take over the galaxy to make up for it.

R2-D2: Bee boo bip!!!

PADMÉ: What's that, R2? Obi-Wan's fallen in the well?

Obi-Wan's Distress Call

PADMÉ and ANAKIN transmit the following message to the Jedi Council on Coruscant:

OBI-WAN HOLOGROBI: So basically they're building a huge droid army over here to attack the Republic, and . . . WAHHHHHH!

YODA: Good, this ain't.

MACE WINDU: Anakin! Stay there! Don't move! And DON'T DO ANYTHING STUPID! Over and out.

PADMÉ: . . .

ANAKIN: . . .

PADMÉ: You ready to do something stupid?

ANAKIN: Rock on.

Some Prison Cell, Geonosis

COUNT DOOKULA: This is terrible! A Jedi held captive! OH, THE HUMANITY!

OBI-WAN: Yeah, because YOU TOLD THEM TO, TRAITOR.

COUNT DOOKULA: Did not! Am not! Oh, if only Qui-Gon were here to vouch for me!

OBI-WAN: He wouldn't join you in . . . whatever it is you're doing!

COUNT DOOKULA: Oh, I beg to diffah. What if I told you that the Republic is now under the control of the Sith?

OBI-WAN: Nuh-uh! The Jedi would know!

COUNT DOOKULA: Darth Sidious has clouded their minds!

OBI-WAN: I don't believe you! 'Darth Sidious'? No one would have a name that dumb!

COUNT DOOKULA: Exhibit A: Me.

OBI-WAN: Touché.

COUNT DOOKULA: You must join me to destroy the Sith and save the Republic!

OBI-WAN: Never! And Senator Amidala thinks you're evil, too!

COUNT DOOKULA: But . . . according to what I'm telling you, she would also be under the control of the Sith.

OBI-WAN: Never! I will never join you and help fight the Sith! Never!

COUNT DOOKULA: But . . . I'm asking you to fight the bad guys.

OBI-WAN: Wait . . . but then . . . and that would mean . . . NEVER!

COUNT DOOKULA: FINE, BE THAT WAY!

296

Palpatine's Office

PALPATINE: What senator would be dumb enough to give me emergency powers?

MAS AMEDDA: Oh, if only Senator Amidala, or someone who could be tricked into voting in her place, were here!

PALPATINE: Yes, indeed.

MAS AMEDDA: Woe.

JAR JAR: Hmm . . .

Senate Chamber, Five Minutes Later

JAR JAR: And so meesa proposen that weesa give Pancellor Chalpatine muy muy power!

PALPATINE: Oh, no, I couldn't possibly, really, you shouldn't have, it's too much . . . But while we're here . . . LET'S CREATE THAT ARMY!

ALL THE SENATORS: YAY!

STAR WARS FANS: Oh, Jar Jar! Now the deaths of all the Jedi in the next movie are indirectly your fault! You so crazy!

Geonosis Droid Factory

PADMÉ, ANAKIN, C-3PO and R2-D2 fall into an old Looney Tunes cartoon. Incredibly tedious hijinx ensue until PADMÉ and ANAKIN are captured and taken away to be executed.

Some Dark Corridor

PADMÉ: Hey, before you wheel us out to be executed, can I just tell him one last thing?

GUARD: Shoot.

PADMÉ [*turning to* ANAKIN]: For some reason, I love you. I love your temper tantrums and your hissyfits and the creepy ways you stare at me. I love your sad little ponytail and your punk-ass braid. I truly, deeply, madly, genuinely, thoroughly, sincerely, honestly, absolutely, entirely, utterly, completely, totally, righteously—

GUARD: STOP STALLING!

PADMÉ: DAMMIT!

The Arena of DOOM

THE GRAND HIGH WHATEVER: Click! Clickyclickyclick!

COUNT DOOKULA [*translating*]: Let the baroque and over-elaborate executions begin!

GEONOSIANS: *do the wave*

[The GEONOSIANS bring PADMÉ and ANAKIN out and chain them up next to OBI-WAN.]

OBI-WAN: Young man, we're having a talk when we get home!

[The executioners bring out a pantherrat, a rhinosaurus and a spidermantis from the planet Harryhausen. PADMÉ has mysteriously sprouted a handcuff key, so, you know, good for her. COUNT DOOKULA, NUTE GUNRAY and the FETTS watch as the three captives proceed to break their chains and/or use them as weapons against the monsters.]

COUNT DOOKULA: You people have really got to get a better chain supplier.

[Despite having a way to unlock her fetters, PADMÉ does not bother to help either of the guys. As karmic retribution, the pantherrat is more than happy to rip the bottom half of her top off.]

FANBOYS: YUSS!

[This does not stop her from kicking the pantherrat in the teeth. Meanwhile, ANAKIN swings by on the rhinosaurus to pick up PADMÉ and OBI-WAN for a mounted Jedi sandwich.]

PADMÉ: Awwww yeah, *this* is what I'm talkin' about.

NUTE GUNRAY: They're not dying! This is not dying! SHOOT THEM!

COUNT DOOKULA [*stomping foot*]: But I wanna see people get EATEN!

[Then a bunch of droids roll out and surround the captives. Game over.]

COUNT DOOKULA: *pouts*

PADMÉ: Look! It's Master Windu!

MACE WINDU: [BLEEP BLEEPING BLEEPERS], this [BLEEP BLEEPING] party's [BLEEP BLEEPING BLEEPER BLEEP] over, [BLEEPING BLEEP BLEEPERBLEEPS]!

[All the paint falls off the GRAND HIGH WHATEVER'S balcony and several Geonosian sailors in the audience faint.]

OBI-WAN: Wow. I didn't even know you could use 'fuck' as a preposition.

[Suddenly a hundred Jedi step out of the audience, completely unnoticed up to this point by ten thousand ugly wingy-things.]

COUNT DOOKULA: You people have the worst security *ever*.

[The mellow, peacekeeping Jedi attack their adversaries gleefully. OBI-WAN slices up the spidermantis with relish. MACE WINDU decapitates JANGO –]

COUNT DOOKULA: Nooooo! Not the guy who looks like Boba Fett!

[– and then the Jedi are outnumbered all over again by an assload of droids.]

MACE WINDU: We will not be your hostages! You'll just have to kill us all!

ALL THE OTHER JEDI: HEY!

PADMÉ: Look! In the sky!

[YODA swoops in on his gunship, the *Deus Ex Machina*, and rescues the ten Jedi who didn't get their asses kicked.]

Empty Arena of DOOM, Ten Minutes Later

C-3PO: I just had the weirdest dream . . . I spent an entire battle wandering around spouting bad puns and being useless!

R2-D2: Bee-boo-bip.

[A forlorn BOBA FETT picks up his father's helmet. And then his father's severed head falls out.]

BOBA: WAHHHHHHHHHHHHHHHHHH!

Attack of the Clones

A frillion clones of JANGO FETT march out and lay waste to Geonosis.

YODA: Their stuff blow up!

ENEMY STUFF: *blows up. A lot*

    [MACE WINDU leads the clone troopers and a handful of Jedi into battle. YODA hobbles from his transporter's handicapped parking spot to the forward command centre.]

THE AUDIENCE: So . . . wait, these are the clones, and this is 'attacking'? WHY ARE THEY HELPING?

    [Meanwhile, COUNT DOOKULA is escaping on a speeder. PADMÉ, ANAKIN and OBI-WAN chase him in a transporter, but they come under fire and PADMÉ falls out of the ship and plummets, like, five thousand feet.]

ANAKIN: AHHHHHHH! MY GIRLFRIEND! I'M STILL A VIRGIN! PUT THE SHIP DOWN!

OBI-WAN: NO!

ANAKIN: YES!

OBI-WAN: NO!

ANAKIN: YES!

OBI-WAN: NO!

ANAKIN: FUCK YOU!

OBI-WAN: GO TO YOUR ROOM!

CLONE OF JANGO FETT: Uh, sir, do you want me to put the ship down or not . . . ?

OBI-WAN: Anakin, what would Padmé do?

ANAKIN: Padmé Prissypants would do her duty and go whale on Dookula.

OBI-WAN: All right then.

Forward Command Centre

YODA: Their asses kicked, I sense my Jedi are about to have. Saddle up!

Bad Guy Headquarters

ENEMY STUFF: *still blowing up*

NUTE GUNRAY: THIS SUCKS!

THE GRAND HIGH WHATEVER: Click! Clickyclickyclick!

COUNT DOOKULA: You're absolutely right. We need to get the Very Secret Plans out of here. Let *me* take them, and leave the rest of you to death and destruction.

THE GRAND HIGH WHATEVER [*holding out Death Star plans*]: Clicky!

The Dunes of Geonosis

PADMÉ falls five thousand feet, breaks every bone in her body and dies.

SOME TROOPER: Oh my God, the Senator is dead!

PADMÉ [*jumping to her feet*]: No, I'm fine! Totally fine! I don't know what Anakin was talking about – sand's not rough and coarse! It completely broke my fall! I'm totally fine!

SOME TROOPER: But you fell, like, five thousand feet—

PADMÉ: Totally fine!

SOME TROOPER: You're not even bruised?

PADMÉ: Totally fine!

SOME TROOPER: You should be dead right now!

PADMÉ: BRAAAAAINS!

SOME TROOPER: What?

PADMÉ: Totally fine!

Hangar of Destiny

ANAKIN: I KEEL YOU!

[COUNT DOOKULA counters with an electric bitchslap that throws ANAKIN across the room.]

COUNT DOOKULA: Son, let the grownups talk.

OBI-WAN: I KEEL YOU!

COUNT DOOKULA: I SCHOOL YOU!

OBI-WAN: OW!

[Just as COUNT DOOKULA is about to finish off OBI-WAN, ANAKIN leaps between them and OBI-WAN throws him his lightsaber so that he can twirl around with two equally useless weapons. We get some Lord-of-the-Dancing in wide shot and then a laser light show in close-up. And then you put your real arm in and your fake arm out; you get your arm cut off and you shake it all about.]

YODA [hobbling into hangar]: Fast so not, Count Dookula!

COUNT DOOKULA: . . . I don't even know what that means.

[YODA and COUNT DOOKULA play tug-of-war with large inanimate objects and shoot lightning back and forth until it becomes clear that they are at a stalemate.]

YODA: Arm wrestle, can we not?

COUNT DOOKULA: But . . . we put aside this huge chunk of budget for a lightsaber battle.

YODA: So be it. HIIIIIIIIYA!

[YODA flips and twirls and spins around like a cracked-out Cirque du Soleil, until finally COUNT DOOKULA is so taken aback that he throws a giant pillar at the two fallen JEDI and makes a run for it.]

YODA [holding up pillar with the Force]: Ughhhhh . . . move over, you must!

ANAKIN: *moans*

YODA: Over, you must roll!

OBI-WAN: *groans*

YODA: DO EVERYTHING AROUND HERE I MUST?

The Evil District, Coruscant

COUNT DOOKULA: So, I tricked each side into fighting the others, because I am actually DARTH SARUMAN.

HOODED FIGURE WHO IS TOTALLY NOT PALPATINE: Eeeexcellent.

The Clone War Begins

OBI-WAN: You know, it's funny how there just happened to be a clone army waiting for us exactly when we needed it.

MACE WINDU: So . . . did we ever figure out who ordered them? The dead Jedi guy, or Count Dookula, or what?

OBI-WAN: Nah, we never did, but I figure, why look a gift army in the mouth?

YODA: *eyeroll*

OBI-WAN: Oh shit.

MACE WINDU: What?

OBI-WAN: I just remembered something – I totally left these two droids on Geonosis.

Deserted Arena of DOOM, Geonosis

C-3PO: Hey, you guys . . . ?

R2-D2: BEE BOO BIP!

Some Wedding Chapel, Naboo

ANAKIN has 'escorted' PADMÉ to Naboo, a word which here means 'convinced her to marry him against all reason, logic, and taste'. The droids have been rescued and reunited with the only people who can stand C-3PO for longer than five minutes.

SOME NABOOVIAN MINISTER: Do you and your mechanical hand take this totally fine senator to be your lawfully wedded wife, until her tragic death at your hands do you part?

ANAKIN: I do.

SOME NABOOVIAN MINISTER: Do you take this jerkawan to be your lawfully wedded husband, until his total transformation into an evil robot henchman for the Dark Side do you part?

ZOMBIE SENATOR PADMÉ: BRAAAAAINS!

SOME NABOOVIAN MINISTER: I now pronounce you antihero and space babe! You may make out with the bride!

R2-D2: Bee boo . . . *sniffle*

C-3PO: Oh, I do love a happy ending!

THE LORD OF THE RINGS (THEATRICAL VERSION) I. THE FELLOWSHIP OF THE RING (2001)

Story Time with Galadriel

GALADRIEL: It began with the forging of the great rings. Three were given to the Elves, immortal, wisest and fairest of all, but none who live now remember it . . .

AUDIENCE: Except for you.

GALADRIEL: Can it, I'm trying to tell a story here. Of the race of Elves in Middle-earth at that time, I was the wisest and the cutest and the most popular. But even the foxiest can misjudge. I was just 1,743 when I met Annatar – he blew into Eregion on his Harley FellBeast XL and after school he'd take me for a ride and I'd hold on tight to his dragonskin jacket and we'd just leave Celeborn holding my books on the sidewalk with that puppy-dog look on his face. Everyone told me Annatar was a 'bad influence', that he came from 'the wrong side of the tracks', and no one even *knew* his family, and after Finarfin grounded me I had to climb down the trellis at night and sneak out to see him, but I didn't care. We broke the speed limit all over Arda with the wind whipping through my hair and one night he looked down at my ring (wrought of *mithril* with a single white stone flickering like a frosty star) and said, 'Baby, I'll give you a *real* ring of power,' and Melian told me boys like that don't go steady but I just *knew* Annatar was the one. And then I got to school the next morning and *everyone had rings of power*. Like, sixteen different people! That cheating JERK! And his real name wasn't even Annatar – it was freakin' *Sauron*! We found out later that he was wanted in three kingdoms for fraud, assault and writing bad cheques! So I went back to Celeborn, who was studying metallurgy at Beleriand U by then, and . . .

AUDIENCE: Are we gonna get to the movie any time soon?

TOLKIEN FANS: Yeah! What about Bilbo and Gollum!

GALADRIEL: Oh, like you haven't worn out three copies of *The Hobbit* already.

TOLKIEN FANS: *hang heads*

GALADRIEL: Anyway. Annatar/Sauron/Jerkface was a cheating lying whore and he had the free peoples of Middle-earth under his thrall, blah blah Alliance of Men and Elves blee, Elendil got his ass kicked blah, Isildur cut the One Ring off Jerkface's hand but he was a moron and didn't destroy it and he lost it and some shriveled froggy creature found it and lost it to a midget, and here we are today. You happy now?

AUDIENCE: . . .

Gandalf's Cart of Exposition

GANDALF rides into the Shire, a happy green place where the men are plump, the women are furry and the children are above average weight. Everyone naps or boozes or frolics in fields of daisies to the tune of a happy flute.

GANDALF [*singing*]:

> Oh give me a home, where the short people roam,
> Where the beer and the golden ale flow,
> Where seldom is heard an uncooked tasty bird
> And the hobbits eat more than they sow. . .

FRODO: Gandalf, I'm so happy to see you! Now that you're here, the movie can start without any more exposition!

GANDALF: . . .

FRODO: . . .

GANDALF AND FRODO: BWAHAHAHAHAHA!

GANDALF: Yeah, I couldn't say that with a straight face, either. How you chillin', Shorty?

FRODO: Fabulous! So, tell me about the place I've lived for years!

GANDALF: Well, it's green, and everyone's happy!

FRODO: Whee!

GANDALF: Fireworks for all the children!

CHILDREN: YAY!

SOME NEIGHBOUR: Oh, that's very fine until someone loses an eye!

GANDALF: What crawled up his ass?

FRODO: Oh, you know. The whole dragon thing – the only dragon folks around here like is the one where they get their beer. Bilbo running off with a bunch of drunk, noisy dwarfs and coming back with foreign gold and magical swords and things . . . kinda made you unpopular around here.

GANDALF: I had nothing to do with any of that!

FRODO: Except for the part where you masterminded the whole thing.

GANDALF: Oh, look! [*Points at giant tent.*] It's A LONG-EXPECTED PARTY!

FRODO: Don't try to change the subject with chapter titles, dude.

Some Hobbit Hole

A sign outside reads 'PARTY BUSINESS ONLY, NO SOLICITORS'.

GANDALF: *knocks on the door*

BILBO: I GAVE AT THE OFFICE, I DON'T NEED ALUMINUM SIDING AND I ALREADY HAVE A PERSONAL RELATIONSHIP WITH JESUS CHRIST, THANK YOU!— Gandalf! It's you! Come on in! Seed cake?

GANDALF: You haven't aged a day since I last saw you! I mean, you're probably going to die from a heart attack at the rate you're carrying on, but still: lookin' good.

BILBO: It's like this all day long. Amway salesmen, Daisy Scouts –

well, the Scouts bring cookies, they're all right – Mormons, relatives of relatives . . . I've got to get out of here, Gandalf. Apple tart? Banana bread? Cinnamon roll?

GANDALF: Thanks but no thanks – I'm on Atkins. What about that camper you wanted to buy, all those road trips you wanted to take?

BILBO: I know, I know . . . I just feel so *tired* these days. So *old*.

GANDALF: Dude, it's probably just indigestion. Lay off the carbs, man. And what about Frodo?

BILBO: I know, I know. Frodo's my favourite . . . uh . . . cousin-brothernephew. But he'll be fine. And he's got that fat little gardener to take care of him.

GANDALF: Yeah . . . that whole scene's a little weird, isn't it?

BILBO: Hey, man, I don't judge. Lemon scone?

Scenes from a Long-Expected Party

BILBO and GANDALF light up on a hilltop overlooking the party preparations. They are smoking a tobacco-like substance that is completely harmless and non-carcinogenic. They are totally not getting high. At all. Never.

GANDALF: Dude, that's some good shit right there.

BILBO: What can I say? Bolger's got a good stash. They don't call him 'Fatty' for nothin', you know.

* * *

SAM: Oh, Rosie is so pretty tonight. I wish I were brave enough to dance with her.

FRODO: Oh, Sam – you and your comical attempts at heterosexuality!

* * *

BILBO: And then the trolls couldn't decide whether to boil us alive seasoned only by our own screams or to break our bones and suck the gory marrow! And then they said, 'Hey, let's do both!' So they stuffed us in a sack with rabid zombie badgers, who started chewing on Bofur's head, and—

HOBBIT KIDS: *run away screaming*

* * *

GANDALF does his part to terrify the children with exploding butterflies and, later, a jig.

PIPPIN: We haven't screwed anything up in five minutes! Come on!

[MERRY and PIPPIN light the biggest firework from GANDALF'S wagon, but an improper detonation technique results in three burnt tents, mass hysteria, a stampede, numerous casualties, blindness and grass stains.]

* * *

While ambulances cart away the dead and firework-wounded, BILBO, nervously playing with the ring in his pocket, gets up to make his big speech.

BILBO: I'm afraid it's time to— OH MY GOD LOOK THE CAKE IS ON FIRE!

EVERYONE ELSE: What?

BILBO: *poof*

EVERYONE ELSE: OMGWTF!

Chez Bilbo

GANDALF: Yeah, that was real funny.

BILBO: You're just mad because you didn't think of it first. Besides, it's not like the fate of the world hinges on this stupid little ring or anything.

GANDALF: Be that as it may, I think you should leave it here with Frodo.

BILBO: Sure, whatever. It's on the mantel.

GANDALF: Dude, it's in your pocket.

BILBO: No it's not.

GANDALF: Yes it is.

BILBO: No it's not.

GANDALF: Yes it is.

BILBO: No it's not.

GANDALF: WHAT KIND OF MORON DO YOU TAKE ME FOR?

BILBO: *wibble*

Chez Bilbo, Half an Hour Later

GANDALF: So, your cousinunclebrother Bilbo's skipped town and left you his ring.

FRODO: What?

GANDALF: Gotta go!

Municipal Public Library of Minas Tirith

GANDALF gallops to some big white city and gets his research on.

LIBRARIANS IN THE AUDIENCE: Beverages in THE RARE BOOK SECTION OH NOES!

THE ACCOUNT OF ISILDUR: Yea, it was precious to me verily, although it looked only like the kind of plain wedding band you would find, ironically, on a bachelor hobbit's finger.

GANDALF: OH SHIT.

After a fulfilling evening of drinking and pretending to like girls, SAM and FRODO stumble home. Once inside his hobbit hole, FRODO realizes he has an unexpected guest.

GANDALF: FRODO FRODO FRODO RING BAAAAAD!

FRODO: Oh no! Well, sit down and tell me about it. Sponge cake? Blueberry muffin? Orange soufflé?

GANDALF [*getting misty*]: Bless.

FRODO: You sure it's a bad ring?

GANDALF: Well, let's test it. Here, I'll throw it in the fire and then you pick it up and look at it.

FRODO: Straight out of the fire?

GANDALF: Yeah.

FRODO: Are you sure this isn't a moron test?

GANDALF: PICK IT UP.

FRODO: Jeez, keep your robes on, Cranky Bear.

GANDALF: So, you see anything?

FRODO: Nope . . . oh. Yeah, here's some mystical flame writing. Probably just says some lovey-dovey crap about 'entwining our love' or something . . .

GANDALF [*reading*]: 'If lost, please return to Sauron the Necromancer, Dark Lord of Mordor, Base Master of Treachery and Maker of Fine Jewellery.'

FRODO: Well, crap. I say we just hide it under the bed, then, or bury it in the back yard or put it in the cookie jar or something. I mean, who would go looking for the ring in Munchkinland?

GANDALF: Yeah . . . about that. Gollum sang like a canary. The minions of the Dark Lord are kind of on their way to get you now. Frankly, I half-expected you to be dead when I got here.

FRODO: AHHHHHHHHH! IT CAN'T STAY HERE! Hey, I know – you take the ring! You're a powerful wizard!

GANDALF: No! If I took it, there would be no movie— I mean, *it would be too great and terrible a temptation*. Yes.

FRODO: So, basically you're saying that I'm going have to stick *my* neck out and run off with it.

GANDALF: That's about the way of it, yeah. Let's pack it up and move it on out.

SOMEONE OUT IN THE BUSHES: UNGFFFHNGH!

GANDALF: WHAT WAS THAT?

SOMEONE OUT IN THE BUSHES: EXTRAUNDERWEAR!

GANDALF: SAMWISE GAMGEE!

SAM: Mr Frodo can't leave without me! He'll never make it on his own!

GANDALF: Now, Samwise, I think Frodo's a big hobbit now. He can undertake this giant, world-altering quest on his own.

FRODO: No, seriously, he's right – I can't. If he's not around to clip my toenails, pretty soon I won't be able to walk at all.

SAM: *beams*

Outside the Hobbit Hole

GANDALF: All right, remember: NEVER PUT IT ON.

FRODO: Right, right.

GANDALF: No, I'm serious. Say it with me: NEVER PUT IT ON.

FRODO: Got it, got it.

GANDALF: Second verse, same as the first—

FRODO: NEVER. PUT IT. ON. I GOT IT.

The Farthest Away from Home That Sam Has Ever Been

FRODO: Sam, we're three blocks from the house. What could possibly happen?

SAM: Well, I mean, I guess minions of the Dark Lord could swoop down, tear you to pieces right here in this cornfield, take the ring and enslave the Earth.

FRODO: . . .

SAM: Or we might run into Merry and Pippin.

MERRY AND PIPPIN: *run into them*

The Tower of Isengard

SARUMAN: You sent the One Ring off with a pack of defenceless munchkins? Clearly, your jones for the halflings' not-weed tobacco-substitute has clouded your mind. And that cloud kind of smells like patchouli.

GANDALF: Oh, put a sock in it, Nancy Reagan.

SARUMAN: Fine, then, I *won't* show you my new Magic 8-Ball.

GANDALF: What? You found one of those? But they're dangerous! We don't know who has the others!

SARUMAN: Well, how else am I going to watch the Nine Black Riders of Ghosty Death gut your little friend like a fish?

GANDALF: THE NINE ARE LOOSE?

SARUMAN: NO ONE CAN WITHSTAND THE WILL OF SAURON.

GANDALF: No one . . . ?

SARUMAN: I am . . . DARTH SARUMAN.

GANDALF: *facepalm*

A Shortcut to Mushrooms

The HOBBITS fall off a cliff and die. The NINE find their bodies, take the ring and SAURON rules the Earth. The end.

PIPPIN: Ow! Hey, look – mushrooms!

[After they run out of mushrooms, the HOBBITS begin to gnaw on each others' toes.]

FRODO: GET OFF THE ROAD! FOR THE LOVE OF LITTLE GREEN APPLES!

PIPPIN: Apples? Where?

[FRODO shoves the other HOBBITS under a tree just as one of the NINE rides up and snurfles around for them. Fortunately, like the T-REX, EVIL ZOMBIE RIDERS apparently can't see you if you don't move.]

MERRY: What the hell was that?

PIPPIN: And I'm *still* waiting for apples.

Bucklebury Ferry

The HOBBITS follow FRODO as he sneaks, sprints, tiptoes, ducks and belly-crawls through the forest.

MERRY: Okay, I call shenanigans. What's *really* going on?

FRODO: I'm being hunted by undead minions of the Dark Lord for a magic ring that could bring about the end of the world.

MERRY: Yeah . . . What you need is a shoddily built raft. To the ferry!

RINGWRAITH: SHREEEEEEEEEEEEEE!

[It turns out that little furry people can really haul it under pressure. SAM, MERRY and PIPPIN start untying the ferry, only to look back and see that . . . FRODO is still at the edge of the forest.]

SAM: Hurry, Mr Frodo! The bad guy's gonna get you!

MERRY: Maybe he'd get away if he'd stop RUNNING IN SLO-MO!

[FRODO eventually gets (1) a clue and (2) his sprint on, making a flying-squirrel leap onto the departing ferry. The RINGWRAITH'S HORSE stamps impotently back on shore.]

PIPPIN: So . . . are these dudes repelled by water, or . . . ?

MERRY: Nah, I think they just don't like to get wet. You ever try to launder thousand-year-old robes of the dead?

The Prancing Pony

FRODO: Excuse me, we're looking for a wizard named Gandalf? He's supposed to meet us here.

INNKEEPER: Hmm . . . tall guy, long beard, giant blue hat, staff like a gnarled tree branch, mysterious red ring that no one knows what it does?

FRODO: Yes!

INNKEEPER: Never heard of him.

[In despair, FRODO sits down and begins to finger his ring. (Ew, not like that.) (Well, maybe like that. He does get kind of into it) while SAM tucks into his grub and PIPPIN goes off to booze with the locals.]

PIPPIN: Frodo Baggins? Why, he's right over there! We've been running from a big scary guy on a black horse all day – Frodo must be carrying something extremely valuable and secret on his small, unguarded person, if you ask me . . .

FRODO: PIPPIN! WHAT ARE YOU DOING?

[FRODO runs to the bar to grab PIPPIN. In his panic, the ring flies out of his hand, up into the air and, in front of everyone and against all odds, right onto FRODO'S finger. No, really. He vanishes.]

THE EYE OF SAURON: PEEKABOOOOOO.

FRODO: *falls down*

[Just when FRODO thinks he's managed to tear the ring off and get out of Ghost World, a giant, angry hand reaches down, jerks him off the floor and hauls him up to a private room.]

FRODO: Really, sir, I'm not that kind of hobbit—!

STRIDER [*sneering*]: Are you scared?

FRODO: Well, now that you're standing over me with a sword bigger than I am, yeah, I'm scared!

[The HOBBITS burst into the room, armed with rustic furnishings.]

SAM: I KEEL YOU, LONGSHANKS!

STRIDER [*sheathing sword*]: Hobbit, *please*.

Later That Night

The BLACK RIDERS find the HOBBITS' room and, with great ceremony, stab them to death in their beds and take the ring. SAURON takes possession of the ring, destroys all that is good and green and takes over the world. Woe. The end.

SAM: Whew! I sure am glad Mr Strider thought to stuff pillows that look just like us under the covers instead!

BLACK RIDERS [*across the hall*]: SHREEEEEEEEEEEEE!

FRODO: What are they?

STRIDER: Nasty-ass bitches who will kill you dead.

FRODO: Oh.

STRIDER: Which is why I'm taking you into the wild, away from all known civilization and aid, away from anyone who might be able to help us.

MERRY: How do you know we can trust him, Frodo?

STRIDER: Well, for one thing, I'm not dumb enough to talk smack about someone WITHIN EARSHOT.

FRODO: He has a point, you know.

Somewhere in the Wild

STRIDER marches them over hill and dale and swamp and marsh and empty lot and car park all day. The moment he turns his back, the HOBBITS try to fire up the Hibachi, much to his dismay.

PIPPIN: But we have to eat! He knows we have to eat, doesn't he?

MERRY: I don't think he cares, Pip.

PIPPIN: But there's a whole *schedule*! He knows about brunch, doesn't he? What about hors d'oeuvres? Pudding? Nuncheon? Tiffin?

MERRY: Dude, *I* don't even know what tiffin is.

The Tower of Isengard

SARUMAN: What do you command, my lord?

THE MAGIC 8-BALL: . . .

SARUMAN: *shakes up the Magic 8-Ball*

THE MAGIC 8-BALL: TRY AGAIN LATER.

SARUMAN: *shakes up the Magic 8-Ball again*

THE MAGIC 8-BALL: CONCENTRATE AND ASK AGAIN.

SARUMAN: * shakity-shakity-shake*

THE MAGIC 8-BALL: BUILD ME AN ARMY WORTHY OF MORDOR.

SARUMAN: Jeez, *finally*. You there!

SOME HIDEOUS SHAMBLING ORC: Yessir?

SARUMAN: Tear down all the trees and stuff. But do it in a montage, because it'll be important later.

Some Big Hilltop That Looks Like a Mushroom

PIPPIN: Mmm, mushrooms.

STRIDER: All right. Here are some rusty old swords that none of you have any idea how to use. I'm going to leave you four halfwits here by yourselves, completely unguarded, while I go scout or brood or something.

MERRY: Rock on.

STRIDER: Now: DON'T DO ANYTHING STUPID.

PIPPIN: *thumbs up*

[Five minutes later:]

MERRY: It's a barbecue and everyone's invited!

SAM: The bonfire needs more wood!

PIPPIN: Merry, I can't get the stereo to work out here.

MERRY: That's because there are no outlets, *Pippin*.

FRODO: WHAT ARE YOU *DOING*?

[Five BLACK RIDERS cruise on up Mount Mushroom and go after the HOBBITS. MERRY, PIPPIN and SAM face them bravely with rusty old swords that they do not, in fact, know how to use, only to get tossed aside like so much dirty laundry. FRODO falls down.]

FRODO: I know I saw the giant flaming eye the last time I put the ring on, but surely that won't happen *again*!

[It doesn't, actually. This time he sees five terrifying white ghosty things who come and stab him when he won't give up the ring.]

FRODO: WAHHHHHH!

[STRIDER magically leaps out and manages to drive off THE WRAITHS with just a sword and a torch.]

STRIDER: DO I HAVE TO DO EVERYTHING AROUND HERE?

The Tower of Isengard

Some moth arrives to help GANDALF, because it is actually an eagle. Or an eagle disguised as a moth. Or a moth that's friends with an eagle. Or something.

EAGLEMOTH: You want me to go get Frodo and take him to Mount Doom?

GANDALF: Nah, that's okay.

EAGLEMOTH: You want me to peck Saruman to death?

GANDALF: Well, not really – I mean, if you just feel like it . . .

EAGLEMOTH: Is there anything I can actually do to help you?

GANDALF: Well, you could take me to Rivendell. I hear it's lovely this time of year.

EAGLEMOTH: *eyeroll*

Some Big Hilltop That Looks Like a Mushroom

STRIDER: Sam! Is there any athelas around here?

SAM: Athewho?

STRIDER: Kingsfoil!

SAM: Foil in the what now?

STRIDER: IT'S A PLANT, SAM. YOU'RE SUPPOSED TO BE A GARDENER.

SAM: Can you eat it?

STRIDER: No.

SAM: Can you smoke it?

STRIDER: No.

SAM: Sorry, can't help you, then.

[While FRODO wails and foams in the background, STRIDER goes foraging and finds . . .]

SOME CHICK WITH A SWORD: Arrrrr . . .

STRIDER: . . . wen!

TOLKIEN FANS: What's this? A character caught out of her storyline?

PIPPIN: Ooo, she pretty.

SAM: WHAT? YOU'RE LETTING SOME RANDOM DAY-GLO CHICK TAKE MR FRODO *WHERE*?

ARWEN: Look, half-pint, I'm the one with the horse. You wanna schlep this kid around on foot for thirty miles with the Faceless Wonders on your tail, you be my guest.

STRIDER: But *I* could take the horse, and—

ARWEN: MY HORSE NOT YOURS!

STRIDER: . . . Have a nice ride!

TOLKIEN FANS: But—! Glorfindel—! AUGH!

Some Ford

THE RINGWRAITHS: GIVE UP THE SHORTSTACK, SHE-ELF!

ARWEN [*raising sword*]: BY THE POWER OF ELBERETH—!

TOLKIEN FANS: *foam at the mouth*

[ARWEN raises the river and the river turns into horses and the horses trample the WRAITHS and FRODO is safe.]

FRODO: *flatlines*

ARWEN: DADDY! FRODO WON'T PLAY WITH ME!

ELROND: Well, sweetheart . . . sometimes things go to sleep and . . . don't wake up. Like that bunny you had, remember?

ARWEN [*crying*]: Noooo! Not like Mr Wiggles!

ELROND: There, there. Let me see what I can do.

The Last Homely House, Rivendell

FRODO wakes up in a lovely wooded retreat/rehab center for One Ring addiction, having been saved by ELROND's Elvish hoodoo.

FRODO: Gandalf! Where were you? We were so scared!

GANDALF: Yeah, see, about that – you see, I was . . .

[GANDALF proceeds to have a flashback in which DARTH SARUMAN is all like, 'JOIN ME OR DIE!', and GANDALF is like, 'NEVER!', and DARTH SARUMAN is like, 'WELL, THEN CLEARLY YOU'D RATHER DIE,' and GANDALF is like, 'WELL, I GUESS SO, THEN,' and then DARTH SARUMAN is like, 'WELL, YOU MIGHT WANT TO GET ON WITH THAT, THEN,' and then the EAGLE-MOTH swings by and GANDALF books it on out of there.]

FRODO: Gandalf? I can't hear your flashback.

GANDALF: Oh. Sorry about that.

Elrond and Gandalf Have a Powwow

ELROND: The ring can't stay here. Look, have Shortcake over there take it for you.

GANDALF: But . . . but . . . he's so *little*!

[Outside, the rest of the cast arrives, and all of them look cranky.]

LEGOLAS: This better be good – I turned down a shampoo commercial for this.

[Back inside:]

ELROND: Well, who do you propose we get to take it, then?

GANDALF: Uh . . . some Men? Who aren't little?

ELROND: Shpfff, *Men* . . . I was there, three thousand years ago, saturated with the stink of the plague of Men . . .

[ELROND flashes back to the moment when he stood on the raging slopes of Mount Doom and was like, 'Isildur, King of Men! Destroy the One Ring in the fire!', and ISILDUR was like, '. . . .', and ELROND was like, 'Seriously, we'll never have a chance like this again! The fire's RIGHT THERE!', and ISILDUR was like, '. . .', and ELROND was like, 'THROW IT IIIIIIIIN!', and ISILDUR was like, 'NO, FOR IT IS PRECIOUS TO ME. MOO HA HA!', and ELROND was like, *facepalm*.]

GANDALF: Really? You don't look a day over twenty-five hundred.

ELROND: Awww, thanks. Anyway, what was I saying? Oh, yes: MEN SUCK.

GANDALF: There is one who sucks less.

ELROND: Yes, well.

The Sword That Was Broken

Extremely obvious extreme close-up: STRIDER is trying to catch up on his reading when some big, self-important guy wanders in and starts manhandling the family heirlooms.

BOROMIR: It's still sharp!

STRIDER: Dude, the sword broke into *shards*, not butter knives.

Bridge of Twinkly Schmoop

ARWEN: I choose . . . a mortal life.

STRIDER: Not like Mr Wiggles!

ARWEN: *brave nod*

STRIDER: I cannot let you do this!

ARWEN [*earnestly*]: I would rather be a bunny with you than face all the ages of this world alone!

STRIDER: This metaphor is a little too weird for me, unless it *also* takes into account the mating habits of rabbits.

ARWEN [*batting lashes*]: Oh, it does.

STRIDER: Oh. Well, rock on, then.

The Council of Elrond

ELROND: So, the ring. Someone who is not me needs to do something with it.

GANDALF: We must destroy it!

BOROMIR: We should use it!

GIMLI: Let's destroy it NOW!

ELROND: Yeah . . . that's not so much going to work.

  [GIMLI tries to chop it in half. It doesn't work.]

ELROND: I told you so.

BOROMIR: Again: totally should be using it.

STRIDER: We must destroy it!

BOROMIR: Ranger, *please*.

LEGOLAS: HE IS ARAGORN, SON OF ARATHORN, AND YOU OWE HIM YOUR PROPS!

THE REST OF THE COUNCIL: OH SNAP.

LEGOLAS: PS – IT MUST BE DESTROYED!

ELROND: Yeah, unmade in the fires of Mount Doom, etc. Any takers?

LEGOLAS: DWARVES SUCK!

GIMLI: DWARVES RULE, ELVES DROOL!

BOROMIR: I HATE ALL OF YOU!

~~STRIDER~~ ARAGORN: *superior eyeroll*

  [Everyone starts arguing and FRODO, who is a sensitive hobbit, starts having a nervous breakdown.]

SEVERAL GIRLS IN THE AUDIENCE: Forget Frodo, who's that dish sitting next to Aragorn?

FRODO: SHUT SHUT SHUT! I WILL TAKE IT!

THE REST OF THE COUNCIL: . . .

FRODO: Even though . . . I don't know where that is. Something about doom . . . ?

GANDALF: Dude, you fall down way too much. I'm going with you.

ELROND: Anyone else?

ARAGORN: You have my scruff.

LEGOLAS: And my pretty!

GIMLI: And my ill-advised one-liners!

SAM: And my slavish loyalty!

MERRY: OI! And our well-meaning ineptitude!

PIPPIN: Merry, what's 'ineptitude'?

MERRY: Something you have a lot of, Pip.

PIPPIN: *beams*

BOROMIR [*sighing*]: Gondor will see your idiocy done.

ELROND: Well, I was hoping we'd round up a fellowship of actual warriors to protect the Ringbearer worth half a damn, but as long as you all get out of my house, you know, whatever.

Bilbo's Parting Gifts

FRODO: So everything's okay here, Bilbo? Food good, weather nice?

BILBO: Oh, it's lovely – and I'm doing really well in RingAnon!

FRODO: Awww, that's great.

BILBO: Before you go, I want to give you my fabulous diamond-crusted plot-point mail shirt, since Elrond says you kids like to 'floss' the 'bling' nowadays.

FRODO: Oooooo!

BILBO: And here's my old Elven sword, Sting! It has a built-in Orc Alert System and Spider-Slashing Action!

FRODO: Aaaaaaaah!

BILBO: Say . . . speaking of RAAAAA GIVE ME THE RIIIIIING!

FRODO: WAHHHHHHHHH!

BILBO [*sniffling*]: Awww . . . this is going to send me right back to Step Number Eight.

GANDALF [*outside*]: FRODO, COME ON! THIS MOVIE'S LIKE

FIVE HOURS LONG ALREADY AND WE HAVEN'T EVEN LEFT YET!

The Hero Shot We Used in the Trailer

Over the mountains, through the woods, to the Dark Lord's Tower we go! Wizard! Ranger! Surly Guy! Elf! Dwarf! Frodo! So-and-So! What's-His-Face! The Tubby One!

SAM: HEY!

GANDALF: Dag, yo – looking heroic is hard work. Time for a break!

A Scene in Which Boromir Is Not a Jackwad

The FELLOWSHIP breaks for sword-fighting and sausages. Somehow, this is not a euphemism for anything dirty.

GIMLI: I say we take a shortcut through Moria!

GANDALF: Don't even go there.

GIMLI: Why not?

GANDALF: Well . . . uh . . . it totally wasn't taken over by thousands of Orcs and a giant fire demon, why do you ask?

GIMLI: Oh, good. You had me worried for a minute there.

A Scene in Which Boromir Is a *Total* Jackwad

FRODO: *falls down*

[ARAGORN helps him up, but in the meantime, the ring has somehow detached itself from the chain around FRODO'S neck and flown off several yards into the snow at BOROMIR'S feet. BOROMIR picks it up and stares at it.]

ARAGORN: Dude?

BOROMIR: . . .

ARAGORN: Dude?

BOROMIR: . . .

ARAGORN: *Dude?*

BOROMIR: All this trouble . . . for such a cheap wedding-band.

ARAGORN: DUDE.

BOROMIR: My dad could totally buy you another one, you know.

ARAGORN: GIVE IT BACK OR I CUT YOU.

PIPPIN: Merry, Mommy and Daddy are fighting again.

MERRY: Shhh, it'll be all right.

Some Snowy Mountain

LEGOLAS skips merrily over the snow while the MEN struggle to carry two HOBBITS apiece.

ARAGORN: A LITTLE HELP HERE?

LEGOLAS: There is a foul voice trying to stop us from crossing the mountain!

BOROMIR: How could it do th—

[Forty tons of rocks and snow fall on the FELLOWSHIP.]

GANDALF: It's Saruman!

BOROMIR: You sure it's not, you know, just the mountain being angry at us? I mean, I hear it's a pretty bitchy mountain—

GANDALF: No, it's Saruman!

ARAGORN: Not Sauron? I mean, he's got a Magic 8-Ball too and all, he can probably see where we are—

GANDALF: No, it's totally Saruman!

BOROMIR: We should turn around and head for the Gap of Rohan!

ARAGORN: HOW CAN YOU THINK OF SHOPPING AT A TIME LIKE THIS?

GANDALF: We'll let the Ringbearer decide!

FRODO: Oh, thanks, *ass*. I can't even decide what to put on in the morning.

SAM: It's true! I pick out all of Mr Frodo's clothes!

[Everyone waits.]

FRODO: I'ma have to pick the option where we don't freeze to death.

GANDALF: Sigh.

The Hidden Doors of Moria

SARUMAN, gloating over his Book of Foreshadowing (illustrated movie tie-in edition), informs us that if the FELLOWSHIP doesn't cross the mountain, there's only one other way they can go, and that way is locked up with magic silver runes.

GANDALF: Shpffff, this is easy.

[*Two hours later:*]

ARAGORN: Gandalf? How's it coming?

GANDALF: I HATE ALL OF YOU.

FRODO: It's a riddle! The password is 'friend'!

PIPPIN: You stole my line!

FRODO: You get plenty later on!

PIPPIN: But dude! This is, like, the only time I get to look smart in the whole book!

MERRY: Look, Pip – something shiny in the water!

PIPPIN: Ooo!

[Meanwhile . . .]

ARAGORN: Sam, let's send Bill back to town. He knows the way back over those fifteen mountain ranges we crossed.

BILL THE PONY: THE HELL I DO!

[The crew peeks inside the Mines of Moria, which are giant and dark and foreboding.]

BOROMIR: Guys, I don't know about this . . .

GIMLI: Oh, come on! It's just really creepy. You'll love it.

FRODO: *falls down*

[. . . in the grip of a giant tentacle, which has popped up and, unerringly picking out the Ringbearer, has started frisking FRODO.]

FRODO: BAD TOUCH BAD TOUCH TENTACLE RAPE HELP!

THE WATCHER: IÄ! IÄ! SAURON FHTAGN!

GANDALF: INTO THE CREEPY PLACE!

[THE WATCHER pulls down the stone doors, trapping everyone inside the lightless, skeleton-littered deathtrap of Moria.]

LEGOLAS [*examining arrow*]: Dead Dwarves! Killed by Orcs!

GANDALF: Thank you for that keen assessment, *Legolas*.

Some Dark Cave

The FELLOWSHIP starts trekking through the mines, until finally GANDALF hits a fork in the caves and doesn't know which way to go. He stops for a smoke break while ARAGORN and BOROMIR argue over whether they should roll a d20 or the rarer d12 to determine GANDALF'S success in choosing the right tunnel. The HOBBITS start chewing each others' sleeves.

GANDALF: Hey, look, it's Gollum.

FRODO: Stupid Gollum. Shoulda killed him.

GANDALF: Now, now. Many that do not die serve as plot points later on. Even the very wise cannot see the ends of all movies.

FRODO: Stupid ring. Wish I didn't have it.

328

[GANDALF gives a poignant and stirring speech about making the most of the time we have that has curious resonance with present-day events.]

FRODO: That's so going to be your Oscar clip, isn't it?

GANDALF: I'm thinking so . . . Hey! It's that way!

FRODO: You remember?

GANDALF: No, but the movie's starting to drag.

The Great City of Dwarrowdelf

GANDALF: Look! The great city of Dwarrowdelf!

LEGOLAS: . . . Made of nothing but columns.

BOROMIR: And there's no shopping here at *all*.

Some Tomb

GIMLI: WAHHHHHHHHH! EVERYONE ELSE HAS BEEN MOULDERING HERE FOR YEARS, BUT I NEVER THOUGHT *MY KINSMAN* WOULD BE DEAD!

[While GIMLI wails and keens over the tomb of BALIN, the FELLOWSHIP gathers around: it's story time!]

GANDALF [*reading from battered book*]: 'We're trapped, trapped! The drums, the drums – we're all going to die in here ACK THEY'RE COMING ARGHHHHHHH!'

ARAGORN: So . . . wait, who buried Balin in this fine commemorative tomb, then?

GIMLI: WAAAUUUUUUAAAAAGHHHHHHH!!!

[Story time is interrupted by PIPPIN nosing around and *BAM BAM BAM* knocking *CRASH BANG SLAM* an armoured skeleton *WHAM BAM BAM* down a conveniently inconvenient well.]

THE FELLOWSHIP: *facepalm*

GANDALF: YOU UTTER FUCKWIT!

PIPPIN: *hangs head*

[A sudden rumbling and tumult and general uproar can be heard coming closer and closer to the tomb. Also, a bunch of arrows hit the door before BOROMIR and ARAGORN can close it all the way.]

LEGOLAS: Orcs!

ARAGORN: NO, REALLY?

BOROMIR: If they've got a cave troll out there, I don't even want to know about it.

CAVE TROLL [outside]: RAAAAAAA!

BOROMIR: Well, *damn*.

[The ORCS eventually hack through the barricaded doors and the CAVE TROLL thunders in after them and there is a lot of shooting and ducking and chain-whipping –]

CAVE TROLL: *whp-chaaaaa!*

LEGOLAS: Okay, you are going to *have* to buy me dinner first if you want to go there—

[– and sworduition and beheaditude and punchitration and stabology. Nobody we like actually gets hurt in any significant way.]

PIPPIN: I'm better with a sword than I thought!

SAM: I'm better with a frying pan than I thought!

FRODO: I'm better at hide and seek than I AUUUUUUUGH.

[Speared by the CAVE TROLL, FRODO falls down.]

GANDALF: OMG!

FRODO KEBAB: AWWWGHHHH . . . !

SAM: OMG!

FRODO KEBAB: UGGGGHHHH . . . !

MERRY AND PIPPIN: OMG!

FRODO KEBAB: WAAAAGHHHH . . . !

[FRODO slumps over, dead. Totally dead. ELIJAH WOOD collects his paycheque and goes home. In grief-stricken rage, the FELLOWSHIP dogpiles the CAVE TROLL and hacks at it until LEGOLAS can shoot it in the head like six times.]

CAVE TROLL: Daaaaa . . . ?

[LEGOLAS shoots the CAVE TROLL in the face. It falls down.]

ARAGORN [*crawling over to* FRODO'S *body*]: Oh, Frodo, no! My scruff failed you, woe!

[Suddenly FRODO sits up, completely unharmed. He opens his shirt to reveal . . .]

FRODO: Hey, I'm fine. Check my bling.

LEGOLAS: Ugh, your slang is older than your chain mail.

GANDALF: Strike up the hero music, we gotta go!

The Stairs to the Bridge of Khazad-Dûm

Just when the FELLOWSHIP seems to be surrounded by ORCS, fire belches through a distant doorway and several thousand ululating chicken-roaches scatter.

BOROMIR: What the shit is this?

GANDALF: It's . . . *a Balrrrrog*.

MERRY: A bal what?

PIPPIN: A rog who?

GANDALF: Elvish for 'You are so screwed'. RUN!

ARAGORN: Go on! I'll stay back here and play clean-up—

GANDALF: THAT MEANS YOU, HERO BOY. GO!

[Unfortunately, parts of the stairs to the bridge are out, if by 'out' you mean 'gaping chasms thousands of feet deep'. The BIG GUYS pitch the HOBBITS over to GANDALF and LEGOLAS, GIMLI jumps, Dwarf-tossing jokes get made (as they do) and finally it's ARAGORN and FRODO'S turn to make the leap. And then half the stairs fall over.]

331

LEGOLAS: That's bad.

GANDALF: YES, WE KNOW.

[Fortunately, ARAGORN is able to save the day through savvy leaning. He and FRODO ride the debris over to the other side of the chasm.]

EVERYONE ELSE: . . .

ARAGORN: Second place, Third-Age Limbo Championship. Good times.

FRODO: Wow, with moves like that, you should've won.

ARAGORN: Nah, lost to some guy called Neo.

The Bridge of Khazad-Dûm

GANDALF: EVERYONE ACROSS THE BRIDGE! I'LL HOLD THE BALROG OFF!

[The BALROG coughs up a ginormous fire belch.]

GANDALF: HEY, WAIT, I'M COMING TOO!

[The FELLOWSHIP races across the extremely high, extremely narrow Bridge of Khazad-Dûm, which is Dwarvish for 'Losing Your Lunch' –]

FRODO: You guys, between the spear and the limbo, I don't feel so good . . .

[– only to turn around at the end and realize that –]

FRODO: GANDAAAALF!

[– GANDALF has parked himself in front of the BALROG.]

GANDALF: I am the servant of the Shakespearean Delivery, wielder of the Really Awesome Tree Branch! The burping of fire will not avail you!

[The BALROG beats down on GANDALF with this totally fearsome fire-sword, but it shatters against GANDALF'S regular old Elven sword, and the BALROG stares at what's left of it like, 'Dude, he broke *fire*?', and GANDALF'S all like, 'THAT'S RIGHT, BITCH!', and the BALROG pulls out his fire-whip but GANDALF stomps on the bridge with his staff and the bridge crumbles and the BALROG falls and GANDALF'S all like, 'YEAH, AND TELL 'EM MITHRANDIR SENT YA!', but then the whip cracks back up and drags GANDALF into the chasm by the foot and before he goes down he's like, 'RUN, FOOLS!', and then he vanishes over the side and the FEL-LOWSHIP just stands there with their jaws on the floor.]

FRODO: NOOOOOOOOOOOOOOOOOOOOOOOOOOOOOOOOO OOOOOOOOOOOOOOOOOOOOOOOOOOOOOOOOOOOOOOOO OOOOOOOOOOOOOOOOOOOOOOOOOOOOOOOOOOOOOOOO OOOOOOOOOOOOOOOOOOOOOOOOOOOOOOOOOOOOOOOO OOOOOOOOOOOOOOOOOOOOOOOOOOOOOOOOOOOOOOOO OOOOOOOOOOOOOOOOOOOOOOOOOOOOOOOOO!!!!!!!!

ARAGORN: Aww, this means I'm in charge now, doesn't it? *Hell.*

Cliff of Manly Weeping

ARAGORN: OH, COME ON! WALK IT OFF!

Some Elfy Forest

The remaining FELLOWSHIP hauls ass into the woods –

GIMLI: They say that a terrible sorceress lives in these woods! And she's an Elf, so you *know* she's got to be a bitch!

SOME TELEPATHIC VOICE: I HEARD THAT.

[– where they are promptly intercepted by an extremely blond, extremely prissy border patrol and taken to a shiny tree village.]

HALDIR: Can't you even wipe your feet before you walk into other people's woods? *Honestly.*

Some Extraterrestrial Treehouse

CELEBORN: Quoth Elrond, nine there were set out from Rivendell, yet only eight stand before me, eight that might be called five and a half due to an unseemly deficit of personal height. Tell me, where is Gandalf? For he has a *lot* of explaining to do.

GALADRIEL: Celeborn? Let me do the talking.

CELEBORN: *pouts*

GALADRIEL: Your quest teeters on the verge of doom, at the brink of a cliff, on the edge of a knife. So much as cross your eyes and it will fail, to the flaming destruction of everyone and everything you love. But don't worry about it too much. Grab some shut-eye. IF YOU CAN.

BOROMIR: *wibbles*

The Ground Beneath the Extraterrestrial Treehouse

PIPPIN: Yeah, we're not so much into the whole 'extreme heights' thing. They put out some nice sleeping bags around the tree roots, though.

[In the trees, the ELVES sing a lament for GANDALF.]

MERRY: What are they saying?

LEGOLAS: I cannot tell you, for there is a strange emotion not unlike your mortal grief that is in great propinquity to my heart—

MERRY: *LEGOLAS.*

LEGOLAS: 'Woe.'

[Elsewhere, BOROMIR and ARAGORN have a heart-to-heart:]

ARAGORN: What's wrong?

BOROMIR: The Lady of the Wood was speaking in my mind, and she said terrible things about my father's rule failing and our people losing faith and our defences falling and I'm *homesick*, man! The White City is so awesome! Have you ever been there?

ARAGORN: Actually, due to the long-lived nature of my people, I was in fact serving the lords of Rohan and Minas Tirith before you were born—

BOROMIR: Look, I'm trying to give an emotional, character-redeeming speech here. Either you *have* or you *haven't*, *show-off*.

[While everyone else sleeps or angsts, FRODO wakes up and follows GALADRIEL to her glade.]

GALADRIEL: Will you look into my mirror, by which I mean 'basin of water with a somewhat reflective surface'?

FRODO: What will I see in there? Bad things?

GALADRIEL: Well, that would be *telling*, wouldn't it?

FRODO: Ma'am? I've had a really hard day.

GALADRIEL: Fine: things that were, things that are, things that used to be, things that might be, things that almost happened, things people thought about a lot but never got around to finishing—

FRODO: I'LL LOOK, OKAY?

[FRODO peers into the basin, where he proceeds to view everything he has ever known and loved being burnt, enslaved and/or destroyed. And then the EYE OF SAURON shows up.]

FRODO: *falls down*

GALADRIEL: So don't screw up, okay? Or it'll be all your fault.

FRODO: You know, really, if it's so important to you, *you* can have the ring. God knows it's not doing me any favours.

GALADRIEL: What?

FRODO: The ring. You can have it. Go on, take it.

GALADRIEL: You're just gonna give it to me.

FRODO: Yeah.

GALADRIEL: Is this a trick?

FRODO: TAKE THE RING.

GALADRIEL: I cannot deny that I have wanted this since the

Second Age, when Annatar offered me this ring—

FRODO: Annatar?

GALADRIEL: Sauron, Jerkface, whatever. And then he totally bailed on me. I was all packed up and ready to run away with him, and he bailed! And now his ring has come to me . . . Instead of staying at home with Verbosity McBottleblond back there, I WOULD BE A QUEEN! QUEEN OF THE NIGHT ON SAURON'S ARM, DANCING UNTIL DAWN! CRAZY-SEXY-COOL AS THE SEA! ALL SHALL LOVE ME AND DESPAIR . . . including Celeborn and . . . awww . . . [*heaving sigh*] I can't do that to him. So . . . I will remain . . . Mrs Lady of the Golden Wood. Woe.

FRODO: Marriage is tough, yo.

The Tower of Isengard

SARUMAN and his HENCH-ORC admire SARUMAN's latest creation, LURTZ THE URUK-HAI:

SARUMAN: Do you know where Orcs came from? They used to be Elves, once beautiful, then kidnapped, tortured and horribly mutilated, a cruel mockery of Ilúvatar's finest creation . . .

SOME SHAMBLING ORC: Thanks for rubbing it in, man.

SARUMAN [*to* LURTZ]: WHO'S YOUR DADDY?

LURTZ: SARUUUMAAAN!

SARUMAN: GO FIND HOBBITS!

LURTZ: RAAAAA!

SARUMAN [*calling after him*]: And they better be UNSPOILED!

A Scene in Which the Fellowship Receive Many Gifts That Will Become Plot Points in All Three Movies

This scene has been cut for time.

GALADRIEL: Bye, you guys!

Some Great River

FRODO: Are we there yet?

ARAGORN: No, it's gonna be a while.

SAM: Are we there now?

ARAGORN: No, we're clearly still on the river.

FRODO: When are we gonna be there?

ARAGORN: LOOK, IT'S THE ARGONATH!

Some Camp by the Great River

LEGOLAS: Something wicked this way comes, I can feel it.

ARAGORN: Man, it's always something evil on the air or in the water or inside the sleeping bags with you, isn't it?

LEGOLAS: No, I mean *really* this time.

ARAGORN: Fine. You hear that, guys? Nobody wander off. Particularly not Frodo, since he's got the fate of the world hanging around his . . . Hey, where *is* Frodo?

[FRODO has wandered off into the woods by himself. BOROMIR has followed him out of the goodness of his heart and a selfless concern for FRODO'S safety. Yes. That is his story, and he is sticking to it.]

BOROMIR:

> so much depends
> upon
> a wide-eyed
> hobbit
> wearing a ring
> of evil.

FRODO: Uh . . . I have to go now.

BOROMIR: Give it to me!

FRODO: No!

BOROMIR: Give it to me!

FRODO: No!

BOROMIR: Give it to me!

FRODO: No!

BOROMIR: You will whine for death before the end!

FRODO: *falls down*

BOROMIR: GIVE IT TO ME!

[FRODO puts on the ring, because we all know how well that's served him before, and manages to escape BOROMIR'S clutches. BOROMIR falls down.]

BOROMIR: Oh my God! This is what it's like to be Frodo all the time! Pitiful and clumsy and weak! I had no idea – Frodo, come back!

[FRODO runs to a big stone thing that is apparently called 'The Seat of Seeing', and then is somehow surprised that there is seeing involved, particularly that of SAURON seeing him. Again.]

FRODO: *takes off ring, falls down*

ARAGORN: Frodo! There you are!

FRODO: The ring got Boromir, oh nos!

ARAGORN: DO YOU STILL HAVE IT? LET ME SEEEEE IIIIIIT.

FRODO: Oh, like I'm falling for that again!

THE RING: *Araaaaagorrrrrn . . . Elesssssarrrrr . . . Dúnadaaaaaaan . . . Eeeeeeestel . . . Thoronnnnngil . . .*

ARAGORN [*closing* FRODO'S *hand over the ring*]: I cannot do this.

THE RING [*muffled*]: *Heyyyy, I'm not doooooooone yet . . .*

FRODO: You see now why I have to strike out on my own, even

though I am small and frail and extremely prone to falling on my ass?

ARAGORN: Godspeed, half-pint. RUN!

[ARAGORN turns to face the snarfling URUK HORDE that has finally caught up to them:]

ARAGORN [*leaping*]: BANZAI!

[Everyone, good and bad, runs around looking for FRODO and/or the battle. LEGOLAS has ARAGORN'S back with his Arrow-Fu. GIMLI . . . chops things. In the crotch, when at all possible. MERRY and PIPPIN divert the ORCS from FRODO (who falls down), only to realize that it's working a little too well:]

MERRY: Didn't think this through! Didn't think this through!

[Fortunately, BOROMIR pops up at the last moment to save their dumb asses. Then he sounds the alarm on the Horn of Gondor, alerting his friends AND EVERY ORC IN A FIVE-MILE RADIUS to the mêlée. Nonetheless, BOROMIR pounds all comers into the dirt, until it finally occurs to LURTZ to shoot him full of arrows from a safe distance. Gobsmacked with sorrow, MERRY and PIPPIN charge the ORCS . . .]

MERRY: FOR THE SHIRE!

PIPPIN: AND THE LOVE OF LITTLE APPLES!!

[. . . and run into the waiting arms of their captors.]

LURTZ: Snerk.

[Just as LURTZ is about to finish BOROMIR off, ARAGORN leaps down from, like, a tree or something. There is a lot of shield-throwing and head-butting and knife-batting and, finally, delimbitation and beheaditude. LURTZ goes down sneering to the last. That taken care of, ARAGORN runs to BOROMIR'S side and starts trying to pull out the giant death arrows.]

BOROMIR: No . . . don't try to save me. I'm totally done for.

ARAGORN: But . . . I have the hands of a healer, and stuff!

BOROMIR: No, it's no use. Know that you were a brother to me, and a captain, and a king.

ARAGORN: Which is why that *athelas* really works! I brought some of it with me and everything—

BOROMIR: *death nod*

ARAGORN [*sniffling*]: May bunnies hop thee to thy rest.

LEGOLAS: I find myself strangely touched by this scene of human mortality, as if I were not quite acquainted with the concept.

GIMLI: *sob*

Some Great River

SAM: Mr Frodo! You're not leavin' without me!

FRODO: Except for the part where I totally am, Sam!

[SAM starts doggy-paddling out to FRODO'S departing boat.]

FRODO: You can't swim!

SAM: *can't swim*

FRODO: SAM!

SAM: *glug glug glug*

[After we watch SAM drown stylishly for a few minutes, FRODO fishes him out and hauls him into the boat.]

SAM: I promised Dead Mr Gandalf that I'd take care of you!

FRODO: Yeah, well . . . you just leave the large bodies of water to me, okay?

[And then they cuddle. What? You laugh like I'm making that up.]

II. THE TWO TOWERS (2002)

- - - - - - - - - - - - - - - - - - -

Previously on 'Lord of the Rings' . . .

The BALROG *coughs up a ginormous fire belch.* 'GANDAAAALF!'
GANDALF *has parked himself in front of the* BALROG. *'I am the ser-
vant of the Shakespearean Delivery, wielder of the Really Awesome
Tree Branch! The belching of fire will not avail you!'* 'Dude, he
broke fire?' 'THAT'S RIGHT, BITCH! AND TELL 'EM
MITHRANDIR SENT YA!' WHP-CHAAAAA! 'RUN, FOOLS!'
'NOOOOOOOOOO OOOOOOOOOOOOOOOOOOOOOO
OOOOOOOOOOOOOOOOOOOOOOOOOOOOOOOOOOO
OOOOOOOOOOOOOOOOOOOOOOOOOOOOOOOOOOO
OOOOOOOOOOOOOOOOOOOOOOOOOOOOOOOOOOO
OOOOOOOOOOOOOOOOOOOOOOOOOOOOO!!!!!!!!'*

Some Desolate Mountainside

FRODO [*sitting up with a jerk*]: Sam! I had this terrible dream!
Gandalf was there, and Boromir was there – and you were there!

SAM: That's because we really were there, Mr Frodo.

FRODO: Oh. Where'd you get that shortbread from?

SAM: Galadriel gave it to me.

FRODO: You sure? I really don't remember that.

SAM: You were *there*, Mr Frodo.

  [After a light snack, the HOBBITS start marching through the
  mountain passes again.]

SAM [*sighing*]: The one place we don't want to go is the place we
have to go, but we can't get there.

FRODO: Well, we're just one rainy day away from an Alanis
Morissette song, aren't we?

  [It rains.]

Later That Night

GOLLUM leaps down on the sleeping HOBBITS like froggy death from above:

SAM: MR FRODOOOO! HE'S CHOKING MNNNNNNGH—

FRODO: LET THE FATTY GO OR I CUT YOU.

SAM: HEY!

[GOLLUM does, and gets a leash of Elven rope for his trouble. He flails around, yowling and gurglewailing like a two year old having a tantrum until . . .]

FRODO: Hey, where'd we get this rope from?

GOLLUM: Nasssty rope, twisted by Elveses! It burrrrrrns, it freeeeezes . . . except . . . that kind of makes it feel like when we puts our handses in the two bowls of water like they made us do in school . . .

FRODO: *Elves?*

SAM: YOU WERE THERE, MR FRODO!

GOLLUM: We swears on the evil, treacherous jewellery to do what you wants! Including but not limited to taking Masster and the fat hobbit to Mordor!

SAM: THIS IS A BAD IDEA. PS – I AM JUST BIG-BONED.

FRODO: You got a better one?

SAM: . . .

FRODO: I didn't think so.

Orcs on the Move

MERRY and PIPPIN are riding along, bound to their captors' backs.

PIPPIN: Oh, if only we had some breadcrumbs to drop!

MERRY: Yeah, but you ate all the breadcrumbs, *Pip*.

PIPPIN: What about pebbles?

MERRY: Yeah, *you* try to reach down there and grab some. Hey – what about your Elven leaf brooch?

PIPPIN: My what?

MERRY: Your Elven leaf brooch! That came with the cloaks Galadriel gave us! We can drop that!

PIPPIN [*looking down*]: Ooo, shiny.

The Legend of the Three Hunters

ARAGORN, LEGOLAS and, to a lesser extent, GIMLI run over the mountains and the plains and the hills and the dales looking for MERRY and PIPPIN. They will run for many blocks. They can run faster than a fox. They will run over many rocks. They should not run in just their socks. They will not stop without their friends. They wish for a Mercedes Benz.

The Tower of Isengard

SARUMAN consults the MAGIC 8-BALL.

SAURON: How's that army coming?

SARUMAN: Pretty good.

SAURON: Sweet.

The Montage of Isengard

SARUMAN: THE MIGHT OF SAURON and Saruman WILL RULE THE EARTH! The world will burn in the fires of industry, where children will work in sweatshops, women will receive less per paycheque than men and SUVs will suck up all our oil reserves!

[SARUMAN'S ORCS cut all the trees of Isengard down, in a scene so important that it is actually recycled from the first movie, so you better pay attention. The shambling ORCS also harvest some more

URUKS from the mud baths. Then SARUMAN goes to rouse the ire of the hairy people.]

SARUMAN: You're Neanderthals, and it's all the Horsey People's fault!

THE HAIRY PEOPLE: RAAAAA!

The Unhappy Land of the Horsey People

PEASANTS: *run around on fire, die*

The Golden Hall

ÉOMER: É! Gonna need a little help here!

[ÉOWYN, the ~~Dark Green Velvet~~ White Lady of Rohan, runs to her brother's aid, only to discover that he has brought their half-dead cousin back from battle.]

ÉOWYN: *Ohhhh.*

ÉOMER: Yeah . . . help me push his intestines back in.

[Some time later, ÉOWYN and ÉOMER go to plead their case to their mysteriously decrepit UNCLE-KING:]

ÉOMER: Uncle! The Neanderthals are burning our villages and the Orcs are killing our people – on *Saruman's* orders!

ÉOWYN: Also, your son is slightly dead.

WORMTONGUE: That's a lie! No villain ever wore white! I mean, *really*.

[ÉOMER tosses down an ORC helmet stamped with SARUMAN'S white-hand device.]

ÉOMER: QED, bitch.

THÉODEN: Apple sauce . . . My oatmeal is too lumpy . . . Where are my dentures . . .?

WORMTONGUE: I don't think your poor, ailing uncle appreciates your *warmongering*, Éomer.

ÉOMER: *WARMONGERING?* I do not think that word means what you think it means.

WORMTONGUE: Well, it . . . refers to the . . . monging of war, right . . . ?

ÉOMER: I think it means I get to kick your ass, and STOP GIVING MY SISTER THE GLAD EYE!

[WORMTONGUE summons his HENCHMEN via telepathy and banishes ÉOMER from the kingdom.]

ÉOMER: You can't do that!

WORMTONGUE: I can so! Your uncle signed a warrant in the extended version!

ÉOMER: DAMN YOU, SNAKE!

The Legend of the Three Hunters, Three Days Later

ARAGORN: running. LEGOLAS: running. GIMLI: somewhat running. Running, running, running. They run into a SCRUFFY CASTAWAY DOCTOR and a FUGITIVE WITH A HEART OF GOLD who looks suspiciously like KATE BECKINSALE.

SCRUFFY CASTAWAY DOCTOR: Not idly do the leaves of Driveshaft fa . . .

  [The two search parties stop dead and stare at each other for a moment.]

SCRUFFY DOCTOR: I say we both turn around and pretend this never happened.

ARAGORN: Agreed.

Night Falls on the Orc Camp

MERRY and PIPPIN sit tied up while the ORCS, who all have names that look like a random handful of Scrabble tiles, argue over dinner:

UGLÚK: The boss said that they have to be UNSPOILED!

SNAGA: Well, if we eat 'em fast, they won't have *time* to spoil!

[UGLÚK deheadifies SNAGA and feeds him to the others.]

PIPPIN: Merry Merry Merry we have to go NOW.

MERRY: Crawl like the wind!

GRISHNÁKH: More for me, then— COME BACK, MAGGOTS!

[Suddenly, the DEUS EX HORSEY PEOPLE arrive and lay a second course of stabnation on the ORCS. MERRY and PIPPIN are trampled to death and never see home again.]

PIPPIN: Wait, we are?

Riders of Rohan

ARAGORN: Legolas! What do your Elf eyes see?

LEGOLAS: A sanguine sun rises. Blood has been—

ARAGORN: Cool it, Tennyson.

LEGOLAS: Hey, you ASKED. Oh, and I also see a large troop of armed cavalry coming. Might wanna hide, and stuff.

[But ARAGORN walks right up to them –]

ARAGORN: Riders of Rohan, what up?

[– and gets a faceful of spear for his trouble. The three are quickly surrounded.]

ÉOMER: What business do an Elf, a Man and a Dwarf have in Horseyland?

GIMLI: I dunno, do they walk into a bar?

[Touchy banter quickly devolves into an armed standoff.]

ARAGORN: COOL IT, ALL RIGHT? Look, I'm the heir of Isildur, Blondie over there's an Elf prince and the Dwarf – well, he's got a lot of personality, let's put it that way. We are friends of the Horsey People and of your king.

ÉOMER: Well, it's not going to do you any good, let me tell you what. He's my *uncle*, and you see how we all ended up. Saruman's gone bad and his slimy little henchman's got my uncle under his thumb and my sister on his mind. I was the only one who stood up to him, so for that, we are banished.

ARAGORN: *Dude.*

ÉOMER: For serious, man. You watch out for the White Wizard. I hear he's wandering around here like he's got nothing better to do. I don't even trust pastels any more, myself [*glaring at* LEGOLAS].

ARAGORN: Look, we're not spies – we're just following some Uruks around looking for our friends. About yea high [*holds hand out very low*], yea wide [*spreads hands out very wide*] . . . ?

ÉOMER: Uh . . . we ran into those Uruks last night. We killed everything on two legs, hacked them up, burnt the pieces and spat on them. So, uh . . . sorry about that?

Some Burning Pile of Corpses

GIMLI pokes around in the smouldering ashes and finds . . .

GIMLI: Their tiny Elven belts! Oh noes!

ARAGORN: Elven belts?

LEGOLAS: You know, the ones they got in the extended version. Which is incontrovertible proof that they're dead, because everyone knows that belts aren't removable, and totally don't have buckles for that purpose.

ARAGORN [*kicking helmet in rage*]: AHHHHHHHHHHHHHH-HHHH!

LEGOLAS: Man, that is some good acting right there.

ARAGORN: AWWWGHHHH . . . !

GIMLI: Okay, dude, we didn't like those guys *that* much.

ARAGORN: WAAAAGHHHH . . . !

LEGOLAS: You okay, man?

ARAGORN: HAGGGHHHHH . . . yeah . . . I'll . . . walk it off . . .

[In the midst of his grief, ARAGORN notices certain telltale tracks and starts dragging himself across the ground to follow them.]

ARAGORN: Look! Right here! [*Draaaaag.*] Tiny footprints . . . [*draaaaag*] that go towards the forest . . . [*draaaaag*].

Fangorn Forest, Some Time Later

TREEBEARD: And soooo . . . I was miiiinding my own buuuuuusiness when these twoooo wooooodchucks—

QUICKBEAM: Woooodchucks?

TREEBEARD: Hooooom . . . maybe they were baaaadgers. Aaaaanyway, these twoooo wooooodchucks were climbing up my faaaaace, and then this Orrrrrrc—

QUICKBEAM: BURRRRARRRRUMAHOOM!

TREEBEARD: I knooooow! He was stuuuuck fuuuuulll of spearrrrrrs like a porcupiiiiine, tooooooo! Heeeeere, help meeeee puuuuuull them out of my rooooooot . . .

PIPPIN [*on* TREEBEARD'S *shoulder*]: Hey, didn't you say you were taking us to a white wizard or something?

MERRY [*on* TREEBEARD'S *head*]: SHUT UP, PIP!

Some Marshes Full of Dead People

GOLLUM: Don't follow the lights. By which we means 'corpses'.

FRODO: Hey, those corpses are remarkably well preserved, considering that . . . [*Falls down.*]

GOLLUM: Is Masster always so bad at following directions?

SAM: Pretty much, yeah.

Later That Night

GOLLUM [*sneering*]: Is Mr Frodo up touching his ring again?

FRODO: Oh, like you have room to talk, *Sméagol*.

[GOLLUM'S nostalgic wibbling over being called by his proper name is interrupted by—]

RINGWRAITH: SHREEEEEEEEEEEEE!

RINGWRAITH'S NEWLY PIMPED RIDE: ROAAAAAAR!

GOLLUM: Wraiths! With *upgrades*!

SAM: I thought the Elf princess drowned them!

GOLLUM: Fat hobbit is new at this, isn't he?

The White Wizard Is Nigh

ARAGORN, LEGOLAS and GIMLI go prowling through Fangorn Forest in search of MERRY and PIPPIN –

ARAGORN: Legolas! What do your Elf ears hear?

LEGOLAS: Really, really bitchy trees, smartass.

[– but instead find that WIZARD ÉOMER was talking about. Sort of.]

SARUDALF: I found the hobbits you seek.

ARAGORN: That's bad.

GANDUMAN: And I let them go.

ARAGORN: That's good.

SANDUMAN: Into a forest full of man-eating trees.

ARAGORN: That's bad.

GARUDALF: In the custody of someone who can help them.

ARAGORN: That's good.

SANDUMALF: That someone is a tree.

ARAGORN: . . .

[The WIZARD ends their confusion by revealing himself to be – TOTALLY NOT DEAD GANDALF!]

GANDALF: I fought my enemy through fire and water, which became steam, which is really good for your pores –

LEGOLAS [*admiringly*]: Really, you look like a new man.

[We see GANDALF and the BALROG on a snowy mountainside, and GANDALF is totally whaling on him with an electrified sword.]

GANDALF: – and then I took by the throat the circumcisèd Balrog and smote him thus!

ARAGORN: I'm not even going to ask how you knew that.

GANDALF: And then I died, and became one with the universe, but then the powers that be sent me back to finish my mission, and I became white instead of grey, and Galadriel hooked me up with all the accessories, and here I am.

ARAGORN: Thanks for narrating that flashback for us.

GANDALF: Well, you know, I learned after the last time.

ARAGORN: Hey, before we leave . . . could you take a look at my foot here . . . ?

A Magical, Sunny Meadow

GANDALF whistles for SHADOWFAX, the Lord of Magical Horses, who comes bounding up in slo-mo, ivory mane rippling in the breeze.

LEGOLAS: I've wanted a horse like that ever since I was a little girl.

GANDALF: What?

Fangorn Forest

TREEBEARD: . . . keeeeeeep those poplarrrrrrs rolliiiin', Barkhiiiiiide!
MERRY AND PIPPIN: *clap along*

The Black Gates

FRODO: Hide! Soldiers are coming!

SAM: Use your Elvish invisibility cloak, Mr Frodo!

FRODO: What? When'd I get one of those?

SAM: Galadriel, dude!

FRODO: Man, did I just sleep through that or what?

SOLDIER 1: You see anything?

SOLDIER 2: Nope, just a cloth rock. Let's go.

Front Porch of Woe

ÉOWYN: Here I am in my pretty white dress, trapped in a tiny mountaintop village full of coarse, dirty people who don't appreciate me—

WORMTONGUE [*inside hall*]: My lady, are you sure you don't want to talk about your dead cousin some more? My neck rubs are famous in times of tragedy!

ÉOWYN: YES, I'M SURE, AND IF YOU TOUCH ME ONE MORE TIME I'M GETTING A RESTRAINING ORDER! [*Sigh.*] Oh, how I wish someone *fine* would come along and sex me up!

   [On the plains below, GANDALF and COMPANY ride up.]

ARAGORN: Who's the babe?

GANDALF: Oh, that's King Théoden's sister-daughter.

ARAGORN: EW.

GANDALF: His *niece*, dude.

ARAGORN: Oh, well, that's different.

GANDALF: Yeah, well, watch out for her. She's, uh, *extremely lonely*, if you know what I mean. If she starts asking about the length of your sword, *run*.

[The COMPANY is met by the dumbfounded stares of several PEASANTS in their best mourning rags. At the Golden Hall itself, they are greeted by an ARMED POSSE.]

HÁMA: I'm afraid you have to check your weapons here. By order of Snaky McEvilpants. You know.

[With much eye-rolling, the BOYS hand over two bows, two quivers, four knives, a bitch-ass long sword, a nail file –]

LEGOLAS: What? You think it's *easy* to maintain a French manicure?

[– and sixteen axes.]

HÁMA: That includes your staff, Mr Gandalf.

GANDALF: Awww, do I have to? I mean, I'm so old and frail, I couldn't *possibly* kick Snaky McEvilpants' ass for you and heal your king and solve all your problems.

HÁMA: Gonna have to take your staff, sir.

GANDALF: I SAID—

HÁMA: No exceptions.

GANDALF: *puppy-dog eyes*

HÁMA: Your staff.

GANDALF [*wave of hand*]: This is not the staff you are looking for.

HÁMA: Totally not the staff. Give my regards to the king!

[Upon entering the hall, they are immediately shadowed by WORMTONGUE'S HENCHMEN. GANDALF leans heavily on pretty, pretty LEGOLAS'S arm.]

LEGOLAS: Oh, that's really smart, acting like you're so old and frail and all.

GANDALF: What? Oh. Yes. Because I'm frail. That's totally why I'm leaning on you. Now, scoot a little closer to Grandpa, would you?

WORMTONGUE: HEY, I SAID NO WIZARDS—!

[The BOYS throw WORMTONGUE and his HENCHMEN a barehanded stealth beating while GANDALF exorcises THÉODEN from the influence of . . .]

GANDALF: *Saruman?*

SARUDEN: MOO HA HA! HORSEYLAND IS MINE!

ÉOWYN [*running in*]: WHAT ARE YOU DOING TO MY UNCLE?!

ARAGORN [*grabbing her close*]: Ma'am, I'm afraid I'm going to have to detain you while the wizard does his thing.

ÉOWYN: Well, I guess if you put it that way . . . Hey, are you wearing Old Spice?

SARUDEN: I DEFY YOU, BROKEDOWN WIZARD!

[GANDALF flings off his grey cloak and stuns SARUDEN with the brightness of his whites and the thorough – but gentle! – cleaning power of his detergent. With a few extra staff jabs, GANDALF sends SARUMAN packing. ÉOWYN runs to her uncle and holds him while SARUMAN'S influence fades, taking several decades of crusty overgrowth with it. THÉODEN takes his sword back in hand for the first time in many months. And then he decides to kick WORMTONGUE'S ass.]

ARAGORN: No, my lord! We're going to need him later for a plot point!

THÉODEN: But it's only going to be in the extended version of the movie! No one's going to miss him! *Come on!*

ARAGORN: But then millions of fans who *will* buy the DVDs will be terribly disappointed when Wormtongue isn't there to do the thing! You know! *The important thing.*

THÉODEN [*putting down sword*]: Hey, who are you, anyway?

GANDALF: Hail, Théoden King!

EVERYONE [*bowing*]: Hail!

GANDALF: You too, Aragorn.

ARAGORN: GAH.

THÉODEN: So, where is my son?

EVERYONE: . . .

THÉODEN: I SAID, WHERE IS MY SON?

EVERYONE: *looks down, kicks dirt*

The Flowery Graves of the Horsey Kings

THÉODEN weeps at his son's grave while GANDALF stands around not being helpful, and stuff.

SOME HORSE: Hey, I've got an order here for two starved kids . . . ?

The Golden Hall

ÉOWYN makes sure that the two REFUGEE KIDS get plenty of bread and soup while the MENFOLK discuss war, because ÉOWYN is a girrrrrrrrl.

SOME HALF-STARVED LITTLE GIRL: . . . and Papa always said that we mustn't ride the big horse but then Mama said that this was special and besides, Mr Wormtongue says Papa can't live here any more so he doesn't have a lot of say in things lately and I don't know why but Mama cries a lot now and Éothain is always telling me to pipe down but I don't see why I can't ask questions or what pipes have to do with it anyway—

ÉOWYN [*stuffing bread in* GIRL'S *mouth*]: Here, kid, eat up.

GANDALF: So: war.

THÉODEN: No dice. All my best men are on the other side of Rohan –

GANDALF: And whose fault is *that*?

THÉODEN: – AND I DON'T WANT ANY MORE OF MY PEOPLE DYING, SHUT UP.

ARAGORN: I think they're pretty much getting mowed down whether you like it or not.

ÉOWYN: I agree with *him*.

THÉODEN: Éowyn? Go make me a pot pie or something.

354

The Stables of Edoras

GANDALF: Grumble grumble run like cowards grumble.

ARAGORN: I know, I know.

GANDALF: I mean, you realize he's holing all his people up in a deathtrap, right? So, if you're still alive five days from now, look to the east and I'll have Éomer's men with me. If I can find them. Oh, and watch out for the lady, if you know what I mean. Shadowfax, away!

ARAGORN: Wait, if *I'm* alive—?

LEGOLAS [*sadly*]: Bye bye, horsie!

Éowyn, Sex-Starved Daughter of Kings

ÉOWYN: I thought you would have a bigger sword than that.

ARAGORN: This? Oh, this is just a knife. I have a much longer sword in my—

ÉOWYN: *raises eyebrow*

ARAGORN: I have to go now.

Exodus from Edoras

All the dirty PEASANTS pile their meagre belongings and best potatoes into wheelbarrows to march on down to Helm's Deep. ÉOWYN does not share her advanced hair-brushing technology with the other REFUGEES.

The Forests of Ithilien

GOLLUM runs on ahead and splashes around in the river and catches himself a fish.

FRODO: Saaaaaaaam, I'm tired . . .

SAM: Just a little further, Mr Frodo.

FRODO: Saaaaaaaam, I'm *hungry* . . .

SAM: Let me dig up some *lembas*, Mr Fro—

FRODO: I'M SICK OF MOLDY FRICKIN' ELF CRACKERS AND I'M SICK OF WALKING ALL NIGHT AND ALL DAY AND I'M SICK OF HIS WHINING AND *I'M SICK OF YOUR FACE*! **WHAT ARE *YOU* LOOKING AT, FISH??**

SAM: Here, Mr Frodo? Have some of my Midol.

The Two Faces of Sméag

Later that night . . .

GOLLUM: Hooooooo, Masster is a cranky Masster.

SMÉAGOL: Can you blame him? I'm sick of fat hobbit's face, too.

GOLLUM: Masster still likes fat hobbit better than you! You're a liar, and a coward, and a thief, and a murderer, and—

SMÉAGOL: Wait, aren't you me?

GOLLUM: Don't change the subject!

SMÉAGOL: Go away!

GOLLUM: But if I *am* you, I can't go away, now can I?

SMÉAGOL: That's not fair! Either you're me or you're not, you can't argue it both ways—

FRODO [*half-asleep*]: Damn, take a Paxil, all right? SOME OF US are trying to SLEEP!

SAM [*waking up*]: Who needs Paxil? I have Paxil!

Lunchbreak in Ithilien

In a desperate bid to be loved, ~~GOLLUM~~ SMÉAGOL has captured the WIDOW WIGGLES and the LITTLEST WIGGLES for FRODO'S nuncheon.

FRODO: Saaaaaam, I'm huuuuungry.

SAM: Here, Mr Frodo, have some of my rabbit stew.

GOLLUM: AIEEEEE! FAT HOBBIT SPOILS THE WIGGLESES!

FRODO: Look over there! Elephants!

[VAGUELY MIDDLE-EASTERN TROOPS are marching through the forest with their ELEPHANTS OF WAR –]

SAM: They're called OLIPHAUNTS, Mr Frodo! *Gah.*

[– when suddenly CAMOUFLAGED STEALTH RANGERS start shooting and a battle breaks out.]

FRODO: Uh, Sam – I think we should— Sam? Dead bodies are falling on me and even Gollum made a run for it and I think we really ought to go now . . . HELP! SAM!

Five Minutes Later

FARAMIR: And you picked these badgers up *where*?

SOME RANGER: Just over there, watching the battle. Clearly they're spies, sir.

FARAMIR: Not very good ones.

SOME RANGER: Touché.

FARAMIR: What is that, stew? Eh, bring 'em along.

Refugees on the March

While THÉODEN and the HORSEY PEOPLE laugh at GIMLI'S hapless, vertically challenged antics, ÉOWYN makes her play.

ÉOWYN: So . . . who gave you the necklace? A girl?

ARAGORN: What makes you say that?

ÉOWYN: Please, it's a *diamond flower*. Either a girl bought that for you, or I'm soooo barking up the wrong tree.

Arwen's Room, Somewhere

ARAGORN meets ARWEN telepathically. Or in a flashback. Or in a dream. Or something. Her lingerie is from Valinor's Secret.

ARWEN [*pressing his hand to her chest*]: Trust in us.

ARAGORN: What, you and your breasts?

ARWEN: No, *you and me*.

ARAGORN: Oh.

ARWEN: . . . and my breasts, sure.

ARAGORN: Yay!

Refugees on the March

ÉOWYN: Aragorn? That explains nothing, because I can't hear your flashback.

ARAGORN: Oh. Yeah. Gandalf said he was going to help me out with that, but . . . had to go save the world and everything. You know.

The Extremely Pissy Wolves of Isengard

GAMLING: WARGS!

HÁMA: Say what?

GAMLING: Giant pissy rodentwolves of unusual size!

HÁMA: Oh, I don't believe they exist.

WARG: *CHOMP!*

[There is charging and snarling and spearing and chewing of heads. The HORSEY PEOPLE win, but just barely.]

LEGOLAS: Where is Aragorn?

SOME DYING ORC: Oh, that dude who fell off the cliff?

358

LEGOLAS [*grabbing* ORC]: How do you know his name? How did you get his necklace? *What happened to him??*

SOME DYING ORC: Dude, he *fell. off. the cliff.*

LEGOLAS: But – they've got a whole other movie named after him! Like, I saw the trailer and everything!

THÉODEN: Them's the breaks, kid.

The Fortress of Helm's Deep

ÉOWYN: Uncle, you've made it back safely!

THÉODEN: Well, almost everyone else got eaten, but yeah, I made it back.

REFUGEE PEASANTS: YAY!

GIMLI [*choked up*]: My lady . . . Aragorn fell.

ÉOWYN: Well, I'm sure we have some Band-Aids around here somewhere—

GIMLI: *Off a cliff.*

ÉOWYN: I'm going to die a virgin, aren't I?

The Tower of Isengard

WORMTONGUE: So . . . you're going to take down the fortress walls *how*, exactly?

SARUMAN: Well, if you don't get that candle out of here, you're about to find out in a big way, is all I'm saying.

WORMTONGUE: Okay, so you break down the walls. What then? You don't have an army of—

SARUMAN: Ten thousand Orcs? Look out the window.

TEN THOUSAND ORCS: RAAAAAAAAAAAA!

SARUMAN: WIPE THE HORSEY PEOPLE FROM THE EARTH!

SPILL THEIR HORSEY BLOOD AND EAT THEIR HORSEY MARROW! TO WARRRR!

[WORMTONGUE realizes that he has betrayed his own race, his own people, and that, thanks to him, none may be left by the next sunrise.]

WORMTONGUE: I'm going to die a virgin, aren't I?

Some River

It is a little-known fact that Elves actually invented the Kiss of Life.

LESS-DEAD-THAN-PREVIOUSLY-SUSPECTED ARAGORN: Will someone explain to me how one moment I'm kissing my ethereal girlfriend and the next moment I'm kissing a horse?

BREGO: Look, you don't want a rescue, I can go back to Rohan by myself.

Arwen's Doom

ELROND: Hurry, Arwen! Everyone's leaving for the ship to the Undying Lands!

[ARWEN is lying on her bed, because reviving your boyfriend with your mind eats up a lot of energy.]

ARWEN: I'm staying, Daddy! I love him!

ELROND: But even if he *doesn't* get killed in the next movie and a half, and even if he *does* live to be, like, two hundred and fifty years old – you're still going to end up alone! In the dark! In the cold!

[She has a vision: QUEEN ARWEN buries AGED KING ARAGORN in a tomb with the marker 'DEVOTED KING, HUSBAND, FATHER AND SON', next to a small crypt bearing the inscription 'LOVING COMPANION, EXCELLENT BUNNY'.]

ARWEN: I still want to stay.

ELROND: NO DAUGHTER OF MINE IS REPLICATING WITH A MORTAL!

ARWEN: *But Daddy!*

ELROND: NOW PUT ON A WARM CLOAK AND MARCH, YOUNG LADY.

Galadriel Calls Elrond Up on the Telepathephone

GALADRIEL: Hey, babe?

ELROND: Yeah?

GALADRIEL: When Finarfin grounded me and forbade me to see Annatar, did *I* listen?

ELROND: . . .

GALADRIEL: Leave a light on for the kid. She'll be back. I'm just saying.

Faramir's Cool Cave Command Center

FARAMIR and his lieutenant MADRIL pore over maps marked with SAURON and SARUMAN'S advancing troops.

FARAMIR: We're screwed, aren't we?

MADRIL: Yeah, pretty much.

The Debriefing Cave

FARAMIR: So, badgers—

SAM: We're not badgers!

FARAMIR: Badgers, groundhogs, whatever. If you're not spies, why are you here, again?

FRODO: We left Rivendell in a Fellowship of Nine Walkers on a

Very Important Mission that . . . I can't really tell you about. Sorry. But Aragorn, son of Arathorn, and Boromir of Gondor came with us, they'd vouch for us. You know either one of them?

FARAMIR: Yeah, I kind of know Boromir. In the sense that we both came from the same womb. So I'd be real interested if you could tell me how he DIED.

FRODO: Died? What? When? Where? How? Why?!

FARAMIR: Look, that's what I'm asking *you*, gopher.

FRODO: Help! What do I say?

SAM: Mr Frodo? I got nothin'.

The Forbidden Pool

MADRIL: Hey! Badger!

SAM [*sleepily*]: Wha . . . ?

FARAMIR: Not the fat badger, the other one.

SAM: HEY!

FARAMIR: You! Come with me if you want the froggy one to live.

[FARAMIR takes FRODO to the edge of the Super Secret Forbidden Pool: GOLLUM is down below, splishing around happily and beating out the brains of some poor fish. After using FRODO to capture GOLLUM, FARAMIR has GOLLUM hauled off to . . .]

The Interrogation Cave

FARAMIR: Okay, woodchucks – I just spent half an hour watching that froggy bastard stroke himself and coo, so you *better* have what I think you have, because that is half an hour of my life that I am never, ever getting back.

FRODO: *cowers*

SAM: Please, Mr Faramir, sir – we're going to Mordor to destroy it! It's made Mr Frodo so sick – won't you help us?

FARAMIR: Ohhhhhh, this is *so* a chance to show my quality.

SAM: I knew you would—

FARAMIR: Madril, get some giftwrap and a bow – Dad's gonna love this. TO GONDOR!

TOLKIEN FANS: *start writing angry letters*

Return of the . . . Not-So-Much-Actually King

ARAGORN staggers into the fortress looking like fifteen kinds of ~~sexy, sexy~~ ass. ÉOWYN is about to jump him when LEGOLAS beats her to the punch and returns ARAGORN'S pretty, pretty pendant. They smile at each other meaningfully.

ÉOWYN: Wow. Wrong tree it is, then. Who knew?

Entmoot, the Mooting of Ents

TREEBEARD gathers all the other ENTS to discuss whether they should help fight SARUMAN.

TREEBEARD: Fellooooooow leaaaaaf-bearrrrrers aaaaaand rooooooot-waaaaaalkers . . . weeeeeeee . . . arrrrrrrrrrre . . . gaaaaaatherrrrrred . . . heeeeeeeere . . . toniiiiiiiight . . .

MERRY: There's going to be a battle in like fifteen minutes! TALK FASTER!

Battle Looms at Helm's Deep

The ROHIRRIM sock all the WOMEN and CHILDREN away in pretty, pretty caves, but not before they've gone through and slapped helmets on anything with a Y chromosome and strong enough to lift a sword. Everyone weeps.

THÉODEN: Éowyn, stay down here with the women and children,

because you're a—

ÉOWYN: I KNOW, I KNOW!

* * *

LEGOLAS would like to register a few complaints before the battle starts – in Elvish, of course.

LEGOLAS: *This is ridiculous! Three hundred Men against ten thousand Orcs!*

ARAGORN: *Well, it was either bring them here or just serve them on platters at Edoras.*

LEGOLAS: *I just heard some old guy ask where he left his battle dentures! That kid's sword is taller than he is! Aragorn, they're going to get slaughtered!*

ARAGORN: *What do you want to do, just leave them here, then? As a future King of Men, I belong here with them!*

LEGOLAS: *We're not going to win, Aragorn!*

ARAGORN: WELL, I GUESS WE'RE ALL JUST GOING TO DIE, THEN, AREN'T WE?

EVERYONE ELSE: . . .

ARAGORN: I didn't say that in Elvish, did I?

* * *

THÉODEN: Come, Gamling, bring my armour. The hour grows late, and I have not yet recited my battle poetry.

* * *

ARAGORN: Lemme see that sword. What's your name?

SOME KID: Some Kid, Son of Some Guy, my lord. The men are saying there's no hope and we're all going to be Orc chow by dawn.

364

ARAGORN: This is a good sword, Some Kid, Son of Some Guy. Trust in yourself, and have courage, and do not despair.

SOME KID: Really?

ARAGORN: Well, no – you're probably going to die, but I figure all the big-name characters will get out all right.

* * *

LEGOLAS: Oh, Aragorn, Aragorn! Those five minutes when we weren't speaking were awful! Let's never fight again!

ARAGORN: Pinky swear!

GIMLI [*in comically oversized mail shirt*]: Hey! Look, I'm still short!

* * *

A troop of ELVES arrive in their best battle velvet – turns out ELROND and GALADRIEL have sent their best warriors.

THÉODEN: Aid comes at so late an hour? How can this be?

LEGOLAS: See? I told you Elves rule.

GIMLI: HEY! If my kin were not all rotting away in the mines of Moria, they would have sent a thousand Dwarves! Each armed with a dozen axes! *Ninja* dwarves! With *rocket launchers*!

HALDIR: We come to honour the Alliance of Elves and Men, as seen at the beginning of this film trilogy, although I wouldn't blame you if you'd completely forgotten about it by now.

ARAGORN: Haldir! *Marry me.*

LEGOLAS: *HEY!*

Entmoot, the Mooting of Ents

TREEBEARD: Theeeeeese wooooooodchucks . . . who we agreeeeeeeeed . . . are not Orrrrrrcs . . .

QUICKBEAM: Woooooooodchucks?

TREEBEARD: The wooooooodchucks who we agreeeeeeeed . . . might be baaaaaaadgers or wooooooodchucks . . .

PIPPIN: We're not woodchucks!

BIRCHSEED: Ohhhhhhh. Definitely baaaaaaadgers, thennnnn.

MERRY: WE'RE NOT BADGERS! WE'RE HOBBITS!

LINDENROOT: Are youuuuu suuuuure they're not Orrrrrrcs?

MERRY: OH GOD NOT THIS AGAIN.

The Battle of the Hornburg

THÉODEN: BRING! IT! ONNNN!

[The URUK-HAI blow up the fortress wall, HALDIR dies to the strains of Barber's Adagio for Elves, all the other ELVES get slaughtered and, worst of all, THÉODEN gets nicked in the shoulder.]

THÉODEN: Take it back! TAKE IT BACK!

Entmoot Decides

MERRY: TALK FASTERRRRR!

TREEBEARD: Nowww, nowww, young baaaaaadger . . .

MERRY: THIS IS A BINARY CHOICE! HELP OR DON'T HELP! YES OR NO!

[The ENTS huddle for a moment.]

TREEBEARD: No.

MERRY: What?

TREEBEARD: No. 'Don't help.' Option B, choice the second.

MERRY: Okay. I'm going to say this real slow, so maybe you'll understand it this time: 'decide faster' means *in our favour.*

THE ENTS: . . .

WOOFBARK: Sooooo . . . whooooo's going to giiiiiive them a ride baaaaaaack?

TREEBEARD: I gueeeeeess I will.

MERRY: ARRRRRRRGH!

The Battle of the Hornburg

THÉODEN: RETREAAAAT!

Pippin's One, Shining Moment

TREEBEARD: Sooooo . . . I'll drop youuuuuu twooooo young wooooooodchucks off on the Horrrrrrsey siiiiiide . . .

PIPPIN: Wait, Treebeard! Turn around and go the other way!

TREEBEARD: But . . . thennnnnn we'll paaaaaaaass Iseeeeeeengarrrrrrrd and Saaaaaaarumaaaaan . . .

PIPPIN: Yes! Because, you see, the closer we are to peril, the greater we are in propinquity to jeopardy while at the same time being more parallel to menace, though we may end up perpendicular to risk.

TREEBEARD: . . .

PIPPIN: . . .

TREEBEARD: Waaaaait . . . where arrrrre we goiiiiiing?

PIPPIN: To Isengard!

TREEBEARD: Ohhhhhhh . . . yessssss.

En Route to Some Big White City

FRODO: Faramir! You've got to let us go! PLEASE! The ring won't help Gondor!

FARAMIR: Gag the squirrel if he gives us any more lip, Madril.

MADRIL: Aye, sir.

FRODO: *FARAMIR!*

The Valley of Isengard

TREEBEARD arrives at Isengard and sees what PIPPIN intended for him to see: the complete wrack and ruin of the forest.

TREEBEARD: WHAT TREACHERY IS THIS? BURRRRAR-RRRUMAHOOOOOM!

Some Big White City

En route to Minas Tirith, FARAMIR and his MEN are diverted to a losing battle at Osgiliath.

SAM: Mr Faramir! You have to let us go! The ring made your brother crazy! He tried to take it and kill Frodo—

[Speaking of which . . .]

RINGWRAITH: SHREEEEEEEEEEEEEEE!

[Rather than actually making the NAZGÛL come down, kill FRODO and take the ring, FRODO is thoughtful enough to climb up on some roof and offer it to him. Only FARAMIR shooting the WRAITH'S FELL BEAST and SAM tackling FRODO prevent the total annihilation of everything green and good.]

FARAMIR: *Dude.* That . . . that was totally messed up.

SAM: So you believe us about the ring now?

FARAMIR: Oh yeah.

The Last Stand of the Horsey People

The LAST SURVIVORS of the battle are holed up in the fortress keep, trying to barricade the last door against the ORCS.

ARAGORN: Is there no way for the women and children to escape from the caves?

GAMLING: Well, there's that one way they could have started on twelve hours ago . . .

ARAGORN: WELL, TELL THEM TO GET A MOVE ON!

The Flooding of Isengard

The ENTS break the dam and flood the valley and stomp on all SARUMAN'S ORCS and kick over his machines.

MERRY AND PIPPIN: Whee!

SARUMAN: And I would have gotten away with it, if it weren't for you meddling trees!

Tales That Really Mattered

SAM: I think I understand now, Mr Frodo. It's not about whether the good guys arrive in the nick of time . . .

[GANDALF and ÉOMER arrive just as ARAGORN convinces THÉODEN to meet the ORCS head on.]

SAM: . . . or if the battle is won . . .

[GANDALF and the ROHIRRIM trample the ORCS utterly.]

SAM: . . . or the villain is defeated . . .

[SARUMAN paces around on his tower balcony, completely trapped by the flood waters.]

SAM: . . . or the guy gets the girl.

[ÉOWYN flings herself at ARAGORN.]

FRODO: What is it about, Sam?

SAM: It's about someone finally making a fantasy film that doesn't look like five dollars' worth of tinfoil – about making people believe in new worlds again, reviving kids' imaginations, using make-believe stories to *teach* people something and give them *hope*, instead of just something to laugh at and brush aside!

EVERYONE: . . .

FARAMIR: That was deep, yo.

III. THE RETURN OF THE KING (2003)

A Green Land, A Long Time Ago

DÉAGOL: Sméag! I just found the most awesome gold ring in the river!

SMÉAGOL [*eyes gleaming*]: You know, it's my birthday, precious . . .

DÉAGOL: I know – I got you a really nice pasta-maker.

A Green Land, Five Minutes Later

DÉAGOL: Sméagol! What are you— Stop! Nooooo! I promise, it's a really nice pasta-mMNNNNNNNGHHHH! [*Dies.*]

Journey to the Crossroads

FRODO: Saaaaaaaam, I'm huuuuungry.

SAM: Here, Mr Frodo, have some of my *lembas*.

GOLLUM: Hurry, hobbitses! To the crossroads!

  [We do not actually see the crossroads.]

The Ruins of Isengard

MERRY: Welcome, my lords, to Treebeard's Snack Shack, established approximately five minutes ago!

PIPPIN: We are *soooooo high*!

MERRY: WOOOOO!

THÉODEN: I've never seen dudes this little before, but I like their style.

GANDALF: Hey, Rockbiter, where's Saruman?

TREEBEARD: Uh . . . he's just . . . ressssting. Yesssss. At a faaar-rrm. We sent him to a faaaarrrrm, where heeeee can play with . . . uh, all the oooooother . . . eeeevil wizarrrrrds.

LEGOLAS: Awww, that's so nice.

PIPPIN: Look! A Magic 8-Ball over there in the water!

GANDALF [*snatching it away*]: MINE NOT YOURS!

PIPPIN: *pouts*

Front Porch of Woe 2: Electric Woegaloo

ÉOWYN: Sigh.

Smoky Hall of the Horsey People

THÉODEN: Hail the victorious dead!

GIMLI: Isn't being dead pretty much the definition of *not* being vic—

ARAGORN: *smacks him*

GIMLI: OW!

ÉOWYN: Themanwholovesmedrinksfromthiscup?

ARAGORN: What?

ÉOWYN: Drink from this cup?

ARAGORN: Sure thing.

ÉOWYN: WOOT!

THÉODEN: I congratulate you on landing Sir Scruffalot.

ÉOWYN [*scribbling on her binder*]: *Lady Éowyn . . . Mr and Mrs*

Aragorn Elessar . . . Éowyn, Queen of Gondor . . .

[PIPPIN and MERRY do-si-do boozily on the tables while GANDALF and ARAGORN watch.]

ARAGORN: So. Sucks to be Frodo right now.

GANDALF: Yeah, pretty much.

ARAGORN: You think he's gonna make it?

GANDALF: Well, it ain't called *Return of the Hobbit*, so . . .

ARAGORN: Yikes.

Night in Ithilien

GOLLUM: The hobbitses are asleep! Let's plot their murder out loud, and at the tops of our voiceseses!

SMÉAGOL: Yes, precious!

SAM: I'LL KILL YOU BEFORE YOU KILL US!

FRODO: No, Sam! We need Gollum's orienteering savvy and fine navigational skills to survive!

GOLLUM: PTHBBBBBBBT!

Pyjama Party at the Golden Hall

Everyone is asleep, except for LEGOLAS and ARAGORN on the front porch . . .

LEGOLAS: I sense a sleepless eye ogling us from behind the veil of the East.

ARAGORN: Yeah? And what does your Elf nose smell?

LEGOLAS: I'm telling you – if you don't quit it, I'm gonna plant my Elf foot up your Man ass.

[. . . and PIPPIN inside the Golden Hall, where he falls prey to the lure of the MAGIC 8-BALL:]

PIPPIN: AHHHHHH! BAD TOUCH! BAD TOUCH!

[Everyone wakes up and starts running around and a game of Hot Potato breaks out –]

LEGOLAS: Grab it, grab it!

ARAGORN: HOT HOT HOT!

[– ending with GANDALF throwing a blanket over the MAGIC 8-BALL.]

GANDALF: YOU TOTAL FUCKWIT—

PIPPIN: *drools blankly*

GANDALF: I didn't mean it, Pippin! *Speak to me!*

[Ten minutes later:]

GANDALF: So the long and short of it is, Pippin's too dumb to give anything away, but he was at least able to glimpse some of Sauron's big plan, which is to attack Minas Tirith next and eventually destroy all mankind, so if the Beacon Alert System goes off, Rohan must be ready to join the fight.

THÉODEN: And I care about Minas Tirith why . . . ?

GANDALF: Because Horsey People are mankind too, *fool*. Oh, and I'm taking the stupid hobbit with me.

PIPPIN: That's a terrible thing to say about Merry!

MERRY: Sigh.

Some Sylvan Glade

FIGWIT: Hi. I'm that guy who had three seconds of screen time sitting next to Aragorn at the council in the first movie. There was such an outpouring of love and admiration for my Elfy self that I now have my own fansite and trading card. I would like to thank all my f—

FANS: Hey, could you move over to the right a little?

FIGWIT: Sure thing, I—

ARWEN: *rides in*

FANS: Oooo, pretty.

SAD ELVISH MUSIC: *is woeful*

> [ARWEN has another vision: ARAGORN will be king, and he will live in Minas Tirith, and he will go grey but still look really studly, and he will have an adorable kid.]

ARWEN: *tear*

KID: *googly Elvish stare*

EVENSTAR AROUND KID'S NECK: *ding!*

ARWEN: OMGWTF THAT'S *MY* KID!

FIGWIT: My lady, the sea that will eternally part you from—

ARWEN: OUTTA MY WAY, I GOT SOME CHILDBEARING TO DO!

FIGWIT'S SCREENTIME: *is over*

FIGWIT: Sigh.

The Last Homely House

ARWEN: All right, let's try this one more time. You looked into my future. What, *exactly*, did you see?

ELROND: Death.

ARWEN: LIAH!

ELROND: *hangs head*

Some Big White City With a Big Ol' Chunk of Stone Sticking Out Of It

GANDALF: So, you know, the whole thing with Frodo and the ring and Aragorn and the Magic 8-Ball and stuff?

PIPPIN: Yeah?

GANDALF: Here's you, right here: *Portrait of a Hobbit Shutting Up*.

PIPPIN: . . .

GANDALF: Lord Denethor: greetings, salutations, and hi. I have been single-handedly keeping Middle-earth's shit together for several months and—

DENETHOR: I HATE YOU AND YOU SUCK!

GANDALF: FUCK YOU TOO!

PIPPIN: Please, Lord Mr Denethor, sir, your son died for us and I'm really really sorry about that and if there's anything my smallness can do for you . . .

DENETHOR: *gives Pippin a wizened stink-eye*

PIPPIN [*to* GANDALF]: You know, this went over a lot better in the book.

GANDALF: *whacks Pippin with staff*

Some Balcony at the Big White City

PIPPIN [*holding up tiny armour*]: You know, I didn't think he'd take me up on it.

GANDALF [*smoking*]: Don't even talk to me, noob.

PIPPIN: What are you so cranky about, anyway?

GANDALF: Well, for one, the fact that Sauron is about to reveal his most terrifying henchman, one that will make you wet yourself and beg for death – the Lord of the Black Riders, the Witch King, the Scary Guy who cannot be killed by any man.

PIPPIN: You mean the one that stabbed Frodo?

GANDALF: Well, I mean . . .

PIPPIN: And that Arwen drowned?

GANDALF: See . . .

376

PIPPIN: And that Aragorn chased off with a torch?

GANDALF: Uh . . .

PIPPIN: And that we've seen several times during the course of the last two movies?

GANDALF: Drop dead, tiny man.

Some Really Dark and Scary Tower on a Dark and Scary Mountain

GOLLUM: Those big statues are the Scary Guy's watchdogses, precious. We climbs the mountain and stays out of their way.

FRODO: *walks right over to them*

SAM: Gollum! You KNOW Mr Frodo can't follow directions!

STATUES: RAAAAAAA!

GIANT GREEN LIGHT: WHOOOOSH!

Some Balcony at the Big White City

GIANT GREEN LIGHT IN THE DISTANCE: *WHOOOOSH!*

PIPPIN: Hold me?

GANDALF: *holds him*

Some Big White City That Is Somehow a Different White City

ORCS sneak up on the other big white city, led by GOTHMOG, a big ORC who looks like the bastard spawn of a tumor and a Circus Peanut.

Some Big White City. No, the Other One.

GANDALF: Pippin! Climb up there and light the beacon! And try not to screw it up!

PIPPIN: . . . Because I have such a good track record with that.

GANDALF: BECAUSE THERE'S NO ONE ELSE TO DO IT! GO!

> [PIPPIN succeeds, but just barely manages not to set himself on fire. The beacon sets off a chain reaction of beacons lighting across the mountains, all the way back to Rohan: the best scene in the whole damn movie, and it's just stuff musically catching on fire.]

Smoky Hall of the Horsey People

ARAGORN: OMGWTFTHEBEACONSARELIT!

> [Everyone looks at THÉODEN.]

THÉODEN: And . . . uh . . . we will answer their call! [*To* ÉOMER]: Shit, we've got some riders around here, right?

ÉOWYN: And I – I mean they – will follow you into battle, even unto death!

THÉODEN: Awww, it's really sweet of you to say so—

ÉOWYN: Not you, *him*.

MERRY: I'm coming too! I'll follow *anyone* into battle!

ARAGORN: Slut.

MERRY: You know it!

Some Big White City That Is Somehow a Different White City

MADRIL: We can't hold them off! The city is lost!

FARAMIR: Dad is gonna *kill* me.

GANDALF: Hurry! We have to go save Faramir and the Rangers!

PIPPIN: Why do *I* have to go?

GANDALF: Because I'm not leaving your dumb ass behind to screw anything else up, is why!

PIPPIN: That's a good reason.

[FARAMIR and his MEN race across the plains to Minas Tirith with the NAZGÛL in hot, shrieky pursuit. GANDALF rides out to meet them with his staff alight, and the bright white beams drive the WRAITHS off. The MEN who were not bowled over like so many tenpins make it safely back to the city.]

PIPPIN: Dude, you can do that? Why are we sitting around twiddling our thumbs if you've got big shiny powers?

GANDALF: Pay no mind to him, Faramir, he's just—

FARAMIR: A badger! Or is it woodchuck? Anyway, I already ran into two of those in Ithilien. Nice critters, so long as you don't mess with their jewellery.

PIPPIN: OMG!

GANDALF: Faramir? Let's go have a talk.

The Secret Stair of Cirith Ungol

GOLLUM leads the HOBBITS up a near-vertical 'stair' in the mountain-side.

FRODO: Why is it never 'The Secret Escalator', or 'The Extremely Well-Hidden Lift'?

GOLLUM: Come, hobbitses, must climb faster!

FRODO: I don't . . . feel so good . . .

SAM: Here, Mr Frodo, have some of my—

FRODO: *Baaaaaaaarrrrrrrrrrrf.*

~~Some Big White City~~ Osgiliath

WITCH KING: COME ON, JUST DO THE SLOTH IMPRESSION FOR ME ONE MORE TIME?

GOTHMOG [*sighing*]: . . . *fine*. 'BAAAAABY RUUUUUUF!'

WITCH KING: HEE HEE HEE.

The Throne Room of ~~Some Big White City~~ Minas Tirith

DENETHOR: Kiss my ring, young midget.

> [PIPPIN glances over at ~~FARAMIR~~ in mild terror. FARAMIR nods and rolls his eyes.]

DENETHOR: Now you have sworn fealty to me, the non-king lord of Gondor, who rewards ass-kissing with love, firstborns with honour and [*pointed look at* FARAMIR] disloyalty with pointless sacrifice.

FARAMIR [*sighing*]: I'll go put on the funeral armour.

Some Perilous Mountain Ledge

GOLLUM: Look! Fat hobbit ate all the Elf crackers!

SAM: DID NOT!

GOLLUM: And he wants the ring for himself!

SAM: DO NOT!

FRODO: I'm sorry, Sam. I'm afraid . . . you're fired. The tribe has spoken. You are the weakest link. Goodbye.

SAM [*bawling*]: As you wish, Mr Frodo!

> [But what FRODO does not know is that 'As you wish' really means, 'How the hell am I supposed to get home from here?!']

Montage of Filial Sorrow

GANDALF: Faramir! Don't throw your life away like this!

FARAMIR: But it is my father's command that I retake Osgiliath, no matter how futile or quixotic a mission it is!

GANDALF: Shpffff, we're not going to be listening to him any more in half an hour anyway! You don't have to do this!

FARAMIR: But I must, because my daddy doesn't love me, and the only way I can ever win his respect is through death.

SOME SOLDIER: Hey, so . . . do the rest of us have to go? I mean, my dad loves me just fine.

GANDALF: You heard the man! Shut up and sacrifice yourself!

SOME SOLDIER'S TEARFUL DAD: Bye, son!

[Meanwhile, back inside the great hall . . .]

DENETHOR: Sing me a song, midget.

PIPPIN:

> Do not slobber gently into that good night,
> Pig, pig against the dying of the light.
>
> Wise men know you are a total bitch,
> But you just want one more sandwich;
>
> Your son is dying in that place,
> While you just want to stuff . . . your . . . faaaaaaace.

DENETHOR: *snarf slobber snuffle crunch*

PIPPIN: *tear*

Mustering the Horsey Troops at Dunharrow

THÉODEN: Riders! Account for your men!

EAST HORSINGTON: We found some farmers who weren't too busy.

WEST PONYVILLE: Uh, we brought three guys and a keg . . . ?

THÉODEN: *facepalm*

[Meanwhile . . .]

MERRY: Whee! I'm gonna go fight with the big boys!

ÉOMER AND GAMLING: BWAHAHAHAHAHA!

ÉOWYN: Why can he not fight for the man he loves? Is he not called to battle by the same bedroom eyes and low-slung hips? WHY DO YOU OPPRESS HIM SO?

ÉOMER: É? We're not really talking about the munchkin, are we?

[Later that night, ARAGORN has a bad dream about ARWEN pining away unto death, yea verily –]

ARWEN'S LAST WORDS: *He was . . . such . . . a good bunny . . .*

[– and wakes up in a cold sweat after he imagines breaking her favourite diamond flower pendant. Fortunately, someone's got a visitor!]

ELROND: Look, Arwen laid this total guilt trip on me about you and her and reforging the Sword Which Once Was Broken and all, and then she called up Galadriel on the telepathephone and – have you ever had to talk to your mother-in-law at three in the morning? Be glad that Celebrían passed over long ago, let me put it that way. So basically, I'm never going to hear the end of it until I give this sword to you and tell you to take the Paths of the Dead, so do me a favour and do that, okay? I'd like to get some sleep already.

ARAGORN: But . . . that's the *scary* way.

ELROND: Son? You're never gonna be king unless you sack up.

Many Goodbyes Are Said

ARAGORN: Before I go to possibly die, Éowyn, I feel like I should tell you that I don't love you, and you, in fact, do not love me. You're just in love with an *image* of me—

ÉOWYN: Yes. And that image? Is *hawt*.

ARAGORN: Focus, Éowyn: I don't love you.

[ARAGORN saddles up and starts riding away with LEGOLAS and GIMLI.]

ÉOWYN: HEY! WHAT'S BLONDIE THERE GOT THAT I DON'T?

ARAGORN: Don't answer that, Legolas.

* * *

GAMLING: Hey! Where's he going?

THÉODEN: Away to the Paths of the Dead, where he must meet his kingly fate.

GAMLING: But – without Aragorn, we're all going to die!

[Everyone waits for words of encouragement.]

THÉODEN: Yeah . . . we *are* gonna die. But we're gonna go down fighting, and we're going to make our fathers proud.

GAMLING: That's totally not what I thought you were going to say, my lord.

* * *

THÉODEN: Beloved niece, before we leave for death and doom and destruction, I would tell you this: if the battle goes ill, you will rule in my place. I mean, assuming it goes *really* ill and your brother dies, too. But, you know, smile for me and move on with life and stuff.

ÉOWYN: You know what? If the battle goes 'ill' and I'm the only one left to rule Edoras while Sauron covers the Earth with darkness, I'm thinking there won't be too much smiling goin' on.

THÉODEN: Look, I'm just saying.

The Paths of the Dead

LEGOLAS: Long ago, the Men of these mountains swore to fight for the last king of Gondor, cross their hearts and hope to die, stick a needle in their eye. But when the chips were down, they turned tail and ran back into the mountains –

GIMLI: They broke the 'stick a needle' oath? Man, that's cold.

LEGOLAS: – and so Isildur, who was not actually the last king of Gondor, but it's the only name any of the viewers will even come close to recognizing, cursed them to walk the Earth in torment, verily, until they said they were very, very sorry.

ARAGORN: Thank you, Lieutenant Exposition.

[They arrive at the end of the Paths of the Dead, and it is scary. ARAGORN and LEGOLAS'S HORSES up and make a run for it.]

ARAGORN: BREGO! WHERE ARE YOU GOING! DIDN'T SAVING MY LIFE MEAN ANYTHING TO YOU?!

LEGOLAS [*sadly*]: Why do pretty horsies always leave?

Rohan Rides Out

THÉODEN and ÉOMER muster all the HORSEY PEOPLE to ride for Gondor, except that ÉOWYN can't go because she's a girrrrrrl, and MERRY can't go because he's a woodchuck.

ÉOWYN [*disguised as male rider*]: Come on, Merry! We won't be left behind! We'll show them all! They'll see!

MERRY: You know, if you're really that upset, I *am* available for therapeutic massage . . .

The Caves in the Mountain at the End of the Paths of the Dead

KING OF THE DEAD: Apple?

ARAGORN: Sorry, I ate back at camp. I have come to tell you to fulfill your oath.

KING OF THE DEAD: Shpffff.

ARAGORN: Fight for me.

KING OF THE DEAD: No.

ARAGORN: Fight for me.

KING OF THE DEAD: No.

ARAGORN: Fight for me.

KING OF THE DEAD: No.

ARAGORN: I KEEL YOU WITH MY GIANT PHALLIC SWORD!

KING OF THE DEAD: OmgpleasedontkillmeIwantto . . . keep . . . being . . . dead . . . ?

ARAGORN: . . .

KING OF THE DEAD: . . .

LEGOLAS: Wait, if you're all supernatural and shit, why couldn't you tell that Aragorn was Isildur's heir when he walked in the cave?

EVERYONE ELSE: . . .

KING OF THE DEAD: Shut it, Swiss Miss.

~~The Only White City Left~~ Minas Tirith

Apparently BREGO had to hoof it over to Minas Tirith to save FARAMIR, because once again a HORSE drags SOME HAPLESS GUY back to safety. But since it is a really long way from the Paths of the Dead to Minas Tirith, FARAMIR is mostly dead by the time he gets there.

DENETHOR: What? MY ONLY SON! OH MY BELOVED SON HOW COULD THIS HAVE HAPPENED TO YOU!

PIPPIN: *massive eyeroll*

[The ORCS catapult the heads of FARAMIR'S slain MEN over the walls of the city, to the horror of all.]

DENETHOR: The son I didn't love is done for! The army I didn't call for hasn't come! O CRUEL WORLD, WHY HAST THOU FORSAKEN ME?!

[In the middle of his rant, he sees the vast armies of ORCS and URUKS and catapults and CAVE TROLLS and some WEIRD TRICERACOW THINGS right at the city gates.]

DENETHOR: FLEE! EVERYBODY FLEE! ABANDON YOUR POSTS! PANIC IN THE STREETS AND WET YOURSELVES LIKE CHILDREN!

[GANDALF intercedes to administer the beatdown of all time:]

GANDALF: STOP SUCKING!

TOLKIEN FANS: *aren't even fazed anymore*

GANDALF: Get back to your posts, bitches!

PIPPIN: What about me?

GANDALF: STAND OVER THERE AND TRY NOT TO DIE.

Shelob's Lair

GOLLUM: Here's the secret way to Mordor, Masster! So nice! So safe!

FRODO: But . . . it's just a big dark tunnel covered in giant cobwebs and . . . what are those, half-gnawed bones?

GOLLUM: Come, Masster! Is the only way!

FRODO: Saaaaaaam, I'm scared . . .

SAM: *is not there*

FRODO: DAMMIT!

[FRODO'S halfway into the Tunnel of Creepy before he realizes that GOLLUM has abandoned him, he doesn't know where he's going and, oh, there's a GIANT SPIDER waiting to eat him. After he's done wetting himself in terror, FRODO manages pull out the phial of starlight that GALADRIEL gave him –]

FRODO: Okay, I actually do remember getting this.

[– and claw his way out of the tunnel to safety. GOLLUM then tries to throttle him again, and FRODO throws GOLLUM into a chasm where he falls to his death.]

TOLKIEN FANS: Wait . . . say what?

[And then FRODO collapses.]

Some Golden Dream-Land

GALADRIEL glides up to FRODO and gives him her hand.

GALADRIEL: Cheer up, emo hobbit!

The Fearsome and Infamous Grond

At the city gates of Minas Tirith, the TROLLS of Mordor slam a giant flaming battering ram while the ORCS chant something over and over.

SOME GONDORIAN SOLDIER: What are they saying?

GANDALF: I'm not entirely sure, but if you know anyone named 'Ron', throw him over the wall *immediately*.

Shelob Redux

FRODO: Hey, look, there's the tower of Cirith Ungol. Good thing I got away from that giant spider – maybe I'll make it on my own after UGHHHHHHH. [*Falls down.*]

[Just when it looks as if SHELOB is going to carry off a FRODO COCOON, here comes SAM with the phial and sword that FRODO dropped.]

SAM: UNHAND MR FRODO, YOU SCUM, OR I'LL –

SHELOB: RAAAAAAAA!

SAM: – run away! Run away!

[SHELOB chases SAM up and down the rocks but finally gets a good bellyful of Sting and scuttles away. This would be a great triumph, except for the fact that FRODO is totally dead. And then a pack of ORCS come along and carry away his body.]

SAM: *weeps*

SOME ORC: I love when Shelob wraps up intruders for us to carry away and interrogate later, because they're totally not really dead.

SAM [*smacking self*]: STUPID, STUPID, STUPID!

Everything Starts to Suck

While PIPPIN is off trying to stop the STEWARD OF THE CITY from slow-roasting his son over an open flame, the HORDES OF MORDOR breach the city wall.

GANDALF: Man, I wish we'd thought to evacuate the women and children before now.

SOME TROLL: *lumbers by eating handfuls of babies*

GANDALF: But hark! What's that?

The Last Great Ride of the Horsey People

The horns of the ROHIRRIM! THÉODEN has come to save the day in one last, great charge of which the generations forever after will sing!

THÉODEN: DEAAATH!

MERRY: No! No death!

HORSEY PEOPLE: DEAAAAATH!

MERRY: Not death! Not death! How about mild discomfort?

THÉODEN: DEAAAAAAATH!

MERRY: Cramps? Sinus congestion?

ÉOWYN: DEAAAAAAAAATH!

MERRY: Let's hear it for migraines!

Somewhere in the Minas Tirith

PIPPIN: OMG Gandalf you have to come right now Faramir's not dead but his father thinks he is and tombs and oil and FIRE BAAAAD!

GANDALF: What?

PIPPIN: LORD DENETHOR, HE CRAZY!

GANDALF: Well, no shit.

PIPPIN: Hey, where's your staff?

GANDALF: Staff? What staff?

PIPPIN: What? You hit me with it, like, an hour ago!

GANDALF: What staff? I never had a staff.

PIPPIN: But—

GANDALF: WE MUST SAVE FARAMIR!

[GANDALF and PIPPIN ride SHADOWFAX to the Tombs of the Stewards, where DENETHOR has already lit a fire under his 'dead' son. GANDALF handles the beatdown end of things while PIPPIN leaps onto the already burning pyre and stop-drop-and-rolls FARAMIR onto the floor. And guess what? Turns out FARAMIR'S still alive after all! Unfortunately, DENETHOR'S whole self-immolation plan is already past the point of no return. He runs screaming down several miles of courtyard . . .]

GANDALF: There passes Denethor . . .

DENETHOR [*falling off city*]: WAHHHHHHHHHHHHHHHHH . . . !

GANDALF: . . . a *great* long-distance runner.

Some Battlefield

VAGUELY AFRICAN-LOOKING GUY: UNLEASH THE ELEPHANTS OF WAR!

[The HORSEY PEOPLE stop and take stock of the situation.]

THÉODEN: LOOSE THE TINY WHITE MICE!

TINY WHITE MICE: DEAAAAAAATH!

ELEPHANTS OF WAR: EEEEEK!

THÉODEN: SPREAD THE BANANA PEELS!

BANANA PEELS: *squish*

ELEPHANTS OF WAR: *slip, fall over each other and crush several thousand enemy soldiers*

ÉOWYN AND MERRY: *fall down*

THÉODEN: Awesome! I sure am glad my niece and the little dude aren't out here getting crushed to death right now!

Gandalf: Inspirational Speaker for the Ages

Having rescued FARAMIR, GANDALF and PIPPIN are holed up behind the second-level barricade waiting to be crushed by incoming TROLLS.

PIPPIN: So . . . we're pretty much going to die and stuff.

GANDALF: Awww, it isn't all that bad. Beyond the Shadowlands—

PIPPIN: Pssst – wrong British writer/professor.

GANDALF: Yikes, sorry about that. Beyond the grey curtain there are white shores and green countries. Or green shores and white countries. I forget exactly. But I was there for a while after that whole thing with the Balrog, and it was pretty sweet.

PIPPIN: Wait . . . isn't that wizard heaven, then? The rest of us don't go to wizard heaven, do we?

GANDALF: Oh . . . well, no, but there's also the Straight Road leading to the Undying Lands . . .

PIPPIN: But isn't that Elf heaven?

GANDALF: Oh. Right.

PIPPIN: So where does everyone else go?

GANDALF: Nowhere interesting enough to merit a pep talk, that's for sure.

Some Battlefield

In the middle of THÉODEN'S troop-rallying, the WITCH KING, LORD OF THE RINGWRAITHS, cruises in on his FELL BEAST.

WITCH KING [*to* FELL BEAST]: SNACK ON HIS SPLEEEEEEEEN.

THÉODEN: Oh, if only I had a torch or a magical river!

FELL BEAST: *chews on his head*

[Just as the WITCH KING comes in for the kill, ~~ÉOWYN~~ 'DERNHELM' leaps between them.]

ÉOWYN: *I will kill you if you touch him!*

[The WITCH KING leans over and starts not-quite-poking THÉODEN, who is lying half-crushed beneath his horse.]

WITCH KING: I'M NOT TOUCHING HIM! I'M NOT TOUCHING HIM! TOUCH TOUCH TOUCH!

ÉOWYN: RAAAAAAAAAAAAAAAAAA!

FELL BEAST'S HEAD: *falls off*

WITCH KING: YOU SON OF A BITCH!

[The WITCH KING chases ÉOWYN around in circles with his giant spiky flail until finally he breaks her shield – and her arm – and she drops her sword. MERRY crawls up and stabs him in the knee before he can flail her in the head.]

ÉOWYN [*tearing off helmet*]: I AM NO SON OF A BITCH! I AM A GIRRRRRRRRRRRRRRRRL!

[ÉOWYN stabs the WITCH KING in the face, and it is awesome.]

MERRY: *Duuuuude.*

Some Wharf

ORCS are waiting at the dock for a shipment of PIRATES. A ship glides up, and out leap . . . a GUY, a DWARF and a BLONDE CHICK? Hey!

ARAGORN: You ordered an ass-kicking?

SOME ORC: I don't think so . . .

ARAGORN: No, I'm pretty sure this ass-kicking's for you.

THE ARMY OF THE DEAD: RAAAAAAAAAAAAAAAAAA!

Some Battlefield

LEGOLAS uses his surfer-chick skills to take down an entire ELEPHANT and its CREW. All the FANGIRLS in the AUDIENCE swoon.

* * *

ÉOWYN: Uncle! You're going to be all right! You're going to make it!

THÉODEN: Hon, I just got crushed by my own horse, and the most sophisticated medical technology we have involves Sir Scruffalot and a handful of weeds.

ÉOWYN: . . .

THÉODEN: . . .

ÉOWYN: Can I have your stereo, then?

* * *

The SCRUBBING BUBBLES OF THE DEAD piranhize a couple of ELEPHANTS, but mostly they're just on clean-up duty now.

GIMLI: Are you sure you want to let the Dead go?

ARAGORN: Yeah, it's cool.

GIMLI: But they can kill anything in, like, two seconds, and we're going up against all of Mordor.

ARAGORN: Yeah, but that would take all the fun out of it.

GIMLI: You sure about this?

ARAGORN: No worries, man. I feel good about it.

GIMLI: I mean, they're dead and all, so they can't be killed, and we're totally killable . . .

ARAGORN: Hey, it's cool. I'm not real fond of those guys in the pointy helmets anyway.

POINTY HELMET GUARD: HEY!

* * *

PIPPIN: Merry!

MERRY [*wounded*]: I think . . . I'm late . . . for tiffin.

PIPPIN: *weeps for joy*

The Tower of Cirith Ungol

SOME URUK: DIBS ON THE SHINY STUFF!

SOME ORC: HEY! YOU TRIED TO STAB ME!

SOME OTHER URUK: HEY, THAT WAS MY EYE!

SOME OTHER ORC: YOU STEPPED ON MY TOE!

YET ANOTHER URUK: HE SANK MY BATTLESHIP!

CHAOS: *ensues*

[SAM takes advantage of the confusion to sneak in, stab a few ORCS and rescue FRODO.]

FRODO: Oh, Sam, they got the ring!

SAM: No, they didn't, Mr Frodo!

393

FRODO: GIMME.

SAM: Well, there's gratitude for you.

FRODO [*putting chain around neck*]: Ahhhhhh. But I'm still naked and alone in the dark, woe!

SAM: Here, Mr Frodo, have some of my clothes!

FRODO: I mean that metaphorically, Sam.

SAM [*looking down*]: No, you also mean it kind of literally.

FRODO: Oh.

The Throne Room of the Minas Tirith

ARAGORN: We must attack Sauron on his home turf to distract him from Frodo and Sam!

ÉOMER: You're assuming they're not already Orc barbecue.

GANDALF: What have I done? I've sent those two defenceless little butterballs to their doom!

ÉOMER: Hey, I'm sure it seemed like a good idea at the time.

ARAGORN: This is what I'm saying, people! We march on Sauron and he'll be too busy pulverizing us to notice the munchkins!

LEGOLAS [*wisely*]: A *diversion*.

ÉOMER: . . .

GANDALF: . . .

ARAGORN: Wow. I think that deserves a promotion to Captain Obvious.

LEGOLAS: *beams*

In the Land of Shadow

FRODO: Saaaaaam, I'm thiiiiiirsty.

SAM: Here, Mr Frodo, take the last of my water.

FRODO: Saaaaaam, I'm tiiiiiiired.

SAM: Well, I am too, Mr Frodo . . .

FRODO: I can't dooooooo this, Saaaaaaaam . . .

SAM: WE DIDN'T COME ALL THIS WAY JUST SO YOU COULD PUNK OUT NOW! I'LL CARRY YOUR WHINY ASS ALL THE WAY UP THERE MYSELF IF I HAVE TO, SO HELP ME GOD!

The Black Gates

ARAGORN gives a rousing speech to the effect of, 'We're all really scared, so let's fight together anyway! Woo!' And then the ORCS and the TROLLS and the NAZGÛL come out to play.

PIPPIN: Look! The eaglemoths are coming!

SOME SPEAR CARRIER: Hey, why didn't Frodo just ride an eaglemoth to Mount Doom in the first pl—

GANDALF ['accidentally' stabbing him]: Oh, will you look at that.

The Cracks of Doom

GOLLUM: I KEEL YOU!

[Oh, come on. You knew GOLLUM wasn't really dead. SAM holds GOLLUM off long enough for FRODO to sprint over to the Cracks of Doom.]

SAM: Throw it in the fire!

FRODO: . . .

SAM: Throw it in the fire!

FRODO: . . .

SAM: Throw it in the fire!

FRODO: . . .

SAM: THROOOOOW IT IN THE FIIIIIIIIRE!

THE DARK LORD FRODO: The ring is MINE.

SAM: You know, it just doesn't have the same oomph as— OW!

[GOLLUM sneaks up and clocks SAM upside the head with a rock. He wrestles with FRODO for the ring, bites FRODO'S finger off and still has to contend with FRODO some more. Ring addiction is tough, yo. And then they fall over the cliff edge into the lava.]

SAM: NOOOOOOOOO!

[Turns out that FRODO is still clinging to the edge. SAM hauls FRODO out while the ring takes its sweet time dissolving.]

The Black Gates

Just as a GIANT TROLL is about to stomp ARAGORN'S face, SAURON'S EYE starts freaking out and the tower crumbles and all his ORCS run away and the EAGLEMOTHS peck the FELL BEASTS to death and the earth swallows up all everything evil and a power shockwave ruins all their electronics.

THE EYE OF SAURON: NOOOOO! MY EMPIRE! MY DOMINION OVER THE EAAAARTH! MY STEREOOOOOO!

EVERYONE ELSE: YAY!

MERRY AND PIPPIN [*cheering*]: FRODO! FRODO!!

[And then Mount Doom blows up.]

MERRY AND PIPPIN [*sobbing*]: FRODO! FRODOOOO!!

Mission Accomplished

FRODO and SAM escape to a tiny island of rock before lava overtakes everything on the mountainside.

FRODO: Well, we did it. We'll never see the Shire again, but we did it.

SAM [*sobbing*]: And I'll never see Rosie Cotton again – I would have married that girl!

THE AUDIENCE: WHAT?

FRODO: You're kidding, right?

[FRODO passes out from sheer incredulity. The next time he opens his eyes, he's being carried by giant EAGLEMOTH claws.]

GANDALF: I *told you* they'd make it!

EAGLEMOTH: Yeah, yeah, you'll get your five bucks.

Some Sunny Recovery Room

FRODO: Cranky! You're alive!

GANDALF: I am Cranky no longer, but rather *Glowy*.

FRODO: Sure thing, Cranky— Merry! Hungry!

[MERRY and PIPPIN leap on the bed and proceed to throw the girliest pyjama party ever.]

MERRY: And then! The lady stabbed the scary guy! IN THE FACE!

PIPPIN: And then—!

[Meanwhile, FRODO has more visitors . . .]

FRODO: Filthy! . . . Girly! . . . KINGLY!

[At the door, SAM pokes his head in.]

FRODO: Awww, Weepy!

ÉOWYN: Hey, guys? Can I—

SAM: NO GIRLS ALLOWED!

FADE: *to black*

THE MOVIE: *is over*

THE MOVIE: *is not over*

GANDALF: I crown thee Edward—

ARAGORN: Wrong Longshanks.

GANDALF: Sorry about that. I crown thee Elessar, King of Gondor!

[The PEOPLE cheer and the rose-petal blower goes into overdrive and everyone is happy . . . well, except ARAGORN, who now has to rule a large, war-torn kingdom by himself for an exceptionally long lifespan.]

ARAGORN: Sigh.

ÉOWYN [*scribbling on her binder*]: *Lady Éowyn . . . Mrs Steward of Gondor . . . Éowyn, Princess of Ithilien . . . Mr and Mrs . . .* Hey, what's your last name?

FARAMIR: What?

ARAGORN: Attention, everyone, attention! Since I'm now without a queen, I have decided to marry the next loveliest maiden in my kingdom – my best friend Legolas.

LEGOLAS: *bats lashes*

ÉOWYN: HEY!

FARAMIR [*turning to* ÉOWYN]: *HEY!!*

ÉOWYN: *looks away, whistling*

ARAGORN: Wait a minute . . . who's that behind . . .

ARWEN [*peeking out from behind banner*]: Hi.

ARAGORN: You're not dead?

ARWEN: No.

ARAGORN: You didn't leave?

ARWEN: No.

ARAGORN: You couldn't RSVP?

ARWEN: Apparently not.

EVERYONE: . . .

ARWEN: I'm really sorry, I know you're not interested any more, I'll just be on my w—

ARAGORN: *snogs*

ÉOWYN: Wait, there really *was* a girl?

EVERYONE: YAY!

ARAGORN: Let's hear it for the half-pints!

EVERYONE: *falls down*

FADE: *to black*

THE MOVIE: *is over*

Some Nostalgic Map

THE MOVIE: *is not over*

[The HOBBITS get back to the Shire and settle down for a good drink in the tavern first thing. And then SAM decides, without so much as a word, to go up to the bar and sweep ROSIE off her feet.]

MERRY: I'll be damned.

PIPPIN: Dude, he's with a *girl*.

FRODO: I know, man.

FADE: *to black*

THE MOVIE: *is over*

Some Grey Harbour

THE MOVIE: *is not over*

GALADRIEL: And so Elrond, Gandalf, Celeborn and I retired from Middle-earth. Our first order of business was to go on a nice, relaxing cruise. Gandalf has turned out to be a crack shuffleboard player, in fact. Elrond keeps showing the cocktail waitresses pictures of his grandkids . . .

WAITRESS: So . . . that'll be one, uh . . . Sex on the Beach for you, sir?

ELROND [*turning over leaf in wallet*]: . . . and here's Eldarion, the future king of Gondor!

GALADRIEL: She doesn't CARE, ELROND! Anyway. Tropical cruise, conga lines, open bar, all is good. And now that What's His Evil Face is out of the picture, Celeborn and I are looking at it as sort of a second honeymoon . . . Oh, and some hobbits came along, too.

CÍRDAN THE SHIPMASTER: ALL ABOARD!

SAM: We'll miss you, Mr Bilbo.

GANDALF: Come on, Frodo, we don't have all day.

HOBBITS: Jigga *whaaaat*?

FRODO: Oh, didn't I tell you? I'm going to the Undying Lands with Bilbo. It's one of those 'hero saves the world but can't enjoy the victory for himself' things. You know.

HOBBITS: *sniffle*

GANDALF: There, there. Let it all out. Not *all* tears are an evil—

SAM: WAAAAAAAAA!

GANDALF: Just yours, you big crybaby.

[FRODO bids each HOBBIT farewell, and after nearly making out with SAM, boards the white ship, which sails into the sunset, and is at peace.]

FADE: *to white*

THE MOVIE: *is over*

Some Hobbit Hole

THE MOVIE: *is not over*

SAM: Finally, I'm home!

LITTLE ELANOR: Daddy!

ROSIE: Well, it took you long enough! I conceived and delivered a second child while you were gone!

THE MOVIE: *is over*

THE CREDITS: We would like to thank the people of New Zealand, the people of Old Zealand, the Maori, the settlers, the inventors of moving pictures and the printing press, God, everyone in Hollywood, their lawyers, their agents, their agents' lawyers and their lawyers' agents, God's lawyer's agent . . .

VOICE FROM THE GRAVE OF TOLKIEN [*muffled*]: HEY!

THE CREDITS: . . . oh, and the late J.R.R. Tolkien, without whom these movies could not have been made, obviously, even though we probably pissed him off to hell and back in the making of them. But hey, at least we're not Disney.

DISNEY: HEY!

THE MOVIE: *is over*

Somewhere in the Shire

SAM: Rosie, why doesn't Baby Gamgee look like me? Rosie . . . ?

FIN.